UCHICAGOCCSR
THE UNIVERSITY OF CHICAGO CONSORTIUM ON CHICAGO SCHOOL RESEARCH

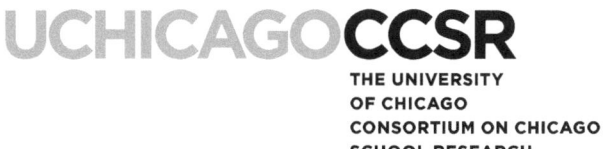

RESEARCH REPORT NOVEMBER 2014

Middle Grade Indicators of Readiness in Chicago Public Schools

Looking Forward to High School and College

Elaine M. Allensworth, Julia A. Gwynne, Paul Moore, and Marisa de la Torre

TABLE OF CONTENTS

1 Executive Summary

7 Introduction

Chapter 1
17 Issues in Developing and Evaluating Indicators

Chapter 2
23 Changes in Academic Performance from Eighth to Ninth Grade

Chapter 3
29 Middle Grade Indicators of High School Course Performance

Chapter 4
47 Who Is at Risk of Being Off-Track at the End of Ninth Grade?

Chapter 5
55 Who Is at Risk of Earning Less Than As or Bs in High School?

Chapter 6
63 Indicators of Whether Students Will Meet Test Benchmarks

Chapter 7
75 Who Is at Risk of Not Reaching the PLAN and ACT Benchmarks?

Chapter 8
81 How Grades, Attendance, and Test Scores Change

Chapter 9
93 Interpretive Summary

99 References

104 Appendices A-E

ACKNOWLEDGEMENTS

The authors would like to acknowledge the many people who contributed to this work. We thank Robert Balfanz and Julian Betts for providing us with very thoughtful review and feedback which were used to revise this report. We also thank Mary Ann Pitcher and Sarah Duncan, at the Network for College Success, and members of our Steering Committee, especially Karen Lewis, for their valuable feedback. Our colleagues at UChicago CCSR and UChicago UEI, including Shayne Evans, David Johnson, Thomas Kelley-Kemple, and Jenny Nagaoka, were instrumental in helping us think about the ways in which this research would be most useful to practitioners and policy makers. We were fortunate to receive substantial feedback and assistance from the UChicago CCSR communications staff, Bronwyn McDaniel, Jessica Puller, and Emily Krone. We thank the Chicago Public Schools for providing us the data that allowed us to do this work. All work at UChicago CCSR is also supported by operating grants from the Spencer Foundation and the Lewis-Sebring Family Foundation. This study was made possible by a grant from the Bill and Melinda Gates Foundation, to which we are very grateful.

This report was produced by UChicago CCSR's publications and communications staff: Emily Krone, Director for Outreach and Communication; Bronwyn McDaniel, Senior Manager for Outreach and Communications; and Jessica Puller, Communications Specialist.

Graphic Design: Jeff Hall Design
Photography: David Schalliol
Editing: Ann Lindner

MIDDLE GRADE INDICATORS OF READINESS

Executive Summary

Across the country, policymakers are raising the expectations for educational attainment. With changes to the economy resulting in dire economic prospects for high school dropouts, high school graduation has become a necessity. In fact, high school graduation is no longer considered sufficient; policymakers are calling on the nation's schools to graduate all students ready for college and careers.

Much of the pressure to improve educational attainment is on high schools, but focus has also turned to earlier grades. There is a very large population of students who struggle with the transition from the middle grades to high school, raising concerns that high school failures are partially a function of poor middle grade preparation. As a result, middle grade practitioners are grappling with questions about what skills students need to succeed in high school, which markers they should use to gauge whether students are ready to succeed in high school and beyond, and whether it is possible to identify in middle grades students who are likely to struggle in high school and college.

This report is designed to provide a detailed picture of the relationship between students' performance in the middle grades (grades five through eight) and their subsequent performance in high school and college among students in the Chicago Public Schools (CPS). Specifically, the report shows:

- Which of many potential middle grade indicators—including attendance rates, grades in specific classes and GPAs, test scores, study habits, grit, discipline records, and background characteristics—are most predictive of high school success. It also shows the degree to which high school readiness is a function of the high school students choose or the middle school they attended. With all of the conflicting messages that policymakers and practitioners hear about what matters for academic success, these findings are intended to clarify which factors are most strongly related to students' educational attainment.

- Which students are likely to be successful in high school—passing their classes, earning high grades that put them on-track for college enrollment and graduation, and achieving test scores at ACT's benchmarks—and which students are at risk of failing to meet those standards. These findings are intended to help schools develop intervention plans and practices around specific students to help them reach particular outcomes. They can also provide a guide for parents about what level of performance their child needs to be likely to graduate from high school and be ready for college.

- The degree to which student performance changes during the middle grades—showing why students leave the middle grades with different levels of readiness. For example, do students need to start the middle grades with high performance to leave middle school with high levels of readiness? Or does students' performance change considerably while they are in the middle grades? These findings are intended to help practitioners and policymakers set realistic goals for improvement.

KEY FINDINGS:

Middle Grade Information Can Be Used to Create Simple Indicator Systems of High School Graduation and College Readiness

Many characteristics of students are associated with their academic outcomes, from background characteristics to test scores, grades, attendance, and discipline records, to noncognitive factors. With so many factors associated with later outcomes, it may seem like practitioners would need complicated models to gauge students' likelihood of success in later years. However, after taking into account just two or three key middle school indicators, other information about students only marginally improves the prediction of later outcomes.

Grades and failures are best predicted by earlier grades and attendance. High school test scores are strongly predicted by earlier test scores. Other information about students provides only negligible improvement in the prediction of their outcomes, beyond the top predictors. Background characteristics, study habits, and grit are not predictive of high school performance, once students' middle grade GPAs, attendance, and test scores are taken into account. Background characteristics (e.g., race, gender, neighborhood poverty, free lunch eligibility, being old-for-grade, and special education status) are all related to high school grades and test scores, but they do not tell us any more about who will pass, get good grades, or score well on tests in high school, once we take into account students' eighth-grade GPAs, attendance, and test scores. Students' misconduct and suspension records in middle school are also not predictive of high school performance, once we take into account their attendance, grades, and test scores. Likewise, students' reports of their study habits in eighth grade, and their responses on a grit scale measuring perseverance in the middle grades, are not predictive of their performance in high school beyond their current grades and attendance.[1]

GPAs from different middle schools are not equivalent, but the differences are generally less than a half of a GPA point. We often hear that grades are subjective—that an A average from one school is not equal to an A average from another school. This suggests that students with the same academic records are more likely to succeed if they came from one school than another. In fact, students with the same grades, attendance, and test score records upon leaving eighth grade are more likely to succeed in high school if they came from some middle schools than from others, net of the effects of which high schools students attend (**see Chapter 3**). At the same time, the differences in success among students with the same grades from different middle schools are small, compared to the differences in success among students with different grades at the same school. As discussed in Chapter 3, an A average from one school represents a better likelihood of success than a B average from any other school. Differences by schools are as much as half a GPA point, at the most.

While it is common for people to believe that grades have different meanings across schools, it also appears that test scores also have different meanings across schools. Students with the same middle grade test scores are more likely to score well on the high school tests if they came from particular middle schools than others (**see Chapter 6**). People tend to see test scores as objective, since everyone takes the same test, but students can be prepared to do well on the middle grade tests in ways that do not necessarily translate into higher performance later on.

Test scores are much weaker indicators of high school grades than middle school grades and attendance. Many high school interventions are based on test score proficiency—meeting standards on tests, or reading at grade level. This is the reasoning behind programs that offer support based on test scores, such as double-dose coursing or grade promotion standards in middle school that delay students' entry into ninth grade based on test scores. However, while middle grade test scores are moderately related to passing classes and getting high grades in high school, most of the relationship between test scores and later performance seems to work through students' grades. That is, students with strong test scores are more likely to get good grades than students with weak test scores, but it is the grades that matter for later outcomes. Grades are based on a number of factors in addition to tested skills, including attendance, assignment completion, and quality of work over the course of an entire semester. Once we account for students' GPAs and attendance in the middle grades, their test scores do not provide much additional information about their likelihood of passing their classes in high school, and they only improve the prediction of getting high grades (As and Bs) in high school among students who also have high grades in middle school.[2]

High test scores also do not inoculate students against poor course performance in high school. Only about a third of students with high test scores in eighth grade (meeting 2013 ISAT standards in reading and math) receive at least a B average in high school, and one-fifth have D averages or lower (**see Chapter 5**).

Whether students are "ready" for high school depends not only on their academic performance in the middle grades but also on the context that they enter into in ninth grade. Students with the same academic records in middle school also have different high school outcomes depending on which high school they attend. Students are more likely to pass their ninth-grade classes, and to make larger test score gains, if they attend some high schools rather than others (**see Chapter 3**). Especially for students with moderate GPAs (between a 1.0 and 3.0), their probability of being on-track at the end of ninth grade is strongly influenced by which high school they attend.

Middle Grade Indicators Can Identify Some Students at High Risk, but High School Warning Systems Are Still Critical

When thinking about how to address problems with high school dropout and college readiness, there are often calls for early intervention (before students get to high school). Some students can be identified as at high risk of poor high school outcomes when they are in the middle grades; early intervention might help them get on a path to high school and college readiness. Many other students, however, do not show signs of poor performance until they get to high school. The change in context across the transition to high school brings new challenges to many students who appear to be doing fine, academically, during the middle grades.

Middle grade attendance and grades can be used to identify a set of students who are at very high risk of failing classes and being off-track in high school, and many of these students can be identified by at least as early as sixth grade. Students with a very high risk of failure in high school are chronically absent in the middle grades or are already receiving Fs in their classes in the middle grades (**see Chapter 4**). The middle grade indicators of very high likelihood of failure in Chicago are almost identical to middle grade indicators that were found to be very predictive of high school dropout in Philadelphia.[3] Many of the students who are at high risk of ninth-grade failure can be identified by at least as early as sixth grade, although some fall into this group as their attendance declines through the middle grade years. Without a dramatic change in their educational experience, these students have very little chance of graduating from high school; they and their future teachers are set up for failure.

While some students can be identified as at high risk of failing in high school, many other students who fail their ninth-grade classes in Chicago do not show signs of being in academic trouble in the middle grade years. The majority of students who fail their ninth-grade courses, and are off-track for graduation in Chicago, cannot be identified precisely in middle school (**see Chapter 4**). While there are calls for early identification of dropouts in middle school, the change in context over the transition to high school makes it difficult to predict exactly who will fail in ninth grade, beyond the students with very high risk. Once students start to show signs of

---

1 See Chapter 3, as well as Appendix E, for models that predict high school grades, pass rates, and on-track status with middle grade variables. See Chapter 6, as well as Appendix E, for models that predict high school test scores with middle grade variables.
2 See Chapter 3 and Appendix E for these comparisons.
3 Neild and Balfanz (2006).

struggle in ninth grade, with absence from classes or low grades, they become at high risk of not graduating.

Students often leave the middle grades looking like they are prepared to do very well in high school, but their grades and attendance drop dramatically in ninth grade. Students without exceptionally high performance in middle school are unlikely to get high grades in high school, and even having a very strong record in middle school does not ensure a student of high grades in high school (**see Chapter 2**). In fact, *40 percent of students who left eighth grade with As or Bs in their classes and ISAT test scores of 310 (exceeding standards) in math earned a C or lower in their ninth-grade math class.* Students who enter high school with strong records but no longer perform well in high school are another group of students ripe for intervention—intervention to make sure they reach their college potential.

Students need at least a 3.0 GPA in the middle grades to be college-bound; a 3.5 GPA gives them at least a 50 percent chance. Prior research on high school predictors of college graduation shows that, by far, the most important predictor of college graduation is students' high school GPA. Only students who graduate from high school with at least a B average have a moderate chance of earning a college degree. Parallel to this finding about college, only those students who leave eighth grade with GPAs of at least 3.0 have a moderate chance of earning a 3.0 GPA in high school. Students who plan to go to college need to get the message that college requires very strong levels of effort and engagement in both the middle grades and in high school.

Attendance Shows More Variation in Growth Over the Middle Grades Than Grades; Test Performance Is Fairly Constant Over Time

Some students show declining attendance and grades over the middle grades; others show improving attendance and grades. On average, GPAs and attendance rates are similar in fifth grade through eighth grade in Chicago. Attendance shows the more variability across students over time than either grades or test scores. In particular, some students' attendance declines considerably in the middle grade years, especially among students who started out with low attendance in fifth grade. GPAs improve or fall for some students by as much as a half of a GPA point as they move from fifth to eighth grade.

All students show growth in test scores over time on the vertically scaled state tests (the ISAT), but their relative performance (e.g., percentile rank) stays about the same, with very little variation in the amount that they grow over time—especially in reading (**see Chapter 8**). There is a push for students to end eighth grade in the *"exceeds"* range on state standards; this point corresponds closely with the college benchmark scores on the high school tests. However, students with average scores in fifth grade would need to improve their test growth by a rate that is well above the highest growth currently observed for these students to meet the *"exceeds"* range at the end of eighth grade, except by random chance.

About half of the changes over time in students' grades, attendance, and test scores can be attributed to which school they attend during the middle grades. At some schools, it is typical for students' grades to improve by about a tenth of a GPA point each year; at other schools, grades tend to decline by a tenth of a GPA point. Thus, students' GPA might end up as much as 0.6 points different by the eighth grade, based on which school they attend for the middle grade years. At some schools, attendance tends to decrease by about one percentage point each year; at others attendance tends to improve by a percentage point a year. At some schools, students' math ISAT scores grow by 15 points a year, and at others they grow at 11 points a year; reading scores grow by 11 points a year at some schools, and nine points a year at others.

Strategies aimed at attendance improvement could likely have as much or more of a pay-off for high school and college graduation as efforts aimed at improving test scores. While there is considerable local and national focus on improving test scores as a mechanism for improving educational attainment, attendance is often seen as a low-level goal. Yet, middle school attendance is much more predictive of passing high school classes than test scores and is as predictive of high grades in high school as test scores. High school outcomes are also higher for students who improve their attendance during the middle grades than for students who improve their test scores. Students who end their middle grade years with strong attendance are much more likely to do well in their high school courses than students with weak attendance, regardless of what their attendance or test scores were in fifth grade (**see Chapter 8**).

Attendance is also the critical factor underlying large declines in student performance in the transition to high school. Students' unexcused absences quadruple in one year, on average, when they go from eighth to ninth grade (**see Chapter 2**). Their study habits also decline. As a result of missing more class time and putting in less effort, students' grades drop by a half of a GPA point, on average. For some students, the drop in attendance leads to high rates of course failure, putting them off-track for graduation. For others, it takes them from being B students to C students, putting them off-track for college readiness. Declining attendance occurs among students with high test scores, as well as among students with low test scores. It is the most critical factor undermining students' educational attainment. This does not mean that schools should focus on attendance instead of on challenging instruction; attendance is the building block that needs to be strong to enable higher-level engagement in school and the development of strong academic skills.

Monitoring high-leverage indicators is not a substitute for improving instruction or creating engaging environments. But by monitoring those indicators that are most strongly associated with later outcomes, school practitioners can make sure that students get the right levels and kinds of support to keep them on-track for high school graduation and college readiness. They can focus attention on indicators that matter the most for later outcomes and they can establish realistic goals for student and school improvement.

INTRODUCTION

Research on Indicators of High School and College Readiness

The expectations for schools have changed over the past 20 years. It is no longer acceptable to graduate only the most motivated students and to prepare only the most academically talented ones for college. Schools are expected to graduate all of their students and to put them on a track for college readiness.

The labor market is grim for students without high school diplomas,[4] and the vast majority of students now aim to attain a four-year college degree.[5] The pressure is on high schools to improve their graduation and college-readiness rates. Educators at the secondary level, however, often contend that students enter high school without the skills they need to be on-track for graduation and college readiness.

While it may seem obvious that students need to enter high school ready to succeed, it is not clear what it means to be ready. There is little research that ties middle grade records to high school outcomes, or that shows how they are related. There is even less work that ties middle school records to college readiness. Such information is needed by middle grade practitioners so that they can gauge students' readiness for later success, set goals for improvement, and provide support for students who are likely to fail. Middle grade practitioners can use indicators of readiness to assess their own success at preparing students for high school and to focus their efforts on those skills and behaviors

> This chapter describes the organization of the study and discusses the prior research on middle school indicators of high school performance and high school indicators of college performance.

School Grade Structures in Chicago: Mostly K-8 Schools

The majority of schools serving middle grades in Chicago are elementary schools that serve grades K-8. Unlike districts that have a middle school structure, most students do not go through a large school transition until the transition to high school. During the 2008-09 school year, 91 percent of the schools that served eighth-grade students were K-8 schools (419 schools). About 4 percent of schools with eighth-graders served only the middle grades—some combination of grades four through eight (20 schools), about 3 percent served middle and high school grades—starting at grade six or seven through 12 (14 schools), and the remainder were schools with other grade configurations.

---

4 Sum et al. (2009); Alliance for Excellent Education (2011); Day and Newburger (2002); Heckman and LaFontaine (2007).

5 National Center for Education Statistics (2007); Roderick et al. (2008).

most crucial for later success. High schools could use better indicators of students' readiness to program students into appropriate classes and target supports as they begin high school.

This report provides the answers to four basic questions about risk and readiness in the middle grade years of fifth through eighth grade. It shows which metrics matter and how schools might use them to identify students for support.

1 *Which middle grade metrics predict ninth-grade failure?*
Based on those metrics, which middle grade students are at risk of failing their ninth-grade classes, and which are likely to pass their classes when they get to high school?

2 *Which middle grade metrics predict earning high grades (3.0 or higher) in high school?*
Based on those metrics, which middle grade students have little chance of earning high grades in high school and which students are likely to do so?

3 *Which middle school metrics predict reaching ACT's college-readiness benchmarks?*
Based on those metrics, which middle grade students are at risk of missing the benchmarks when they get to high school and which students are likely to meet them?

4 *How does students' performance on key indicators change during the middle grades, and what are the implications for high school success?*

In this chapter, we describe the prior research that set the stage for the study and how this report provides new information. Each of the subsequent chapters provides specific pieces of information on middle grade indicators. Some readers may be more interested in particular chapters than others. We offer the following as a guide to the content of the report, which can point readers to the information of most interest to them:

Chapter 1: **Issues in Developing and Evaluating Indicators.** This chapter addresses some of the issues to consider when deciding which measures of performance to focus on in early warning indicator systems, how many to use, and the implications of using different cut-offs for identifying risk.

Chapter 2: **Changes in Academic Performance from Eighth to Ninth Grade.** This chapter provides a picture of how Chicago students' academic performance changes from eighth to ninth grade and provides context for understanding the indicator predictions shown in later chapters.

Chapter 3: **Middle Grade Indicators of High School Course Performance.** This chapter evaluates potential indicators of high school grades, showing how well students' personal characteristics and their academic performance in the middle grades predict their grades in ninth and eleventh grade. It also evaluates which combinations of indicators provide the best predictions.

Chapter 4: **Who Is at Risk of Being Off-Track at the End of Ninth Grade?** This chapter shows students' risk of failing, based on their middle grade records. This information could be used by school practitioners to identify students who are at high risk of failure and can be used to discuss goals for student performance with students and their families.

Chapter 5: **Who Is at Risk of Earning Less Than As or Bs in High School?** This chapter shows students' likelihood of earning high grades in high school—grades that will make them eligible for college and likely to succeed, once there. The information in this chapter could be used to discuss goals for student performance with students and their families.

Chapter 6: **Indicators of Whether Students Will Meet Test Benchmarks.** This chapter evaluates potential middle grade indicators of performance on high school tests. It compares predictions of performance on subject-specific tests and composite test scores. It also examines the differences in predictions, based on which middle or high school students attend.

Chapter 7: **Who is at Risk of Not Reaching the PLAN and ACT Benchmarks?** This chapter shows the levels of performance in the middle grades that give students a chance of meeting PLAN and ACT benchmarks in ninth and eleventh grades.

Chapter 8: **How Grades, Attendance, and Test Scores Change.** This chapter addresses the degree to which students show different amounts of growth and decline in attendance, grades, and test scores over the middle grade years.

Chapter 9: **Interpretive Summary.**

> ### The Ninth-Grade On-Track Indicator
>
> The ninth-grade on-track indicator simply shows whether students are making sufficient progress in ninth grade to be likely to graduate. A student is on-track if she ends ninth grade with at least five full-year credits and no more than one semester F in a core course (English, math, science, or social science). Ninth-grade on-track is highly predictive of eventual graduation (80 percent correct prediction).[A] It is more predictive of graduation than any other middle or high school predictor, other than the combinations of predictors that include twelfth-grade performance (i.e., those that are measured during the year of graduation, rather than several years prior), based on comparisons of studies from across the country.[B]
>
> A Allensworth and Easton (2005, 2007).
>
> B Bowers, Sprott, and Taff (2013).

Prior Research Shows Passing Classes and Earning High Grades in High School Are Essential for High School and College Graduation, While Test Scores Matter for College Access

There is often a perception that students' performance on tests is what matters for high school and college graduation. While there are innumerable studies showing significant relationships between test scores and educational attainment, grades are more strongly and consistently found to be related to educational attainment than test scores.[6] Furthermore, the relationship of test scores to high school and college graduation becomes small, once we take into account students' GPAs.[7] It is students' grades that ultimately matter more for high school and college graduation than their test performance because grades capture more of the factors relevant for student achievement than test scores. This does not mean that test scores are irrelevant—it is easier for students with higher tested skills to get good grades—but a focus on test scores as the dominant factor affecting college readiness would be misplaced. For this reason, this report focuses on more than just test scores as indicators of preparation for high school and college.

There is also a fairly widely held perception that students' background factors are more deterministic of whether they graduate than their grades. However, while background factors (e.g., race, gender, and economic status) are related to high school graduation, once we take into account students' course grades, background factors and test scores do little to further predict students' future educational attainment.[8]

Passing classes is essential to graduate high school. To obtain a diploma, students need to accumulate credits. That means they need to pass their classes. For most dropouts, the pattern of course failures begins in the ninth grade; failures then accumulate in later grades, until they are so far behind that they cannot catch up. As a result, a simple indicator of whether students are on-track or not in ninth grade, based on failures in the ninth-grade year (see box above; *The Ninth-Grade On-Track Indicator*), is very predictive of eventual graduation, and accounts for almost all of the differences in graduation rates by students' race, gender, economic status, and other background characteristics, including test scores.[9] Each semester course that a student fails in ninth grade lowers the probability of graduating by 15 percentage points.[10] For this reason, passing ninth-grade courses is one of the key outcomes examined in this report.

High grades in high school are essential for college graduation. While passing courses is critical for graduating from high school, it is not enough to be ready for college. Students who are likely to succeed in college

---

6 Rumburger and Lim (2008); Allensworth and Easton (2007).
7 Geiser and Santelices (2007); Roderick et al. (2006); Bowen, Chingos, and McPherson (2009); Allensworth (2013).
8 Allensworth and Easton (2007); Allensworth (2013).
9 Allensworth and Easton (2007); Allensworth (2013).
10 Allensworth and Easton (2007).

are not merely passing courses; they are working hard and earning high grades. Research in Chicago, and across the country, has found that students' high school grades are, by far, the most important predictor of getting into college and eventually graduating—more important than ACT or SAT scores or high school coursework.[11] A student who earns at least a B average in high school has a 50/50 chance of getting a four-year college degree (**see Appendix A** for more information).[12] Therefore, we focus on students' probability of earning high grades as the leading indicator of college readiness. Test scores also play a role in college graduation, particularly in giving students access to more selective colleges.[13] College selection matters for graduation because students with the same high school records are more likely to graduate at some colleges than others.

High test scores help students get access to college. When colleges make entrance decisions, they usually rely on both students' grades and their scores on college entrance exams (the ACT and SAT). For this reason, higher scores on the college entrance exams help students gain access to more selective colleges and programs (**see Appendix A** for more information). High test scores also can help students obtain scholarships. In Chicago, all students take the ACT college entrance exam in the spring of their junior year, as part of the state testing system. They can use those scores for applications to college. They also take ACT-aligned EPAS exams in earlier years—the EXPLORE in the fall of their eighth- and ninth-grade years and the PLAN in the fall of their tenth-grade year. These tests include ACT college-readiness benchmarks—scores that ACT has determined give students a 50/50 chance of earning grades of B or better when they get to college, if they continue to make normal progress. Therefore, we also include scores on ACT's EPAS tests as outcomes in this study.

Prior Research Shows Links Between Students' Middle Grade Performance and High School Outcomes

There are many studies that have shown relationships between students' middle grade performance and later outcomes.[14] However, researchers often identify significant relationships between middle and high school factors, without considering whether the middle school indicators are actually good predictors of later performance, for example, showing how many students are correctly identified as likely to succeed/fail in their classes or on their tests in high school. A few studies have specifically tried to discern the predictiveness of middle school indicators for high school performance. These studies provide a good starting point for considering the types of middle grade indicators that should be examined as indicators of high school readiness. They also allow us to compare patterns in Chicago to other places, which gives us a sense of whether the same indicators matter in different places.

Chronic absence or failure in middle school indicates high risk for eventual dropout. There is a growing body of work, across multiple cities, that consistently shows middle school attendance and course failures are strong predictors of whether students eventually obtain a high school diploma. Research on middle grade indicators in Philadelphia, Baltimore, New York, and three school districts in California (San Francisco, Fresno, and Long Beach) all found that, among the measures that were studied, course failures and low attendance in the middle grades were the strongest predictors of high school course failure or dropout.[15] As shown in Chapter 3, this is similar to what we find in Chicago. Studies in Philadelphia and Baltimore, which examined students' sixth-grade records, also found that an out-of-school suspension in sixth grade was highly predictive of not graduating from high school. Most of the studies also examined test scores and demographic characteristics—showing that, while they were related to high school graduation or on-track rates, they were less predictive than attendance or grades.

There are also a number of studies that link students' test scores to later grades and high school graduation and suggest that test scores can be used as early indicators of high school performance. These studies often fail to note the low predictive power of test scores, however, and rarely include students' grades and attendance in the models for comparison. One example of this is a study by ACT, Inc., which

Research Consistently Links Absence and Failures in Middle School to High School Dropout

Philadelphia: Neild and Balfanz (2006) examined eighth-grade indicators, while Balfanz, Herzog, and MacIver (2007) examined sixth-grade indicators to determine whether they could identify students with a very high probability of eventual dropout. At both grade levels, they found that students with Fs in math or English, less than 80 percent attendance, or an out-of-school suspension (in the sixth-grade study) were at high risk of not graduating. Students' demographic characteristics and their test scores were not as predictive as grades and attendance.

California: Kurlaender, Reardon, and Jackson (2008) examined the relationships between seventh-grade achievement indicators and high school graduation. Attendance was not one of their indicators; but they found that, among indicators studied, course failures in middle school were the strongest predictors of eventually not graduating among those they studied. Test scores, retention in the elementary and middle grades, and the timing of when students took algebra were similarly related to graduation—but not as strongly as course failures.

New York: Kieffer and Marinell (2012) examined students' fourth-grade test scores and attendance as predictors of being on-track for graduation in ninth grade, as well as changes in attendance and test scores from fourth through eighth grade. Course grades were not included in this study, but researchers found that both attendance and test scores in the early grades were predictive of being off-track for graduation in the ninth-grade year, along with declining attendance or test scores. Declining attendance through the middle grade years was particularly indicative that students were at elevated risk of not graduating.

Baltimore: The Baltimore Education Research Consortium (BERC, 2011) showed that chronic absenteeism, course failures, and suspensions in sixth grade were strongly associated with not graduating within one year of the expected date. Chronic absenteeism had the strongest relationship of all the indicators.

---

showed that students' eighth-grade EXPLORE exam could predict low grades in students' ninth-grade year, using data from 24 school districts that participated in their EPAS testing system. The study found that 22 percent of the variation in low ninth-grade GPAs could be explained by eighth-grade EXPLORE scores (ACT, Inc., 2008, p. 27).[16] Unfortunately, the study did not include indicators of middle grade attendance or course grades to compare with exam scores as indicators of later performance. Yet, the study did use an interesting set of measures of academic behaviors, from surveys of students, to determine whether self-reports of conduct, discipline, and relationships with school personnel improved the prediction. They found that those three self-reported student characteristics combined doubled the precision of their prediction of low GPAs, beyond test scores alone. Thus, while the authors conclude that test scores predict future grades, their analysis actually shows that factors other than test performance are critical for passing classes; while the focus of the study was on the predictiveness of test scores, the relationship was modest and dwarfed by other factors.

---

11 Bowen, Chingos, and McPherson (2009); Geiser and Santelices (2007); Roderick et al. (2006).
12 Roderick et al. (2006); Allensworth (2006); Bowen, Chingos, and McPherson (2011).
13 Roderick et al. (2006).
14 For example, Alexander, Entwisle, and Kabbani (2001); studies cited in Rumburger and Lim (2008).
15 The studies in Philadelphia (Neild and Balfanz, 2006; Balfanz, Herzog, and MacIver, 2007), Baltimore (BERC, 2011), and California (Kurlaender, Reardon, and Jackson, 2008) predicted high school graduation/dropout, while the New York study (Kieffer and Marinell, 2012) predicted ninth-grade on-track rates.
16 The 22 percent rate is calculated using the percent variance explained for ninth-grade low GPAs provided in the footnote to Figure 8. Figure 8 states that the EXPLORE composite explains 53 percent of the explained variance, while the footnote states that 52 percent of the total variance is explained.

Low test scores in the middle grades foretell low test scores at the end of high school. While test scores are not strongly predictive of students' later grades, students' test scores in the middle grades are highly predictive of their test scores at the end of high school. In California, for example, Zau and Betts (2008) examined whether indicators from grades four to nine could predict success on the California exit exam (CAHSEE); Kurlaender, Reardon, and Jackson (2008), likewise, examined the relationship between seventh-grade indicators and risk of failure on the CAHSEE. Both found that students having very weak test scores in the early grades were at high risk of failing the exit exam. Zau and Betts (2008) showed that they could predict students' California exit exam passing almost as well in fourth grade as they could in ninth. These two studies also found that students' course grades, behavior, and attendance in the primary grades could predict passing the CAHSEE. It is not clear from these studies the extent to which students' grades and attendance improve the prediction of CAHSEE failure, beyond prior test scores, as the variables were entered together in their statistical models. However, each was predictive.

ACT, Inc., has shown a strong relationship between their eighth-grade EXPLORE exam and student performance on the corresponding eleventh-grade ACT exam. Furthermore, they have shown that prior test scores eclipse other factors in predicting ACT scores. Entering eighth-grade test scores are far more predictive of eleventh- and twelfth-grade ACT scores than students' coursework, grades, or background characteristics during high school.[17] In their words, *"the level of academic achievement that students attain by eighth grade [their EXPLORE score] has a larger impact on their [ACT score] by the time they graduate from high school than anything that happens academically in high school."* Their interpretation of this relationship is that early intervention is important. They do not study early intervention, however, to see if this makes a difference in later performance.

All of these findings, however, could also suggest that exam performance may not be strongly malleable. If students' test scores at the end of high school can be predicted as well in fourth grade as in ninth grade, and if students' high school experiences matter little for their ACT scores compared to their prior test scores, how much do students' experiences in school actually matter for test scores at all?

As we show in this report, we find only small differences in students' test score growth across the middle grade years. No students with low performance in fifth grade make up enough ground to have average performance by eighth grade, especially in reading. The same pattern can be seen in Kieffer and Marinell's (2012) study in New York, described earlier. They observe very little variation in test score growth from fourth through eighth grade, relative to the size of the gaps that exist initially. We find that, while there is substantial year-to-year variation in gains, differences tend to even out when multiple years are considered and are modest relative to the differences in test scores that students start out with in the early grades. This brings up questions about how effective interventions around test score growth can be for reducing inequities in performance, even if students are identified as at risk early on, as long as all schools have similar resources, incentives, and approaches.

This Study Extends Prior Research on Middle Grade Indicators

This study builds off prior research and extends the analysis of middle grade performance by asking questions that have not been addressed before:

Should schools consider a broader range of indicators, beyond test scores, grades, attendance, and discipline, such as grit and test score growth? Prior studies have found relationships of middle school test scores, grades, attendance, and discipline records with high school outcomes, so we include these as potential indicators of high school success. We also include change during the middle grade years in these indicators, since Kieffer and Marinell (2012) found them to be predictive in New York. Prior research in Chicago, and elsewhere, has shown that it is not just students' absolute skill levels that are related to passing classes and getting good grades, but their skills relative to classroom peers; even students with above-average achievement are at elevated risk of failure if their classroom peers have much higher skill levels.[18] Therefore, we include indicators of students' skills relative to their school cohort peers.

We also expand the indicators under consideration to include two noncognitive factors—students' self-reported grit (or tenacity) and their study behaviors in the middle grades. The concept of academic tenacity has received considerable attention in recent years as an important factor behind students' academic achievement.[19] Duckworth and her colleagues have found that grit, or perseverance to pursue long-term goals over the long-term, shows relationships with the grades of high-achieving students above and beyond their test scores (Duckworth et al., 2007). We include a subset of the grit scale used by Duckworth and colleagues as one of the indicators of middle grade performance. We also include a measure of students' study habits in the middle grades. Prior research on ninth-grade indicators found students' study habits predict ninth-grade pass rates and grades, above and beyond their attendance (Allensworth and Easton, 2007). We might expect that students' study habits in middle school predict their success when they get to high school.

Table 1 provides a list of the middle school indicators included in this study, and **Appendix B** lists the definition of all the indicators.

Which indicators are the most critical indicators to track? Many variables are related to later outcomes, but not all indicators are useful or necessary for an effective indicator system. With the wide array of data that are now available, practitioners often feel that they are drowning in data. It is important to critically analyze the ways which indicators are related to later outcomes, if practitioners are to focus on the best indicators to enact change. Chapter 1 discusses some of the issues to consider when evaluating indicators.

Do the indicators depend on where students attend middle and high school? Students' success in ninth grade is determined not only by their preparation but also by their experiences in the ninth grade. The structure and climate of the high school they attend will moderate the relationships between readiness indicators and ninth-grade outcomes. It could be, for example, that students of all skill levels are likely to fail in some high schools. Other high schools might have very strong student support systems in place, leading students to succeed who would have been at risk if they attended other schools. Thus, which indicators are most important, and the levels of those indicators that indicate risk, might depend on which high school students attend. The Kurlaender et al. (2008) study that compared three California districts found, for example, that while course failures and test scores were predictive of later outcomes in all districts, the timing of algebra was not. One can also see from their analysis that the threshold that puts students at risk of failing the CAHSEE varies by which district students attend—with students in Fresno at risk if they are simply *"below basic"* levels on the eighth-grade assessment, but students in the other districts at risk only if they are *"far below basic"* levels.

It is also possible that the predictiveness of indicators depends on which middle school a student attends. There is a prevailing belief that GPAs are not comparable across schools, meaning that two students with the same grades attending different middle schools may not be equally ready for high school. Often, concerns are raised that GPAs are easily manipulated. Yet the same could be said of many other potential indicators. For example, some schools seem to manipulate test scores, over-preparing students for the types of questions asked on the standardized assessment in a way that would not translate to different examinations taken in later years.[20] Thus, there may be a different threshold of risk for an indicator, based on which middle school a student attends.

Who is at risk for not being college-ready, as well as for not graduating? Prior work on middle school indicators has primarily focused on minimum expected levels of performance—graduating, passing classes, and passing exit exams. Middle grade educators also want to be

---

[17] ACT, Inc. (2008).
[18] Nomi and Allensworth (2013); Farkas, Sheehan, and Grobe (1990); Kelly (2008).
[19] The importance of perseverance for academic success gained considerable attention in a *New York Times Magazine* article (Tough, 2011), through a manuscript commissioned by the Bill and Melinda Gates Foundation (Dweck, Walton, and Cohen, 2011). We recently included it as one of a number of important noncognitive factors affecting grades in a UChicago CCSR report (Farrington et al., 2012).
[20] Luppescu et al. (2011); Koretz (2005, 2008).

TABLE 1

Middle Grade Indicators Included in the Study

	Middle Grade Indicators (Grades Five through Eight)
Course Performance	• Average grades in all core classes (both semesters combined in each year) • Average grades in English/language arts classes (both semesters combined in each year) • Average grades in math (both semesters combined in each year) • Number of course failures in core courses (both semesters combined) • Growth in GPA from grades five through eight * Grades are measured on a 4-point scale, where F=0 and A=4.
Attendance	• Attendance rate (number of days attended out of number of days enrolled in a given year) • Growth in attendance rates from grades five through eight
Test Scores	• Reading score on the ISAT in the spring of each year, grades six through eight • Subscales in the reading test in eighth grade: Vocabulary development, reading strategies, reading comprehension, literature, and extended-response results • Math score on the ISAT in the spring of each year, grades six through eight • Subscales in math test in eighth grade: Number sense, measurement, algebra, geometry, data analysis, statistics and probability, and extended-response results for mathematical knowledge, strategic knowledge, and explanation results • Average gain in test scores (reading and math) from grades six through eight • Relative skills: difference in reading/math score from average of eighth-grade peers in the same school * Middle grade test score indicators are based on the Illinois Standards Achievement Test. Information on these tests is available in ISBE (2012).
Suspensions and Misconduct	• Number of days suspended during the eighth-grade year • Number of serious (levels 4-6) infractions committed during the eighth-grade year * Serious infractions include battery/fighting/aggravated assault; theft/burglary/robbery; disorderly conduct; trespassing on CPS property; gang activity; use of firearm; arson; use of alcohol, narcotics; murder.

Noncognitive Factors	Measures obtained from surveys when students were in the seventh or eighth grade:
	
	Grit (Individual-level reliability in grades six through eight is 0.86.)
	To what extent do the following describe you:
	
	    A. I finish whatever I begin.
	    B. I am a hard worker.
	    C. I continue steadily toward my goals.
	    D. I don't give up easily.
	
	Not Like Me At All, Not Much Like Me, Somewhat Like Me, Mostly Like Me, Very Much Like Me
	
	Study Habits (Individual-level reliability in grades six through eight is 0.83.)
	How much do you agree with the following:
	
	    A. I set aside time to do my homework and study.
	    B. I try to do well on my schoolwork even when it isn't interesting to me.
	    C. If I need to study I don't go out with my friends.
	    D. I always study for tests.
	
	Strongly Disagree, Disagree, Agree, Strongly Agree

Background Characteristics	• Race, gender, special education status, neighborhood poverty level, neighborhood socioeconomic status, free/reduced price lunch status, and whether student entered high school older than age 14 • Neighborhood characteristics come from census data at the block group level on male unemployment, percentages of families below the poverty line, mean education levels, and median family income. Other characteristics are derived from school administrative data.

Note: See Appendix B for more information on data used for this study.

able to assess whether their students' performance puts them on a path to potentially succeed in college. To be on-track to college readiness, students should be making appropriate gains in learning the skills required for acceptance to college. These are generally measured by tests such as ACT's EPAS system. In Chicago, all students participate in the EPAS tests and take the ACT in eleventh grade. Even more importantly, they need to be performing at sufficiently high levels in their high school classes to earn high grades. Therefore, we examine readiness for high school in three ways: Ready to pass their ninth-grade classes; ready to meet college-readiness benchmarks at the end of ninth grade; and ready to earn high grades (As and Bs).

What is students' level of risk, who is at high risk, and who might go either way? It is useful to be able to identify students who have an extremely high risk of failing to meet an outcome (e.g., high risk of being off-track, not graduating, missing test benchmarks) because school personnel know with a high degree of certainty that the students they target are very likely to drop out—they are not wasting resources on students who will graduate without any intervention. These are *"high-yield"* indicators that very accurately identify students who will likely fail without falsely identifying students who will not fail.[21]

At the same time, there are limitations to just considering intervention plans for students at very high risk of failure. Students at very high risk of failure may not be very amenable to change. If a student has a 90 percent chance of dropping out, it will take a very substantial intervention to get that student to graduate. Yet, a student with a 50 percent chance of dropping out could go either way. A more modest intervention might be enough to get that student to succeed. Even though interventions would need to be targeted to a larger group, those interventions might be more effective and potentially less costly.

This suggests that indictor systems might want to identify students at moderate risk, as well as those at high risk, so that schools can design tiered intervention systems that match the level of support to the level of risk. It is also helpful to know students' general level of risk, given their middle grade performance, to help students and their families understand the connections between students' current progress and their likelihood of success in later years and to set goals that will encourage high levels of performance. These issues are discussed in more detail in Chapter 1.

How We Answered Questions About Middle Grade Indicators

To examine the ways in which middle grade indicators are predictive of high school success, we followed a cohort of students in the Chicago Public Schools from fifth to eleventh grade, using their academic records, survey data, and census information on their residential neighborhood. The report focuses on the cohort of students who were first-time ninth-graders in 2009-10, and who should have been in the eleventh grade in the 2011-12 school year. **See Appendix B on p.106** for a description of the cohort samples used in each analysis. The analyses focus on performance in the ninth-grade year, showing whether middle grade factors were related to performance when students arrived in high school. We include some eleventh-grade outcomes to show whether it is likely students will eventually graduate and to show the achievement levels that give students access to college.

We examine the predictiveness of each middle grade indicator for each ninth-grade outcome. We examine them alone and in combination—whether each adds new information for predicting the outcome beyond the others, or depends on values of others. We try to determine what minimal combination of predictors is the most accurate. We also examine the precision in the prediction—who can be identified for intervention or success with high certainty, and how accurately we can predict students' later performance from their middle grade records. Finally, we examine to what degree the predictions depend on which middle school or high school students attend.

---

21 For more information on high-yield indicators, see a summary in Heppen and Therriault (2008). *Developing Early Warning Systems to Identify Potential High School Dropouts*. Retrieved from: http://www.betterhighschools.org/pubs/documents/IssueBrief_EarlyWarningSystemsGuide.pdf.

After determining the best predictors of each outcome, we examine the degree to which the best indicators change across the middle grade years. We examined student performance from fifth through eighth grade, whether performance tended to change on average, and the degree to which some students showed more growth or decline than others. We also examined the extent to which these changes could be attributed to the school that students attended.

Finally, we discuss the implications of this work for middle school and high school practitioners. The findings in this report suggest that simplistic calls for *"early intervention"* may not be the best solution. Students' experiences in high school moderate the degree to which students succeed, above and beyond their qualifications upon leaving middle school. Many students who perform well in the middle grades do not graduate from high school ready for college. High schools could make use of middle grade indicators to make sure students are reaching their potential.

CHAPTER 1

Issues in Developing and Evaluating Indicators

There are myriad studies that show relationships between students' academic performance, family characteristics, neighborhood factors, and personal factors in the elementary and middle grades with their academic performance in high school. Many characteristics of students in the middle grades are related to their performance in high school, but it is difficult for practitioners to track a large number of indicators and develop intervention strategies for all of them. It is also inefficient to focus efforts on factors that have only weak, indirect, or spurious relationships with the high school outcomes, when similar amounts of effort could have a bigger pay-off if focused on factors with stronger direct relationships with high school outcomes. An effective early warning indicator system focuses attention on factors that have strong and direct relationships with later performance, and that also are malleable with school practice.

> This chapter discusses issues to consider when designing indicator systems—which indicators to use and how many, as well as implications of different cut-offs for identifying risk. This chapter also explains how to read the graphs that are used in subsequent chapters to compare indicators.

Which Indicators Produce the Most Accurate and Simple System?

The simpler an indicator system, the easier it is to track the indicators and develop intervention plans. Many potential indicators are correlated with high school outcomes, but it is not necessary to track all of them. If a small number of indicators is just as effective at indicating students' risk of later outcomes as a larger number of indicators, school practitioners do not need to monitor the myriad elements that may be related to the outcome. Thus, one issue to consider is how to get the best prediction of later outcomes with the smallest number of indicators.

Another issue to consider is whether the indicator is useful only for prediction, or whether it also could be used as an intermediary outcome to drive change in the later outcome. For example, in Chicago, schools use ninth-grade attendance and failure rates as indicators of eventual high school graduation; they provide fairly accurate predictions of students' risk. However, they are strongly related to high school graduation because they directly affect it—when students miss class and fail classes they do not accumulate the credits they need to graduate. Therefore, Chicago designed student monitoring systems around the ninth-grade indicators of attendance and course failure, and schools used those systems to improve attendance and pass rates in the ninth grade. This provided a mechanism for driving improvements through use of the indicator system itself.

In contrast, other indicators are correlated with high school outcomes simply because they are related to other factors—their relationship with the outcome is spurious and would not be a good lever for moving student outcomes. Other factors have an indirect relationship with the high school outcome—affecting it by affecting some other factor that has a direct relationship. For example, poverty status is related to high school graduation, but the relationship is indirect—poverty affects students' attendance rates and grades, and their grades affect whether students graduate.

Efforts to track and improve indicators that directly affect the outcome will generally be most effective for improving the outcome, because no other intervening variable has to change as a result of the intervention. Efforts to change indicators that have indirect relationships could also improve outcomes, but only to the extent that the mediating factor also changes. Often practitioners are frustrated when the results of their efforts do not translate into improvements in the outcomes that were targeted for improvement; this occurs when their efforts are aimed at indicators that are only modestly or indirectly related to the targeted outcome.

It is standard practice for researchers to enter potential predictors of an outcome into a statistical model and then determine which of them show significant relationships through the regression coefficients, controlling for other predictors in the model. However, because the predictors are correlated with each other, it is not possible to use regression coefficients to decide which predictors are actually the best to track.[22] This approach results in unnecessarily complicated indicator systems that include predictors that do not necessarily improve the prediction of the outcome beyond all of the others. Instead, the model statistics (R^2) are much more useful than significance levels on coefficients for determining which potential indicators produce the simplest indicator system.

The first step in selecting the best indicators is to identify which has the strongest relationship to the outcome. The easiest way to do this is to compare correlation coefficients; although, as discussed in the next section, researchers should also consider the predictive power of the indicators and issues of sensitivity and specificity, as well as cut-off levels that are meaningful for predicting later outcomes. Once the strongest predictor is identified, the next issue is whether the prediction could be improved by considering other indicators. Model statistics on the amount of variation in the outcome that is explained by the predictors (e.g., the R^2 or pseudo-R^2), along with changes in the accuracy of predictions (e.g., the percentage of students correctly classified), can be used to determine whether the prediction is significantly better with any given additional predictor. If the model does not explain more variation, and the percentage of students correctly predicted to succeed or fail does not significantly improve, then the additional indicator is superfluous. Appendix C describes the methods used for comparing indicators in this study.

To some extent, this approach also makes it likely that indicators that are most directly related to the later outcome will be chosen over indicators that have indirect or spurious relationships with the outcome. Indicators that have direct relationships with the outcome will often—but not always—have the strongest relationships with the outcome, because no other intervening factor must change. Indicators with direct relationships will also continue to add to the prediction when other variables are included, because their relationship is not dependent on a third factor. Factors that have indirect or spurious relationships with the outcome will no longer contribute to the prediction, once the intervening variables (in the case of indirect effects) or prior variables (in the case of spurious relationships) are included in the model.[23] At the same time, just because an indicator has a strong relationship with an outcome does not necessarily mean that it has a direct effect; such an interpretation would depend on theory and on research designed to get at questions of causality. Furthermore, a predictor that has an indirect or spurious relationship with an outcome can still be useful in an indicator system if it adds to the prediction of the later outcome.

Chapters 3 and 6 show the strength of the relationships of each potential middle grade indicator with each of the high school outcomes, and the degree to which combinations of potential indicators improve the prediction above and beyond predictions that use smaller numbers of indicators. Tables of potential indicators and combinations of indicators are included so that readers can compare the strength of the relationship of each potential indicator with the high school outcome, and see how it changes the prediction. In all cases, prediction models that use just two or three indicators are almost as predictive as models that use all possible indicators. Even though many factors are related to high school achievement, most are indirectly related to high school achievement through some combination of middle grade GPAs, attendance, or test scores.

---

22 The regression coefficients will potentially be strongly affected by multicollinearity. The distribution of shared variance could be arbitrarily attributed to two factors, when one factor is the most directly related, depending on which other variables are in the model. Some variables may be significant predictors of the outcome, but not add significantly more explanatory power beyond the other variables.

23 For more information on these issues, see Davis (1985).

How Accurate Are the Predictions That Result from the Indicators?

Often, researchers identify factors as related to later outcomes, without showing the accuracy of predictions based on the indicator system—the degree to which students at risk are correctly identified or misidentified using the indicators. Although an indicator may be correlated with an outcome, the indicator might not substantially improve the prediction of that outcome beyond what would occur if we just assumed that all students were at risk or not at risk. This often occurs if an outcome is either very rare or very common. If an event is rare, even a student with an elevated risk is unlikely to experience it; the opposite is true for outcomes that almost all students achieve. An indicator may be able to precisely identify a subset of students who are at risk of not achieving an outcome—so that all of the students who are identified will fail to reach the outcome without intervention—but miss the majority of students who fail to achieve the outcome because too few students were identified as at risk.

When deciding which indicators to use and how to use them, researchers consider two primary issues. The first issue is the proportion of students who fail to meet an outcome who would be identified by the indicator as at risk of failure. This is known as the sensitivity of the indicator; a highly sensitive indicator of dropout would identify a large proportion of the students who drop out. The second issue is the false-positive or *"false alarm"* rate—the percentage of students who do not fail who are identified as at risk of failure by the indicator. This is also known as the false-positive proportion.[24] If only 60 percent of students flagged by an indicator actually fail, then there is a high rate of *"false alarms"* because 40 percent of students would succeed without any intervention. Indicator systems with a high false-positive rate have the potential to waste valuable resources.[25]

The false-positive issue was the primary driver of the indicator work done in Philadelphia by Neild and Balfanz (2006) and Balfanz, Herzog, and MacIver (2007) to identify high-yield indicators of dropout; students flagged with high-yield indicators had at least a 75 percent likelihood of dropping out. Using data on Philadelphia schools, the researchers looked to see whether they could find indicators of eventual dropout using data on students' performance in the middle grades. Using the 75 percent criterion, they found that an F in English or math and attendance lower than 80 percent were signals available in middle school that could be used for precise targeting of students at very high risk of not graduating. The Philadelphia indicators are highly useful because practitioners do not need to worry that students who are identified with these indicators will succeed without intervention.

High-yield indicators are useful for targeting interventions that are expensive or require substantial resources. Their high degree of precision among students who are flagged as at risk, however, comes at two potential costs. The first issue is the sensitivity of the indicator—the percentage of students who actually fail but are not identified with the high-yield indicator. In general, there is a trade-off between minimizing false positives (false alarms) and missing true positives (students who really will fail). This is a very substantial issue for Chicago, when we try to apply the high-yield indicators from Philadelphia. In Philadelphia, just over half of eventual dropouts were identified using the high-yield indicators.[26] But in Chicago, only a small percentage of eventual dropouts are identified with middle school high-yield indicators, as discussed in Chapter 3. If all strategies were based around students with a very high likelihood of failure, then the majority of students at risk for dropout would be missed in Chicago.

The second limitation of high-yield indicators is that interventions to change the outcome may be very resource-intensive, and there may not even be any known intervention that can get the students who are identified as at risk to eventually succeed. For example, if a student has a 90 percent chance of failing to graduate, an intervention that successfully lowers her risk by 30 percentage points still would not be enough to make

---

24 This is calculated as one minus the specificity, which is one minus the proportion of students who succeeded who were identified as succeeding.

25 For a description of these issues, see Bowers et al. (2013).

26 Neild and Balfanz (2006) correctly identified 54 percent of dropouts with their eighth-grade indicators.

her likely to graduate. On the other hand, a student who had a 50 percent risk of failing could go either way, and a modest intervention might be enough to make him succeed. Schools would not want to put an expensive intervention into play for students with a 50 percent risk, because half of the students would succeed without intervention, but these students would not be in need of a major intervention.

As school districts design strategies to address high school and college success, they can think about strategies for students with different levels of risk for failure or for not meeting college readiness goals. Similar to the Response to Intervention (RTI) approach, interventions with different levels of intensity could be targeted to students with different levels of risk. Students with moderate risk are in need of modest interventions, while most students at high risk will need very intensive interventions if they are to succeed. Thus, indicator systems might identify students with different levels of risk to match them with appropriate supports.

The chapters that follow use figures that compare the sensitivity of indicators with the false-positive rate.[27] Figure 1 provides a description of how to interpret these charts. Each dot on the chart represents the ability of an indicator, or a set of indicators, to accurately predict a later outcome. Indicators, or sets of indicators, that are able to identify all of the students who end up failing have a high sensitivity, and are represented by dots at the top end of the chart (where the sensitivity gets close to 1.0). Indicators, or sets of indicators, that correctly identify students who are at risk of failing without falsely identifying students as at risk who will succeed are represented by dots at the far left of the figure.

FIGURE 1
Chart for Comparing the Ability of Indicators to Predict Later Outcomes

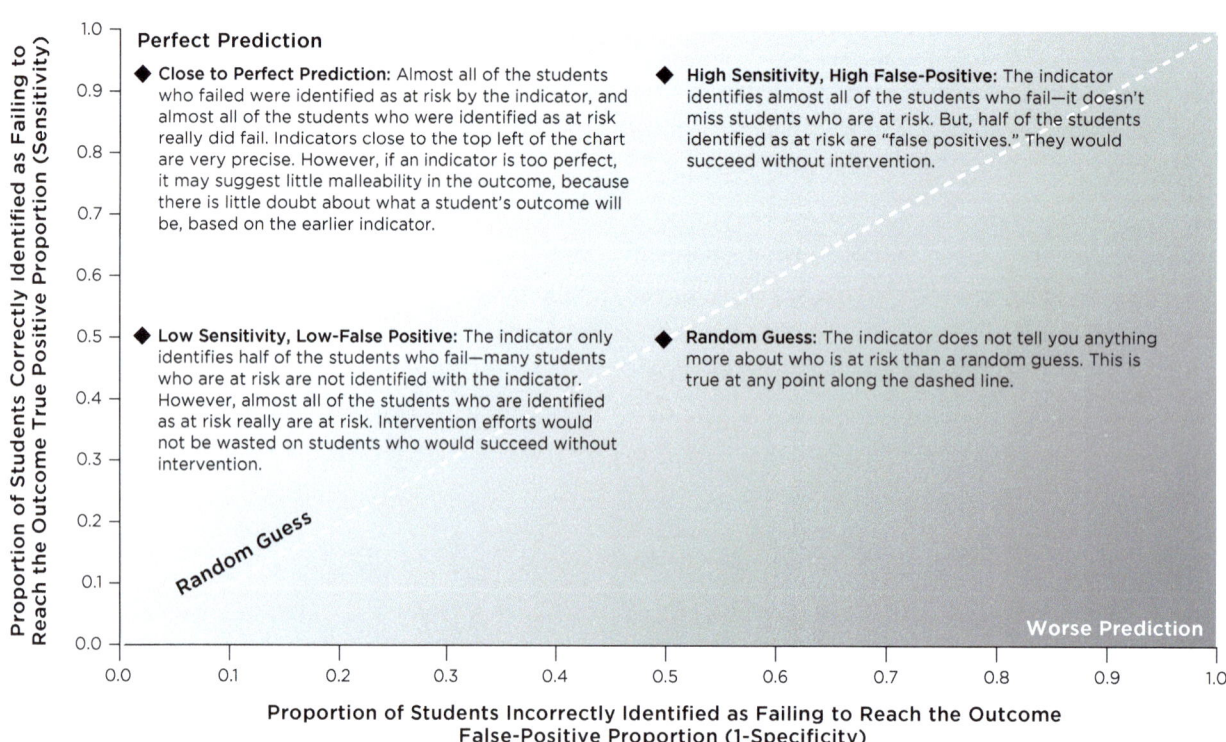

27 See Bowers et al. (2013) for more information about using this type of chart to compare the predictions of different indicators of high school dropout.

How Malleable Are the Indicators?

Another issue to consider is the extent to which the indicator is malleable and whether there are known strategies for moving it in a school. Indictors do not have to be malleable to be useful for identifying students' risk; non-malleable indicators may be very useful for targeting students for interventions if they are highly predictive. However, if indicators directly or indirectly affect the outcome, and if there are known ways to influence the indicators, they not only allow school practitioners to identify students' risk of failure but also give them an intermediate outcome to work on for moving the later outcome. For example, the ninth-grade early warning indicators used in Chicago around attendance and grades have been effective for getting more students on the path to graduation because schools have been able to develop effective strategies for actually improving students' ninth-grade attendance and course performance.

Indicators that are not within the power of practitioners to change cannot be used to improve school practices. For example, students' gender, age at entry into high school, and race might be associated with their performance in high school, but high school practitioners cannot develop strategies to change these background characteristics. A final question, then, is the extent to which there is evidence that schools can change the indicator to a degree that such efforts could have a substantial impact on the final outcome.

Chapter 8 begins to get at questions of malleability by examining the degree to which the best indicators of high school outcomes actually show different rates of growth across students over the middle grade years. If no student shows substantial change on an indicator over time, or if all students show the same amount of growth or decline over time, then there may not be known strategies to substantially change that indicator. If so, tracking the indicator may not be an effective means of improving the later outcome, compared to other indicators that are movable and also related to the later outcome.

In the end, the indicators that are likely to have the most potential to improve high school outcomes are those that have strong, direct relationships with high school outcomes, which identify students at risk with a high likelihood of precision, and which can be changed through intervention. Some of the most commonly used indicators that are in use today for decisions about who to target for interventions, and that have been identified by research as predicting later outcomes, do not meet these criteria, as discussed in subsequent chapters.

CHAPTER 2

Changes in Academic Performance from Eighth to Ninth Grade

Students' experiences in high school are often very different from their experiences in middle school. During the middle grades, student behavior is more closely monitored by teachers and other adults in the school than in high school. In some K-8 schools in Chicago, students have the same teacher for most of their classes. In these schools, there is no need to move from classroom to classroom, making it difficult to skip class. Even if a middle school is departmentalized, students are often accompanied from one class to another by a teacher. Once students enter high school, they experience much more freedom. They change classes and go to lunch and the library by themselves, with no adult supervision. They may see each teacher for less than an hour a day, making it less likely they will have an adult looking out for them throughout the day. As a result, it becomes easier for students to skip classes and students are less likely to have teachers notice when their grades start to slip. This has implications for their academic performance.[28]

Students' grades and attendance tend to decline considerably when they move from eighth to ninth grade. This is a pattern observed in many places across the country.[29] In Chicago, on average, GPAs go down by about half of a point when students move from eighth to ninth grade. As shown in **Figure 2**, only about 5 percent of students who were in eighth grade in the 2008-09 school year had failing GPAs (less than 1.0). One year later, almost one-fifth of these same students (18 percent) had GPAs of less than 1.0 when they were in ninth grade in the 2009-10 school year. In eighth grade, three-fourths of students had between a 2.0 and 4.0, which is a C, B, or A average. But by ninth grade, just over half had at least a C average (2.0) and less than a quarter (23 percent) received GPAs of 3.0 or higher in ninth grade.

This chapter shows how Chicago students' academic performance changes from eighth to ninth grade. There are dramatic decreases in school attendance and grades when students move into high school. Testing standards also change in ninth grade.

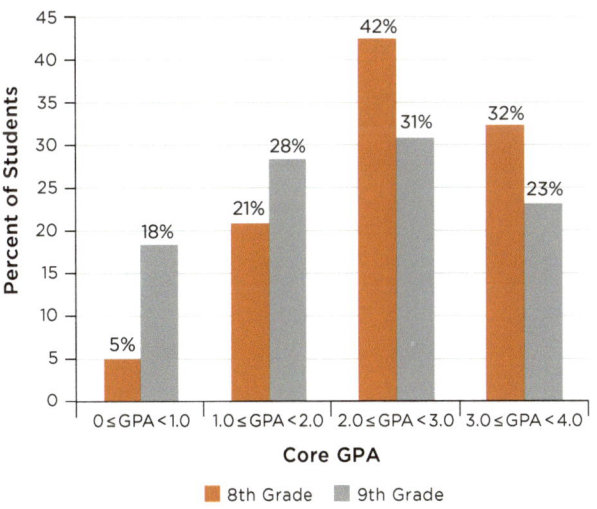

FIGURE 2

GPAs Decline from Eighth to Ninth Grade

Note: Average GPAs for students entering ninth grade in 2009-10 who were eighth-graders in 2008-09. The same set of students is represented in each year (eighth and ninth grade).

Grades decline across all types of students—both boys and girls, across race/ethnicity, and among students with high as well as low test scores (**see Table 2**). Both boys and girls show a decline in GPAs of about half a grade point. The decline also is similar

---

28 For further information about why students' grades and attendance fall when they enter high school, see the UChicago CCSR research series, *Free to Fail or On-Track to College*.

29 See Benner (2011) for a review of literature on the high school transition.

TABLE 2
Average Decline in GPA from Eighth to Ninth Grade by Subgroup

	Average Decline in GPA Points
Girls	-0.5
Boys	-0.5
African American	-0.5
Latino	-0.5
White	-0.5
Asian	-0.2
Top Quartile ISATs	-0.6
Bottom Quartile ISATs	-0.4

among African American, Latino, and white students. Only Asian students show a smaller decline in grades, with GPAs falling by 0.2 points instead of half of a point. One might think that students get poor grades in high school because they lack sufficient academic skills to handle high school courses. Students with high test scores, however, actually show slightly larger declines in grades over the high school transition than students with weak test scores, declining by 0.6 points versus 0.4 points, respectively.

One of the main reasons that students' GPAs fall when they enter high school is the change in students' attendance. Many students stop attending every class every day when they are in high school.[30] In eighth grade, only 5 percent of students had less than 80 percent attendance (**see Figure 3**); one year later, in ninth grade, a quarter of these same students had less than 80 percent attendance. A student with 80 percent attendance is missing, on average, one day of school a week. In eighth grade, 60 percent of students had attendance rates of 96 percent or higher. In ninth grade, only 37 percent of students attended at least 96 percent of the time. In just one year, students' attendance drops dramatically; this occurs when they transition into high school.

The main driver of the increase in absence rates comes from unexcused absences. Unexcused absences

FIGURE 3
Attendance Declines Dramatically from Eighth to Ninth Grade

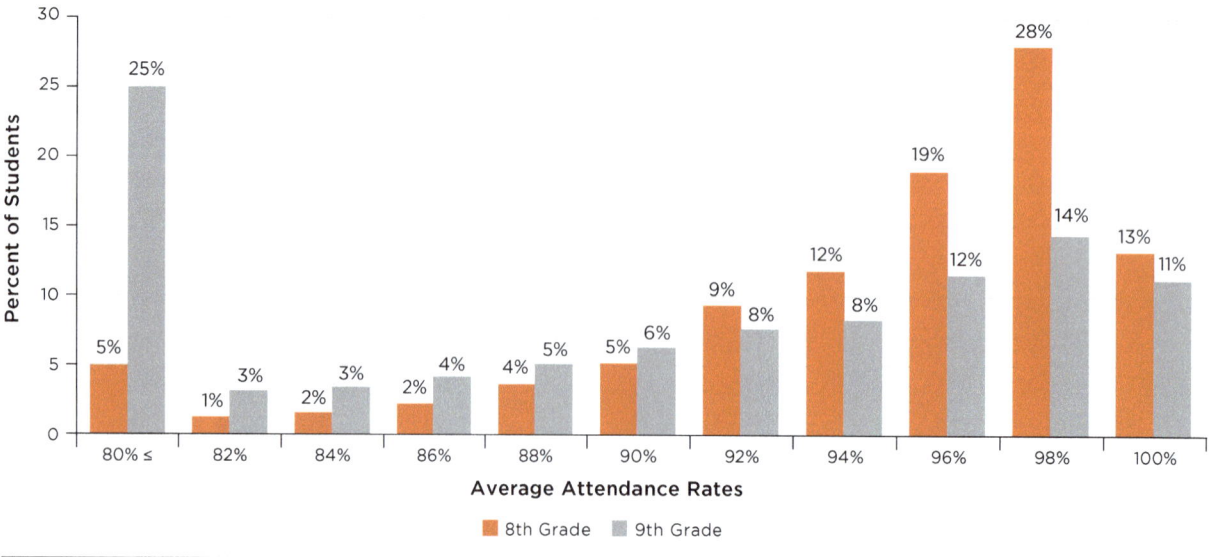

Note: Average attendance rates for students entering ninth grade in 2009-10 who were eighth-graders in 2008-09. The same set of students is represented in each year (eighth and ninth grade).

---

30 For an analysis of the reasons grades drop from eighth to ninth grade, see Rosenkranz et al. (2014).
31 For more information, see Rosenkranz et al. (2014).
32 Rosenkranz et al. (2014) used regression equations to predict students' grades in eighth grade and ninth grade with a series of variables that included test scores, demographic variables, attendance in each grade and students' reports of study habits. Study habits explained 14 percent of the decline in English grades and 13 percent of the decline in math grades. Attendance explained an additional 72 percent of the decline in English grades and 78 percent of the decline in math grades, beyond study habits. Together, these factors accounted for 86 percent of the decline in English grades and 91 percent of the decline in math grades.

quadruple from eighth to ninth grade, from five days to 21 days, on average.[31] At the same time, students also report putting less effort into studying and making sure they get their work done. According to the CPS student connection survey, 27 percent of seventh-graders in spring 2007 said they *"strongly agree"* that they *"try hard on schoolwork even if it is boring"*; two years later, in 2009 when they were ninth-graders, only 18 percent of the same group of students strongly agreed to the same question. There were also declines in the percentage of students who said they set aside time for homework and studying and the percentage of students who said they always study for tests. The changes in attendance and study habits account for most of the decline observed in students' grades; statistical models show that almost all of the gap in GPAs between eighth and ninth grade can be explained by students' attendance and study habits.[32]

Test Benchmarks Change, Making It Look Like Test Performance is Lower in High School

It can be difficult to compare students' performance on standardized tests from eighth to ninth grade because the tests that students take in middle school are different from the ones taken in high school. **Figure 4** visually compares students' performance, showing math scores for the same set of students and comparing the distribution of eighth-grade scores on the ISAT to the distribution of scores they received on the PLAN at the beginning of tenth grade. The distributions are placed above and below each other so that the average is at the same place and the range of scores, from the fifth to the 95th percentile on both tests, is shown in the figure. This allows us to compare the general distribution of scores across all students who take both tests.

One important difference between the two tests is where the benchmark is placed. As shown in **Figure 4**, the high school test standards (on the PLAN exam) are higher because schools are aiming towards ACT's college-readiness benchmark. Eighth-grade standards are based on the ISAT benchmarks set by the state, which are based on grade-level expectations.[33] In 2009, this same group of students was much less likely to reach PLAN benchmarks in high school than to meet the state standards in eighth grade, because it is set at a higher level. The benchmark for meeting state standards on the eighth-grade ISAT was raised in 2013, but it is still below the high school standard.

While the average eighth-grade student (the average math ISAT score is 267) met the eighth-grade math ISAT standards (based on 2013 standards as well as previous standards), the average tenth-grade student failed to meet the PLAN benchmark at 19 (the average math PLAN score is 16). The ISAT-score benchmarks are provided for each grade level in **Appendix D**. The PLAN exam is the middle test in ACT's EPAS sequence and benchmark scores indicate that students are performing at a level that gives them a 50 percent chance of achieving a B in college math, if they continue to make normal progress through the remainder of high school. EPAS-benchmark scores are also provided in **Appendix D**. It is most common for CPS students to have PLAN scores that are four to six points behind the benchmark (in the 13 to 16 point range). Most students gain just over a point a year on the EPAS system; thus, most students' PLAN scores are about four to six years of learning behind ACT's benchmark for the tenth grade on the math PLAN exam. As is the case with math, few students reach the benchmarks in reading and science (with benchmark scores of 17 and 21, respectively); it is more likely that students will reach the English benchmark on the PLAN, where the benchmark score is only 15.[34]

---

33 State standards shown in Figure 4 reflect the previous standards and the 2013 standards. Throughout the report we will focus on the performance levels defined by the cut scores in 2013, when the Illinois State Board of Education raised the performance levels. Appendix D shows the range of ISAT scores for each performance level for all grades before and after 2013.

34 In September 2013, ACT revised the ACT college readiness benchmarks with more recent data. This has resulted in changes to the reading and science benchmarks; the reading benchmark went up a point (from 17 to 18) and the science benchmark went down a point (from 21 to 20) for all tests in the EPAS series. For tests taken in 2013 and later, ACT will apply these revised benchmarks.

FIGURE 4

Test Score Standards and Score Distributions Are Very Different in Eighth Grade Than in High School

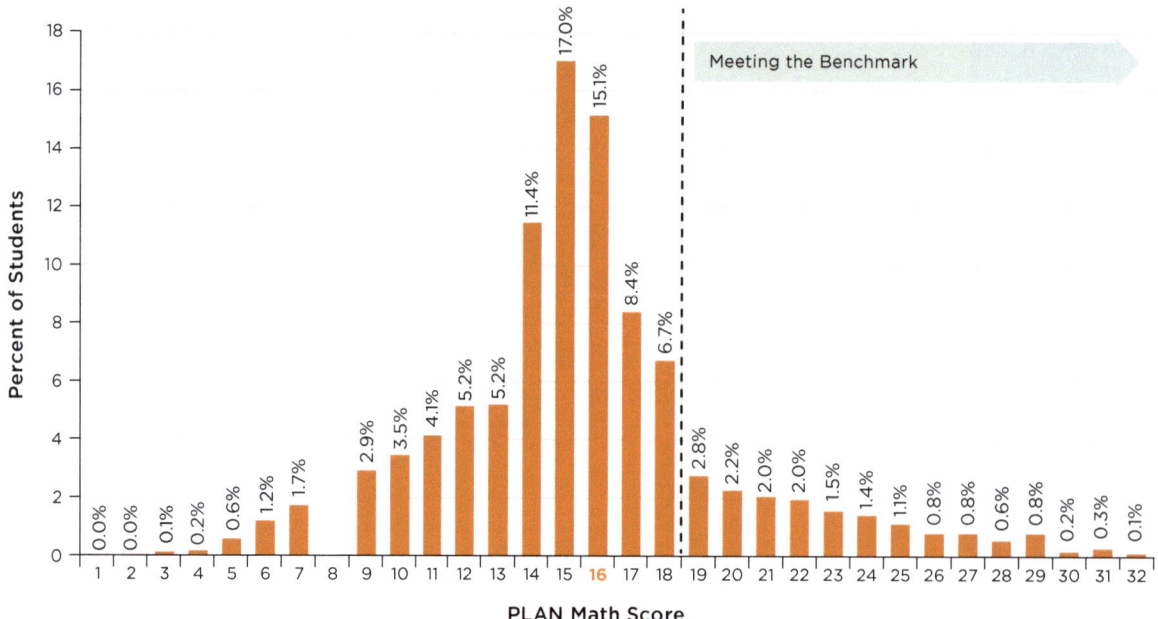

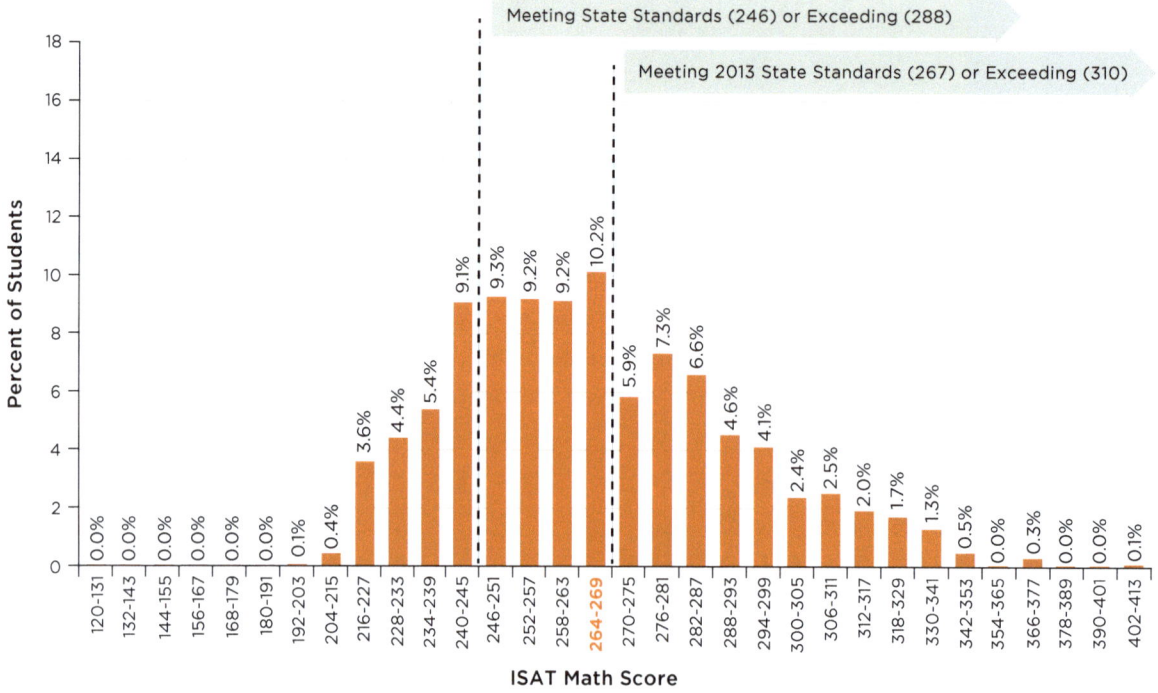

Note: Test score distributions for students entering ninth grade in 2009-10 who were eighth-graders in 2008-09 and had data for both test scores. ISAT scores come from the spring of 2009 when students were in eighth grade. PLAN scores come from the fall of 2010 when students were in tenth grade. The distributions are lined up so that the average scores are in the same horizontal location as well as the 5th and 95th percentiles. The orange highlighted numbers in the X-axis represent the average scores for this cohort of students: 16 for PLAN; 267 for ISAT.

In the top panel, no students scored an "8" on the PLAN, therefore there is no bar for that score category.

New ISAT Performance Levels

In 2013, the cut scores that define the ISAT performance levels were raised to better align with the more rigorous standards of the Common Core State Standards. The old cut point defining "meets standards" was 231 in reading and 246 in math in eighth grade, while the "exceeds standards" was 278 in reading and 288 in math. The new cut points that define "meets standards" went up to 248 in reading and 267 in math. These cut points are very close to the average scores in the district. The new cut points that define "exceeds standards" went down to 271 in reading and up to 310 for math. Prior to the change in the cut points for meeting and exceeding state standards, the *"exceeds standards"* point in reading was much harder to reach compared to the math *"exceeds standards"* point, with very few students exceeding standards in reading while many more were able to exceed standards in math in eighth grade.

Throughout this report, we focus on the performance levels defined by the cut scores in 2013 when the Illinois State Board of Education raised the performance levels.

Appendix D shows the performance levels before and after 2013.

Summary

Students' academic performance declines considerably between the middle grades and high school. They are missing many more days of classwork due to a large increase in unexcused absences, and they are less likely to exhibit strong study habits. Their grades decline by half of a GPA point from eighth to ninth grade, and the decline is exactly what would be predicted based on the change in attendance and study habits. Only about a quarter of students end their ninth-grade year with at least a B average, which means the vast majority are not on-track to be likely to succeed in college. Test scores are difficult to compare across assessments. Because the standards are much higher in high school, however, most students are far away from meeting the expected scores for their grade level at the start of tenth grade, while most were meeting state standards in eighth grade.

CHAPTER 3

Middle Grade Indicators of High School Course Performance

Passing high school classes is an essential step toward graduating from high school. When students fail one or more classes, they miss opportunities to accumulate credits needed for graduation. Each semester F that a student receives in ninth grade lowers their probability of graduating by about 20 percentage points (Allensworth and Easton, 2007). But merely passing classes is not sufficient for ensuring that students are prepared to succeed in college. Students with Cs and Ds in high school are very unlikely to succeed in college. In fact, only those earning average grades of B or higher (a 3.0 GPA) have close to a 50/50 chance of getting a four-year college degree (Roderick et al., 2006; Bowen, Chingos, and McPherson, 2009).

Unfortunately, many students receive very low grades in their ninth-grade classes. Around one-third (32 percent) of first-time ninth-graders in 2009 were *off-track* by the end of ninth grade, meaning they failed one or more core courses and did not accumulate enough credits to be promoted to tenth grade. Only one-quarter of all first-time ninth-graders (23 percent) had a GPA of 3.0 or higher by the end of the ninth grade. This sets the stage for poor grades throughout high school, as shown later in this report.

Advocates for improving high school graduation and college enrollment rates often ask if it is possible to intervene before high school and identify students in the middle grade years who are at risk of failure or of earning low grades in high school. In this chapter, we show the predictiveness of middle grade indicators for being on-track and earning As or Bs in ninth grade and whether a combination of indicators improve the prediction of each outcome. In addition, we look at how school effects influence the predictiveness of eighth-grade indicators for being on-track and earning high grades—whether the indicators work differently based on what school a student attends. Finally, we examine the predictiveness of middle grade indicators for being on-track and earning high grades in eleventh grade.

> This chapter shows how well students' academic performance in the middle grades predict their grades in high school and which combinations of indicators provide the best predictions. It examines predictions of ninth-grade on-track rates and ninth-grade GPAs, eleventh-grade progress to graduation and eleventh-grade GPAs, and grades in ninth-grade English and math classes.

Eighth-Grade Core GPA as a Predictor of High School Outcomes

Of all indicators tested, eighth-grade core GPA is the best predictor of being on-track at the end of ninth grade and of passing particular subjects. Each potential middle grade indicator was examined to determine how well it could predict whether students were on-track in ninth grade, based on its correlation, variance explained, and correct prediction rate. We also looked to see whether indicators had nonlinear relationships with on-track rates (where the indicator was more predictive at low or high levels), and whether combinations of indicators provided much better predictions. **Table 3** provides a partial list of the indicators that we examined; a complete list is provided in **Appendix E**.

Out of a large array of indicators of middle grade performance that we examined as potential indicators, the strongest predictor of being on-track at the end of ninth grade is students' eighth-grade core GPA.[35] However, the relationship is only moderately strong, with a correlation of 0.43 and a pseudo-R^2 of 0.18.

> ### What Is the R-Squared Statistic?
>
> The R-squared (R^2) statistic describes the proportion of variance explained in a linear regression model. Stated differently, it is a measure of how well a predictor, or a set of predictors, explains variation in an outcome. When there is only one predictor, the R-squared statistic is equal to the square of the correlation between the predictor and the outcome. In this study, we use R-squared statistics to tell us how well combinations of middle grade indicators predict high school outcomes. An R-squared statistic can range from 0 to 1, with higher values indicating a better prediction; a value of 0 means the indicator does not predict the outcome at all, while a value of 1 means it produces an exact prediction. Although there is no strict agreement on what constitutes a strong or weak R-squared, we used the following generally accepted guidelines in this project. **R-squares under 0.10 indicate a poor prediction** of the outcome; there is considerable variation in the outcome that is not explained by the indicators. This would be equivalent to a correlation of about 0.3 or less, if just one indicator were used as a predictor. **R-squares between 0.11 and 0.30 indicate a moderately good prediction** for the outcome (equivalent to a correlation of about 0.3 to 0.5 for a single indicator). **R-squares above 0.30 indicate a very good prediction** for the outcome (equivalent to a correlation of over 0.5 for a single indicator). An R-squared above 0.6 represents an extremely strong prediction (equivalent to a correlation of about 0.8 for a single indicator). A prediction level that is extremely high means that schools could very accurately predict students' later outcomes based on the indicators, which might suggest it is useful for targeting interventions. However, if the prediction is extremely high, it also means that the outcome might not be sufficiently malleable for interventions to be effective.

Seventh-grade core GPA is similarly as predictive of being on-track in ninth grade as eighth-grade core GPA; the correlation is 0.41 and the pseudo-R^2 for is 0.17.

Eighth-grade math and English grades are each slightly less predictive of ninth-grade on-track status than core GPA in either seventh or eighth grade (**Table E1 in Appendix E**). It is not surprising that core GPA, a measure of students' overall performance in eighth-grade core classes, is more predictive of on-track, also a measure of overall performance, than subject-specific GPAs. But, *core GPA is also more predictive of whether students pass their English or math classes and of their overall grades in both math and English than their prior grades in either subject.* (**Table E1 in Appendix E** shows the relationship of middle grade indicators with the probability of passing particular subjects—English and math—and with earning high grades in those subjects.) This suggests that course performance depends more on general learning behaviors—academic and noncognitive skills—rather than skills or interest in a particular subject. A student's grade in a single class contains less information about these learning behaviors and skills than grades across multiple classes, measured by core GPA.

After grades, eighth-grade attendance is the next most predictive indicator of passing ninth-grade classes (the pseudo-R^2 is 0.12 and correlation is 0.35) followed by the number of core course failures in eighth grade (the pseudo-R^2 is 0.10 and the correlation is -0.33), and subject-specific ISAT scores (the pseudo-R^2 between math ISAT and on-track is 0.08; the pseudo-R^2 between reading ISAT and on-track is 0.05).[36, 37] Combining math and reading ISAT scores does not improve the prediction of on-track rates. None of the other test-based metrics, such as growth in test scores over the middle grade years or relative rank on test scores compared to school peers, were even moderately predictive of passing ninth-grade classes.

---

35 Core GPA is calculated from the grades students receive across all core courses (i.e., math, English, science, and social science).

36 Including a squared term for attendance improved the prediction of on-track rates slightly; the pseudo-R^2 increases from 0.12 to 13. Including squared terms for GPA, as well as for reading and math ISAT scores, did not improve the predictiveness of these indicators.

37 We also examined ISAT subtest scores to determine if particular skills in math or reading were especially important to pass ninth-grade classes. (In math, subtests include algebra, analysis, geometry, measuring, and number sense. In reading, subtests include composition, literature, strategy, and vocabulary.) However, these subtests are no more predictive of ninth-grade pass rates than their overall test score in each subject. The overall score provides a more reliable estimate of students' skills as it is determined by a larger number of test items.

TABLE 3

Relationships of On-Track and Earning High Grades in Ninth Grade with Selected Middle Grade Variables

See Appendix E for the relationships of ninth-grade on-track and grades with more middle grade variables and combinations of variables, and with English and math grades.

Single Indicator	On-Track at the End of 9th Grade			Earning As or Bs in 9th-Grade Core Classes		
	Correlation	Pseudo-R^2	% Correct	Correlation	Pseudo-R^2	% Correct
8th-Grade Core GPA with Squared Term	0.43	0.18 0.18	0.74 0.74	0.44	0.21 0.21	0.81 0.81
8th-Grade Math GPA	0.38	0.14	0.72	0.38	0.15	0.79
8th-Grade English GPA	0.40	0.15	0.73	0.40	0.18	0.80
8th-Grade Core Course Failures	-0.33	0.10	0.72	-0.22	0.08	0.77
8th-Grade Attendance with Squared Term	0.35	0.12 0.13	0.73 0.73	0.23	0.08 0.09	0.77 0.77
8th-Grade Math ISAT with Squared Term	0.27	0.08 0.08	0.68 0.68	0.35	0.11 0.11	0.78 0.78
8th-Grade Reading ISAT with Squared Term	0.23	0.05 0.06	0.68 0.68	0.29	0.09 0.09	0.78 0.78
8th-Grade Suspensions	-0.24	0.06	0.71	-0.14	0.04	0.77
8th-Grade Misconduct	-0.16	0.03	0.70	-0.09	0.02	0.77
8th-Grade Grit[1]	0.08	0.01	0.72	0.06	0.00	0.74
8th-Grade Study Habits[1]	0.13	0.02	0.72	0.17	0.03	0.74
7th-Grade Core GPA	0.41	0.17	0.73	0.42	0.18	0.80
7th-Grade Attendance	0.29	0.08	0.71	0.21	0.07	0.77
7th-Grade Math ISAT	0.25	0.07	0.69	0.33	0.10	0.78
7th-Grade Reading ISAT	0.22	0.05	0.68	0.28	0.08	0.78
Combining Two 8th-Grade Indicators						
8th-Grade Core GPA + Attendance		0.21	0.75		0.22	0.81
8th-Grade Core GPA + Math ISAT		0.18	0.74		0.21	0.81
8th-Grade Math + Reading ISAT		0.08	0.68		0.12	0.79
Combining Three or More 8th-Grade Indicators						
8th-Grade Core GPA + Math ISAT + Reading ISAT		0.18	0.74		0.21	0.81
8th-Grade Core GPA + Attendance + Math ISAT + Reading ISAT		0.21	0.75		0.22	0.81
Background Characteristics[2]		0.06	0.70		0.09	0.78
8th-Grade Core GPA + Attendance + Math ISAT + Reading ISAT + Background Characteristics		0.21	0.76		0.24	0.81
8th-Grade Core GPA + Attendance + Math ISAT + Reading ISAT + Course Failures + Suspensions + Misconduct + Background Characteristics		0.21	0.76		0.24	0.81

TABLE 3: CONTINUED

Relationships of On-Track and Earning High Grades in Ninth Grade with Selected Middle Grade Variables

See Appendix E for the relationships of ninth-grade on-track and grades with more middle grade variables and combinations of variables, and with English and math grades.

Single Indicator	On-Track at the End of 9th Grade			Earning As or Bs in 9th-Grade Core Classes		
	Correlation	Pseudo-R^2	% Correct	Correlation	Pseudo-R^2	% Correct
Adding in 7th-Grade Indicators						
8th-Grade Core GPA + Attendance + Math ISAT + Reading ISAT + Seventh-Grade GPA		0.23	0.76		0.23	0.82
All 7th- and 8th-Grade Indicators		0.22	0.77		**0.25**	**0.82**
Adding in School Effects						
All 7th- and 8th-Grade Indicators + School Effects		0.33	0.79		0.34	0.84

Notes: 1) Grit and study habits are calculated from students' responses to items on UChicago CCSR's annual survey of CPS students. The elementary/middle grade student survey had a response rate of 59 percent in 2009. Because not all students answer the survey, the sample size for these models is smaller than the sample sizes for the other models included in this table. The percent of students who are on-track or earn high grades is slightly higher in this smaller sample resulting in a somewhat higher correct prediction rate for these two variables. 2) Background characteristics include race, gender, special education status, neighborhood poverty level, and socioeconomic status, free reduced price lunch status, and whether a student was older than 14 when entering high school. 3) The bolded numbers represent the best indicator or combination of indicators in each group.

Noncognitive skills in eighth grade, including grit and study habits, are not very predictive of whether students are on-track at the end of ninth grade. The pseudo-R^2 between study habits and on-track is only 0.02; the pseudo-R^2 between grit and passing math is zero. Although study habits and grit have been shown to be predictive of course performance during the same semester,[38] we do not find that they are very predictive of course performance one year later. This is consistent with research in other places showing weaker longitudinal relationships between grit and subsequent achievement than between grit and achievement measured at the same time.[39] This may be because students' demonstration of high levels of perseverance, as well as the demonstration of academic behaviors, is often context specific.[40] Students can show a great deal of perseverance in one area or context, and very little in another area (e.g., getting homework done but giving up on the mile run, showing up on time for one class but not another). Because the transition from middle school to high school involves moving from one kind of school context to a very different kind, it may be that the demonstration of some noncognitive factors, such as study habits and perseverance, do not necessarily carry over into high school when students have different teachers and a very different environment.

Prior research in Philadelphia found that serious behavior infractions and suspensions in middle school were related to later high school dropout, (Balfanz, Herzog, and MacIver, 2007), but we did not find these relationships to be strong in Chicago. The relationships were modest whether we examined infractions and suspensions in fifth or in eighth grade. The differences in prediction power between Chicago and Philadelphia may be due to differences in disciplinary practices, or record keeping around discipline, in the different cities. It is possible that there is less consistency in disciplinary practices across schools in Chicago than in Philadelphia, leading it to be an unreliable predictor.

Students' background characteristics were much less predictive of ninth grade on-track status than students' academic performance in the middle grades. Even when we combine many background factors together (e.g., race, gender, special education status, neighborhood poverty level, socioeconomic status, free or reduced priced lunch status, and age when entering high school), the prediction was less predictive (combined pseudo-R^2

FIGURE 5

On-Track Rates by Eighth-Grade Core GPA and Attendance

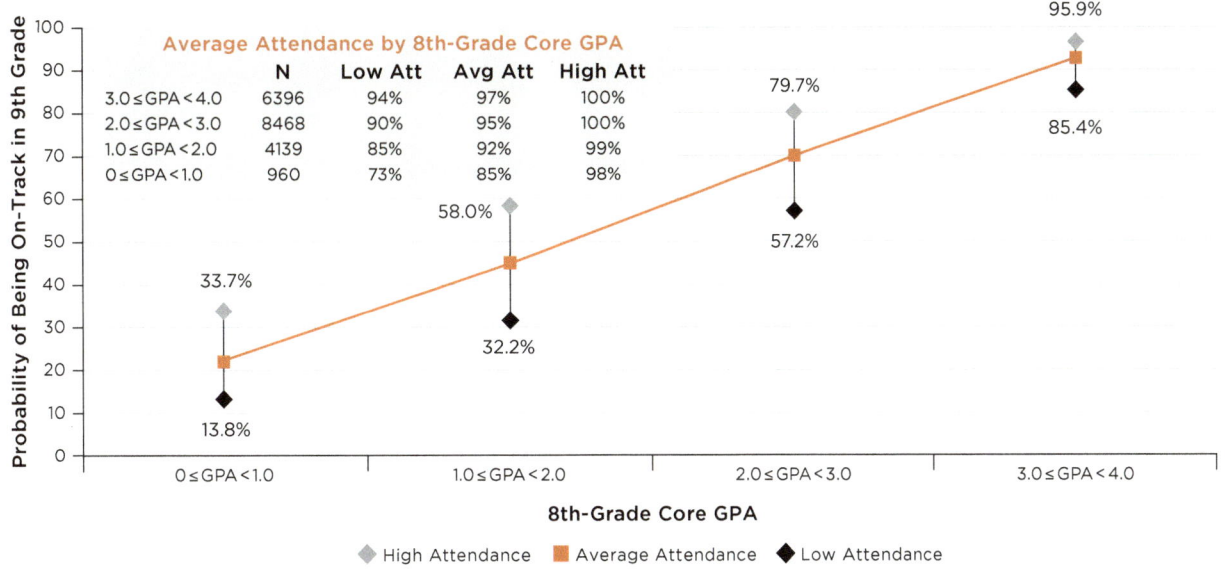

Note: These figures show students' predicted probability of being on-track based on their eighth-grade core GPA and either their attendance (see Figure 7) or math ISAT scores (see Figure 8). The orange squares in each figure show the predicted probability of being on-track for students with the same core GPA who have average attendance (or average ISAT scores). The gray diamonds show the predicted probability for students with the same eighth-grade core GPA who have above-average attendance (or ISAT scores). The black diamonds represent the predicted probability for students with below-average attendance (or ISAT scores). The table inside each figure shows how high, average, and low attendance or ISAT scores were defined for each level of core GPA.

=0.06) than when using any one of the middle grade academic indicators alone or in combination (eighth-grade GPA, test scores, or attendance).

Eighth-grade GPA combined with attendance provides a better prediction of who will be on-track than either alone; adding other indicators only marginally improves the prediction. Combining eighth-grade core GPA with eighth-grade attendance gives a better prediction of who will be on-track at the end of ninth grade than core GPA alone.[41] The pseudo-R^2 increases from 0.18 to 0.21 when attendance is used in addition to core GPA to predict ninth-grade on-track. Attendance also improves the prediction of who will pass their ninth-grade English and math classes than GPA alone (**see Appendix E**). **Figure 5** shows ninth-grade on-track rates by students' core GPA and attendance rates in eighth grade.[42, 43] At each GPA level less than 3.0, ninth-grade on-track rates are about 20 to 30 percentage points higher for students with high attendance rates in eighth grade than students with the same eighth-grade GPA but low attendance. For example, among students with

---

38 Allensworth and Easton (2007); Duckworth et al. (2007); Duckworth and Seligman (2005, 2006).
39 The correlations found between grit and students' grades in studies where both were measured concurrently are higher than those where grit is measured in the prior semester, and the prior year. See Duckworth et al. (2007); Duckworth and Seligman (2005, 2006).
40 See Farrington et al. (2012) for a discussion of noncognitive factors that affect students' course grades.
41 The pseudo-R^2 columns in Table 3 can be used to compare predictions using multiple indicators.
42 Figures 5 and 6 are based on statistical models in which core GPA and either attendance or ISAT scores are used to model the probability of being on-track at the end of ninth grade. We used the distribution of students at each level of core GPA to determine the high (1 standard deviation above mean), average, and low (1 standard deviation below the mean) attendance or ISAT scores were. Using these values and also coefficients from the model, we calculated the probability of passing for three groups of students at each level of core GPA.
43 Because attendance and grades are related to each other, high and low attendance are not defined in the same way at each GPA level. No students with high grades have very low attendance because low attendance interferes with getting good grades. The inset table in each figure shows what level of attendance is low, high, or average for students with particular GPAs. Low attendance is defined as one standard below the mean for students at each level of GPA; high attendance is one standard deviation above the mean. For students with above a 3.0 GPA, 94 percent attendance is low. Yet, 92 percent attendance is typical for students with a GPA between 1.0 and 2.0; for these students, low attendance is defined as 85 percent.

FIGURE 6
On-Track Rates by Eighth-Grade Core GPA and Math ISAT Scores

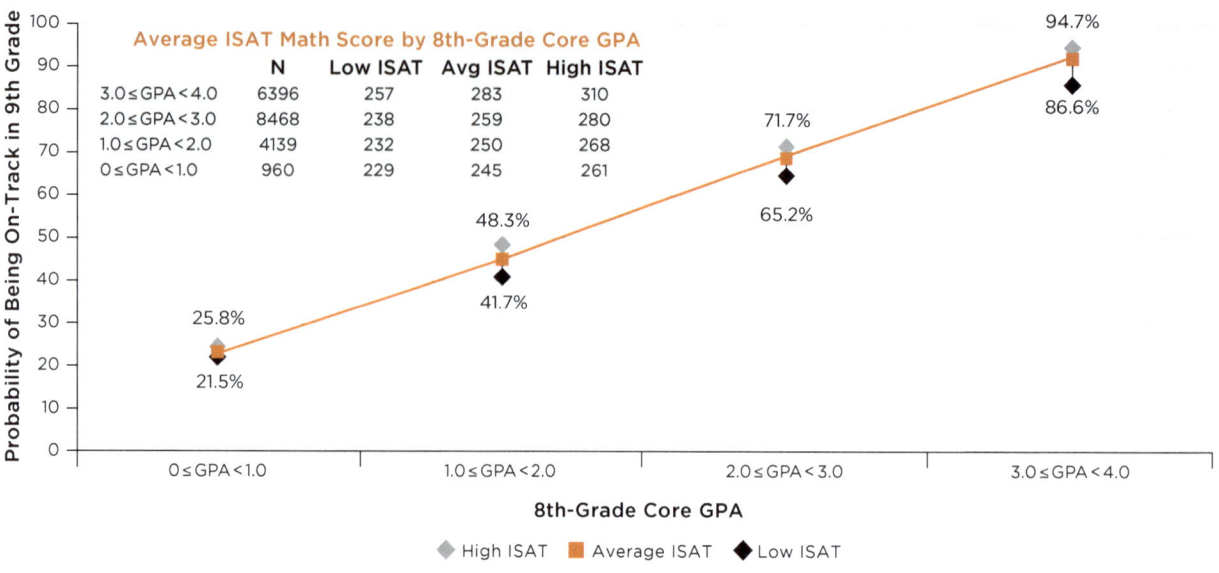

Note: These figures show students' predicted probability of being on-track based on their eighth-grade core GPA and either their attendance (see Figure 7) or math ISAT scores (see Figure 8). The orange squares in each figure show the predicted probability of being on-track for students with the same core GPA who have average attendance (or average ISAT scores). The gray diamonds show the predicted probability for students with the same eighth-grade core GPA who have above-average attendance (or ISAT scores). The black diamonds represent the predicted probability for students with below-average attendance (or ISAT scores). The table inside each figure shows how high, average, and low attendance or ISAT scores were defined for each level of core GPA.

GPAs between 1.0 and 2.0, those with strong attendance have a 58 percent likelihood of passing their ninth-grade math class, compared to a 32 percent likelihood for students with the same eighth-grade GPA but poor eighth-grade attendance.

Combining math ISAT scores with core GPA does not improve the prediction of who will be on-track at the end of ninth grade compared to GPA alone (**see Table 3**). As **Figure 6** shows, there is very little difference in on-track rates between students with high test scores and students with low test scores at each level of core GPA. Furthermore, the differences that do exist disappear when we incorporate attendance in the model, or if we use more nuanced versions of GPA (rather than 1-point differences). Once we know the grades and attendance of students in middle grade, their test scores provide almost no additional information about whether they will be on-track. At the same time, grades and attendance improve the prediction of who is on-track among students with similar test scores—**see Appendix C** for figures that show the contribution of grades and attendance to predicting on-track rates among students with similar test scores.

Combining other eighth-grade predictors, including student background characteristics, with eighth-grade core GPA and attendance does not improve the prediction of on-track rates beyond what is achieved from only using core GPA and attendance. However, the prediction can be improved somewhat by combining seventh- and eighth-grade GPA and eighth-grade attendance; the pseudo-R^2 increases to 0.23. But the improvement in the prediction that comes from using three indicators is not that much higher than the prediction that comes from using only two (eighth-grade core GPA and attendance). Adding in seventh-grade data also requires an extra year of data. The improvement in prediction may not warrant the increased complication in the indicator system.

Figure 7 graphically shows the degree to which individual predictors and combinations of predictors can identify students who are at risk of being off-track by the end of ninth grade (Y-axis), while also showing whether predictors are falsely identifying students as off-track (e.g., identifying students who are actually on-track as being off-track, X-axis). A predictor that is able to perfectly identify everyone who is off-track, while never falsely identifying anyone as being on-track, would appear in the upper left corner of the figure. ISAT

FIGURE 7

Sensitivity and Specificity of Eighth-Grade Indicators for Being On-Track at the End of Ninth Grade

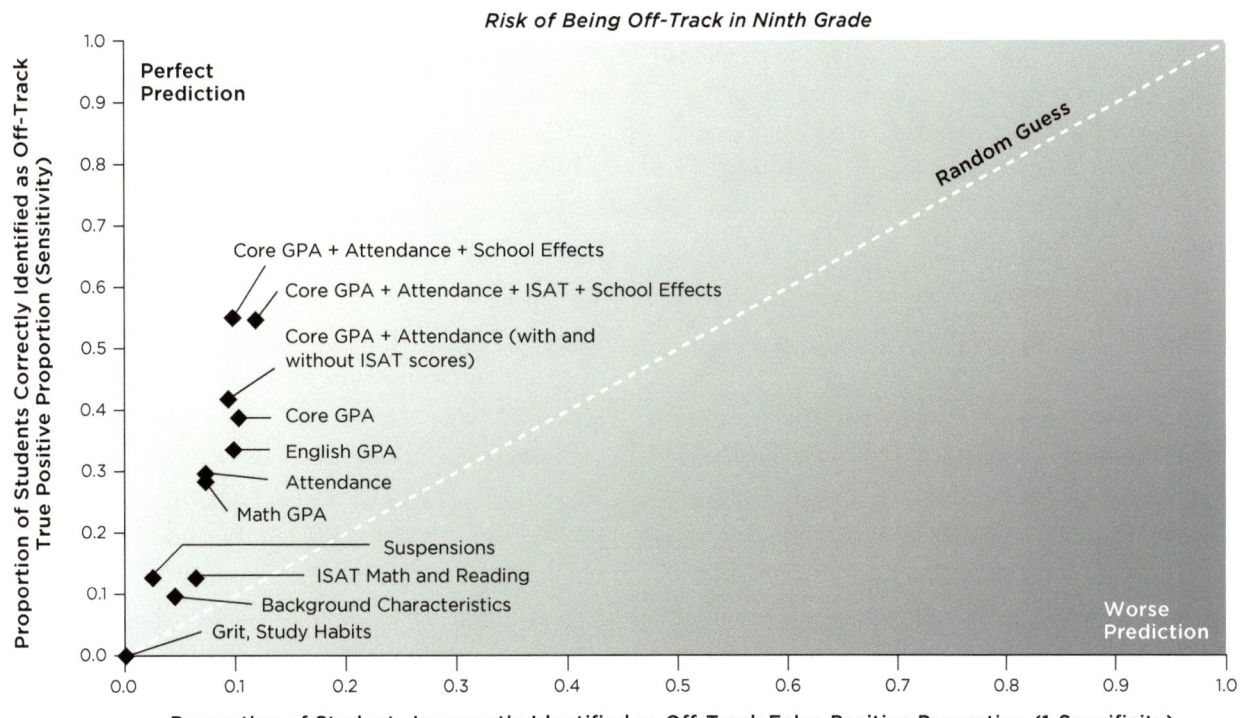

math and reading scores are in the bottom left of the chart—they only correctly identify about 10 percent of off-track students, but they do not misidentify many as off-track who are not. Only a small number of students would be identified as at risk of being off-track using test scores alone. Attendance is much better, identifying 30 percent of off-track students; eighth-grade core GPA is the best single predictor, identifying almost 40 percent of off-track students. GPA and attendance together identify 44 percent of off-track students, without misidentifying many as off-track who are not. Adding together all information about students prior to high school does not substantially improve the prediction beyond just using core GPA and attendance.

Eighth-grade core GPA is also the best predictor of earning high grades, followed by test scores and attendance. The best indicators of students' readiness to excel in high school classes are similar to those predicting the likelihood that students will pass their high school classes. Eighth-grade core GPA is the strongest predictor of whether students earn As or Bs in ninth grade (pseudo-R^2 is 0.21). Eighth-grade core GPA is also the best predictor of earning As or Bs in specific subjects, more so than students' grade in that particular subject (ninth-grade English and math classes; **see Table E1 in Appendix E**). Although core GPA is somewhat more predictive of earning high grades than being on-track, the relationship between core GPA and high grades is still only moderately strong. Seventh-grade core GPA is slightly less predictive than eighth-grade core GPA of earning high grades (pseudo-R^2 is 0.18), as are math and English GPAs (pseudo-R^2s are 0.15 and 0.18, respectively).

After middle school grades, ISAT scores in seventh and eighth grades are the next-best predictors of earning As or Bs in ninth grade. Eighth-grade math ISAT scores are associated with high grades with a pseudo-R^2 of 0.11, which is stronger than the relationship with on-track (pseudo-R^2 is 0.08). Combining eighth-grade math and reading ISAT scores slightly improves the prediction of earning high grades (pseudo-R^2 of 0.12). Seventh-grade math ISAT scores are associated with earning high grades with a pseudo-R^2 of 0.10. Math ISAT scores are a better predictor of high school grades than reading ISAT scores; they are much more predictive of math course grades and are even slightly better at predicting English course grades (see Appendix E).

Attendance and also the number of courses failed in eighth grade are somewhat less predictive of earning high grades than ISAT scores, with pseudo-R^2 scores of 0.08 each. Other eighth-grade metrics, including suspensions, grit, and study habits, are either only weakly or not at all associated with earning high grades in high school.

Attendance or ISAT scores improve the prediction of earning As or Bs beyond core GPA, but only among students with strong middle school grades.

Combinations of indicators only modestly improve the prediction of who earns As or Bs in high school beyond eighth-grade core GPA. This is because the improvement in prediction is only evident among high-achieving students. For example, combining eighth-grade attendance with core GPA differentiates substantially among students who earn a 3.0 or better in eighth grade but does not differentiate at all among students who earn less than a 2.0. Among eighth-graders with a GPA of at least 3.0, students with perfect attendance (100 percent) are 20 percentage points more likely to earn As or Bs than students with 94 percent attendance (see Figure 8). Among students who earn less than a 2.0, there is no difference between students with high versus low middle grade attendance in their likelihood of earning high grades in ninth grade.

Combining eighth-grade math ISAT scores with eighth-grade core GPA also differentiates among students who earned a 3.0 or better, but does not differentiate among students who earned less than a 2.0 in eighth grade. For example, eighth-graders with at least a 3.0 and high ISAT scores (310) are around 20 percentage points more likely to earn As or Bs than students with the same grades but low ISAT scores (257) (see Figure 9). But among students with less than a 2.0 GPA in high school, higher ISAT scores increase the probability of high grades by less than three percentage points. While test scores do not strongly differentiate who will earn high ninth-grade grades among students with the same middle school GPAs, middle school GPAs do strongly differentiate who earns high ninth-grade grades among students with the same test scores. These differences, along with the combination of test scores with attendance, can be found in Appendix C.

FIGURE 8

Probability of Earning As or Bs by Eighth-Grade Core GPA and Attendance

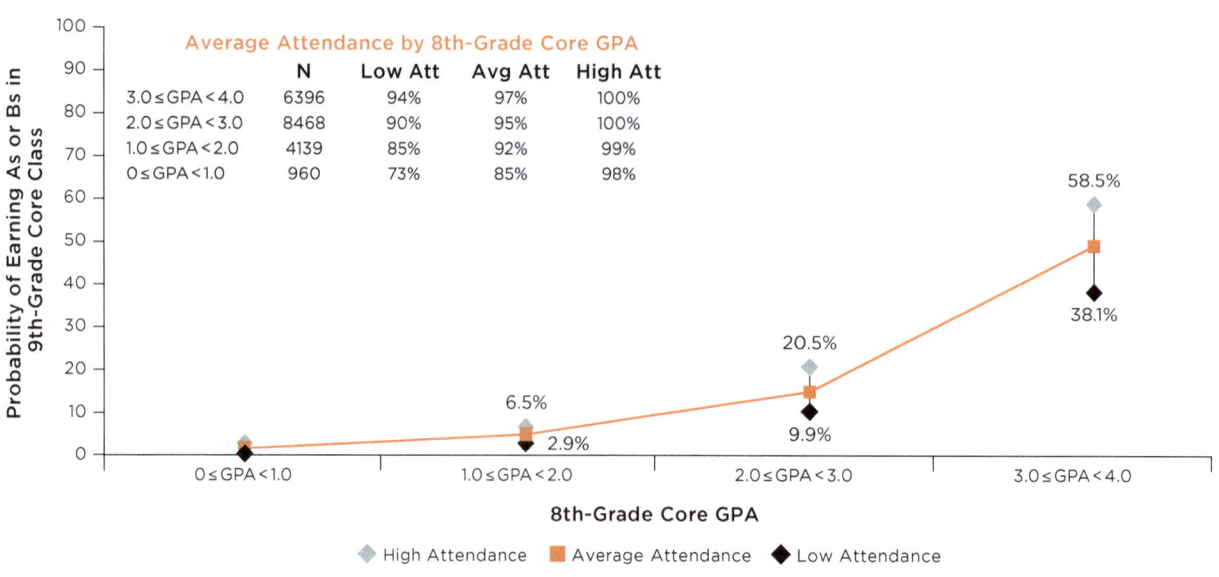

Note: These figures show students' predicted probability of earning high grades based on their eighth-grade core GPA and their attendance or math ISAT scores (see Figure 9). The orange squares in each figure show the predicted probability of earning high grades for students with the same core GPA who have average attendance (or average ISAT scores). The gray diamonds show the predicted probability for students with the same eighth-grade core GPA who have above-average attendance (or ISAT scores). The black diamonds represent the predicted probability for students with below-average attendance (or ISAT scores). The table inside each figure shows how high, average, and low attendance or ISAT scores were defined for each level of core GPA.

The prediction of who earns high grades can be improved further if background characteristics or seventh-grade GPA are also included as predictors along with core GPA and attendance (pseudo-R^2 increases to 0.24 by adding in background and to 0.23 by adding in seventh-grade core GPA. **See Table 3 on p.31.**). However, the improvement in prediction may not warrant the increased difficulty of bringing in data from a prior grade. Using all seventh- and eighth-grade indicators together yields only a slight further improvement in prediction (pseudo-R^2 is 0.25).

Figure 10 graphically compares the predictive ability of individual indicators, and their combination. Many of the indicators can correctly identify over 90 percent of students who earn a GPA of less than 3.0, but these predictions come with a relatively high rate of false positives. The fact that the majority of ninth-graders are not earning a GPA of at least 3.0 makes a true-positive prediction an easy task; the difficulty is in reducing the proportion of false-positive predictions (i.e., the proportion of students incorrectly identified as earning low grades). A model using eighth-grade attendance as a predictor suffers from a false-positive proportion of roughly 90 percent. A model using eighth-grade core GPA as a predictor improves that proportion to roughly 60 percent and is the best single indicator to predict the likelihood that a student will earn a GPA of less than 3.0 in ninth grade. Adding eighth-grade attendance rates and/or ISAT scores, as well as, core GPA reduces the proportion of false positives slightly. Adding all other potential indicators only marginally further improves the prediction.

Students with the same middle grade performance have different probabilities of being on-track or earning high grades in high school, depending on which schools they attend. Often, there is a perception that the same academic records may indicate different levels of performance if students come from one school versus another. For students with middle grade performance that is either very high or very low, middle grade performance predicts similar levels of success regardless of where they attended the middle grades. Students with particularly weak eighth-grade performance (i.e., GPA of 1.0 or below and attendance of 80 percent or below) are unlikely to either to be on-track or to earn high grades in ninth grade,

FIGURE 9

Probability of Earning As or Bs by Eighth-Grade Core GPA and Math ISAT Scores

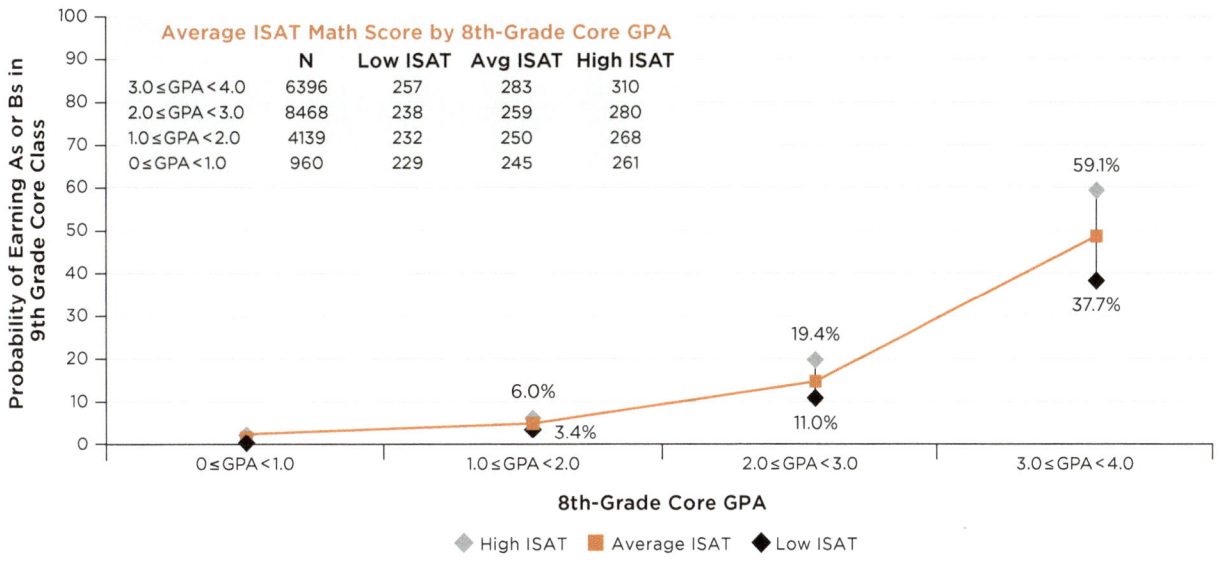

Note: These figures show students' predicted probability of earning high grades based on their eighth-grade core GPA and either their attendance (see Figure 8) or their math ISAT scores. The orange squares in each figure show the predicted probability of earning high grades for students with the same core GPA who have average attendance (or average ISAT scores). The gray diamonds show the predicted probability for students with the same eighth-grade core GPA who have above-average attendance (or ISAT scores). The black diamonds represent the predicted probability for students with below-average attendance (or ISAT scores). The table inside each figure shows how high, average, and low attendance or ISAT scores were defined for each level of core GPA.

FIGURE 10

Sensitivity and Specificity of Eighth-Grade Indicators for Earning As or Bs in Ninth Grade

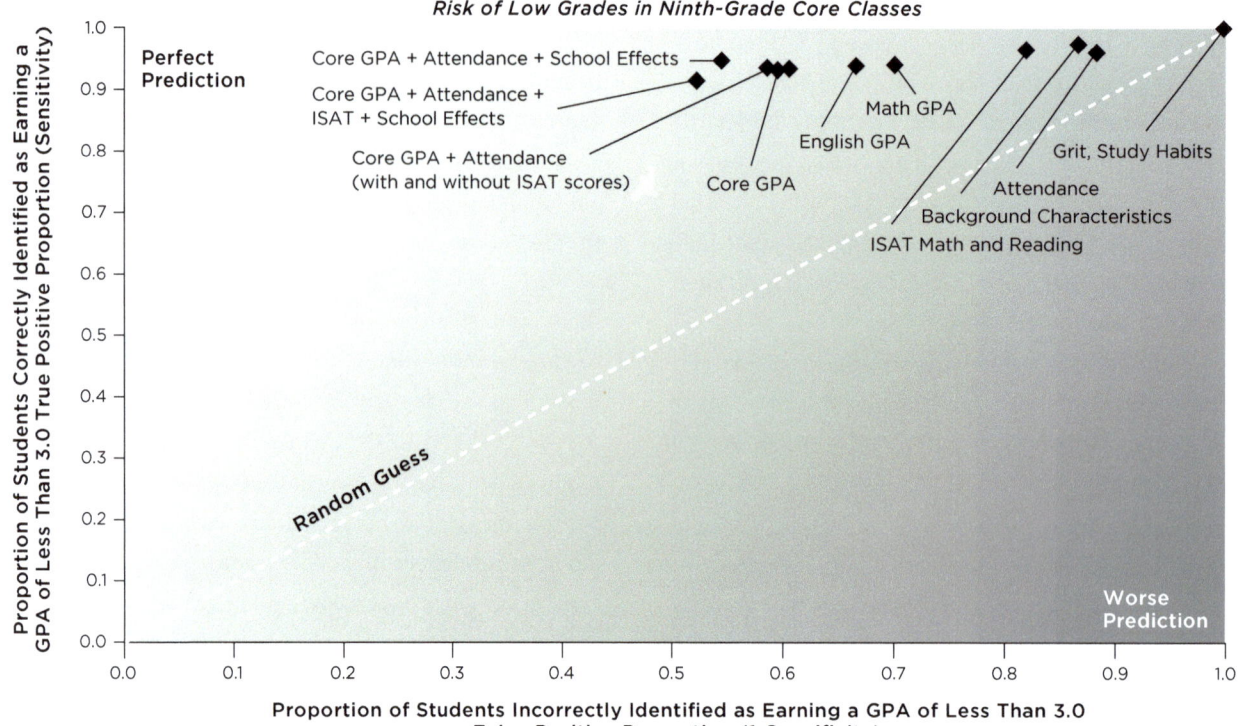

regardless of where they earned those low eighth-grade grades. (**See Figure 11, left panel; and Figure 12, left panel.**)[44] Students with strong eighth-grade performance (i.e., GPA 3.0 and above; attendance of 97 percent or better) are very unlikely to be off-track, regardless of where they attended middle school (**see Figure 11, left panel**). They are also very likely to earn high grades in high school, regardless of which school they attended for the middle grades. (**See Appendix C** for the methods of determining differences in outcomes by school.)

For everyone else, the likelihood of being on-track or earning high grades is different depending on which middle school they attended, comparing students with similar middle grade GPAs, attendance, and test scores. For students with a moderate chance of being on-track, based on eighth-grade indicators, their actual on-track rates can range from 41 to 66 percent, a difference of 25 percentage points, depending on where they went to middle school, net of any high school effects. For students with a moderate chance of earning high grades, their chances of earning high grades can vary from 47 to 72 percent, which is also a difference of 25 percentage points, depending on the middle schools they attended.

The middle grade schools where students perform better than would be expected in ninth grade tend to be schools that are generally higher-performing, and are serving more economically advantaged students.

---

44 How we calculated school effects: We first calculated each student's overall likelihood of being on-track using a logistic regression equation in which the outcome was modeled as a function of students' eighth-grade core GPA, attendance, and ISAT scores. The predicted value from this model was entered as a student-level predictor into cross-nested models, with observations simultaneously nested within students' middle school and their high school, predicting whether students were on-track or earning high grades in ninth grade. These models produce estimates of school effects on on-track rates for each middle and high school, net of the effects of the other school the student attended. The variance components from these models were used to determine school effects, net of students' individual qualifications and any effect of the other school the student attended (middle school effects net of high school effects and vice-versa). Figures 8 and 9 graphs school effects that were one standard deviation above and below the mean. The same procedure was used to determine school differences in the probability of earning As or Bs. More details on the models are provided in Appendix C.

FIGURE 11
Middle and High School Effects on the Probability of Being On-Track in Ninth Grade

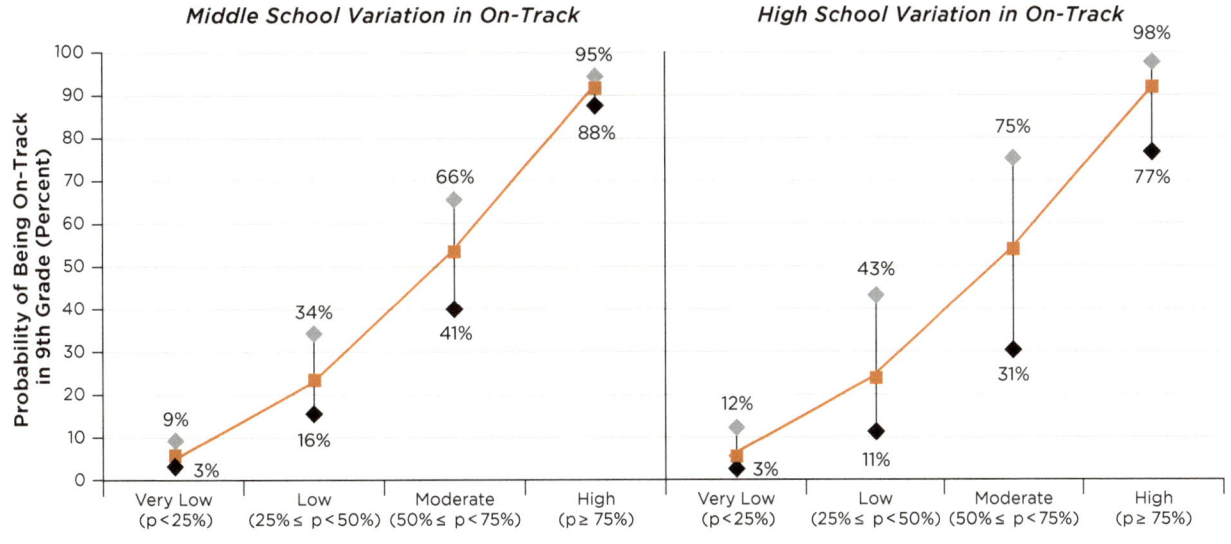

FIGURE 12
Middle and High School Effects on the Probability of Earning As or Bs in Ninth Grade

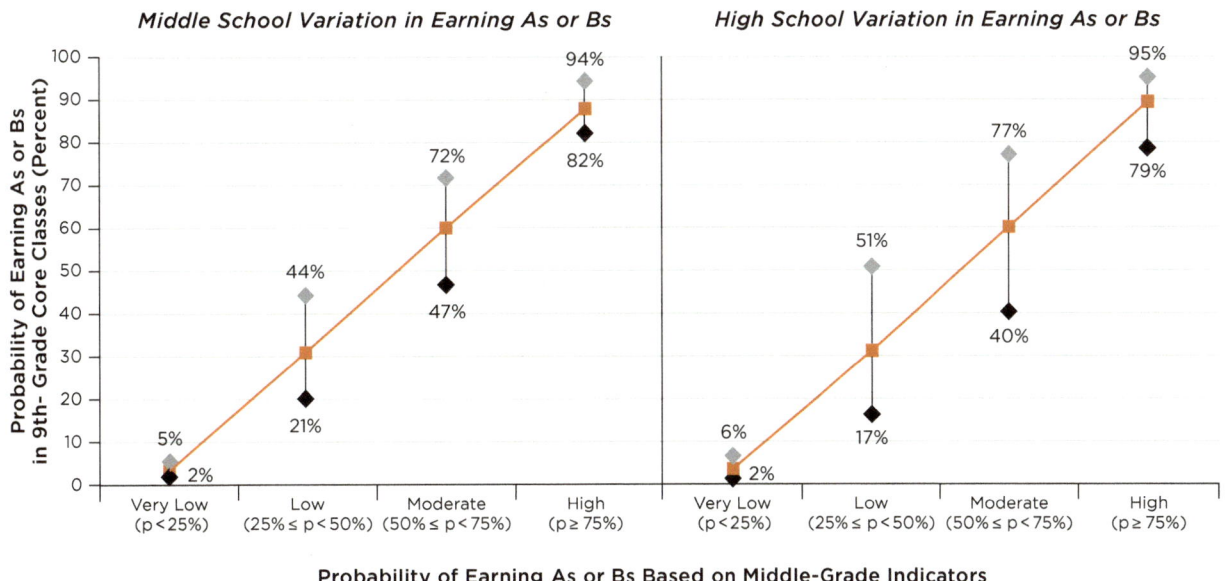

Note: These figures show the likelihood of being on-track (see Figure 11) and earning high grades (see Figure 12), depending on which elementary/middle school (left panel) or high school (right panel) students attend. The figures are based on cross-nested models in which students are nested in their elementary/middle school and also in their high school; see Appendix C for additional details. The orange squares in each graph represent the average predicted probability of being on-track or earning high grades based on students' eighth-grade core GPA, attendance, and math ISAT scores. The gray diamonds above the orange squares represent the predicted probability for students with similar levels of eighth-grade preparation attending schools with strong positive effects on the probability of being on-track or earning high grades. The black diamonds below the orange squares represent the predicted probability for students with similar levels of eighth-grade preparation attending schools with strong negative effects.

TABLE 4

Correlations Between School Characteristics and School-Level Residuals from Models Predicting Ninth-Grade On-Track and Earning As or Bs

	9th-Grade On-Track			Earning As and Bs in 9th-Grade Core Classes		
	Column A	Column B	Column C	Column D	Column E	Column F
	Correlations with Middle School Residual Incorporating High School Effects	Correlations with High School Residual Incorporating Middle School Effects	Correlations with Middle School Residual without Incorporating High School Effects	Correlations with Middle School Residual Incorporating High School Effects	Correlations with High School Residual Incorporating Middle School Effects	Correlations with Middle School Residual without Incorporating High School Effects
ISAT Math	0.21***	-0.26***	-0.03***	0.27***	-0.65***	0.09***
ISAT Reading	0.23***	-0.26***	-0.01	0.30***	-0.65***	0.09***
% Latino	0.04***	-0.15***	-0.11***	0.16***	0.012	0.22***
% African American	-0.16***	0.24***	0.08***	-0.31***	0.20***	0.28***
% White	0.23***	-0.24***	-0.01	0.34***	-0.49***	0.16***
% Over Age	-0.18***	0.24***	0.04***	-0.23***	0.56***	-0.08***
Percent Special Education	0.00	0.07***	0.05***	-0.04***	0.49***	-0.02**
Average Concentration of Poverty	-0.23***	0.29***	0.05***	-0.29***	0.45***	-0.14***
Average SES	0.09***	-0.03***	0.08***	-0.02*	0.31***	-0.18***
General	-0.13***	0.21***	-0.07***	-0.09***	0.42***	-0.01
Magnet	0.13***	-0.19***	0.05***	0.10***	-0.51***	0.01
Vocational	NA	-0.13***	NA	NA	-0.05***	NA
APC	NA	0.16***	NA	NA	0.12***	NA

Note: To generate the correlations above we ran four separate analyses. Two analyses modeled the probability of being on-track and two modeled the probability of earning high grades. For each outcome, we first modeled the probability of that outcome (either being on-track or earning high grades) using a cross-nested model in which students were nested in their middle grade school and in their high school. Columns A, B, D, and E are correlations between the school level residuals from these models and school characteristics. We then modeled the probability of each outcome using a hierarchical model in which students were only nested only in their middle grade school. Columns C and F report the correlations between school level residuals and school characteristics from these two models.

Among students with the same eighth-grade GPAs, attendance, and test scores, those who went to a high-achieving middle school (with higher average ISAT scores) with fewer students living in poverty are more likely to be on-track and earn high grades in ninth grade than students who went to a low-achieving middle grade school, with many students living in poverty (**see Table 4, columns A and D**). Going to a higher-performing, economically advantaged middle school seems to confer some benefits that are not picked up through grades, attendance, and test scores. It is possible that grading standards may be higher at high-achieving middle schools than low-achieving middle schools, so that an A from a high-achieving middle school might mean stronger course performance than an A from a low-achieving middle school. Or it may be that peers in high-achieving middle schools provide support, social capital, or other types of influence that help students be more successful in their classes the next year. It is also possible that high-achieving middle schools do a better job preparing students for the responsibilities and demands of high school in ways that are not reflected on tests, such as teaching students how to manage their workload or write term papers.

While students' probability of being on-track or of earning high grades depends on which middle school they attended, the school effects do not outweigh the predictiveness of the indicators themselves. Grades and attendance during the middle grades are important regardless of which school students attend; strong grades and attendance at a low-performing middle school suggest a higher degree of readiness than average grades and attendance at a high-performing school.

Figure 13 shows the extent to which there are differences in the expected "return" from students' eighth-grade GPAs, in terms of their ninth-grade GPAs, based on which middle school they attended. We use the term *"return"* to describe the idea that similar students with the same eighth-grade GPAs from different middle schools can earn different GPAs in ninth-grade; thus one student receives a higher return on his eighth-grade GPA than the other student. On average, students with a 3.0 eighth-grade GPA (a B average) earn a 2.5 GPA in ninth grade. However, students with a 3.0 eighth-grade GPA from *"high-return"* middle schools tend to earn a 2.9 GPA in ninth grade, while students with a 3.0 eighth-grade GPA from *"low-return"* middle schools tend to earn a 2.2 GPA in ninth grade, net of differences attributable to high schools. The difference between a B average at one middle school and a B average at another middle school is smaller than the difference between a B average and a C average at any school, in terms of students' performance in their high school classes. For example, while a student with a B average at a *"low-return"* middle school is predicted to earn a 2.2 GPA in ninth grade, a student with a C average from a *"high-return"* middle school is predicted to earn only a 1.9 GPA in ninth grade. While there may be differences in exactly what that B means, the fact that a student has earned a B average—and not an A or C average—is a better indicator of their success than knowing from which school the B average was earned.[45]

FIGURE 13

Students' Predicted Ninth-Grade GPA by Students' Eighth-Grade GPA: Differences Attributable to their Middle School

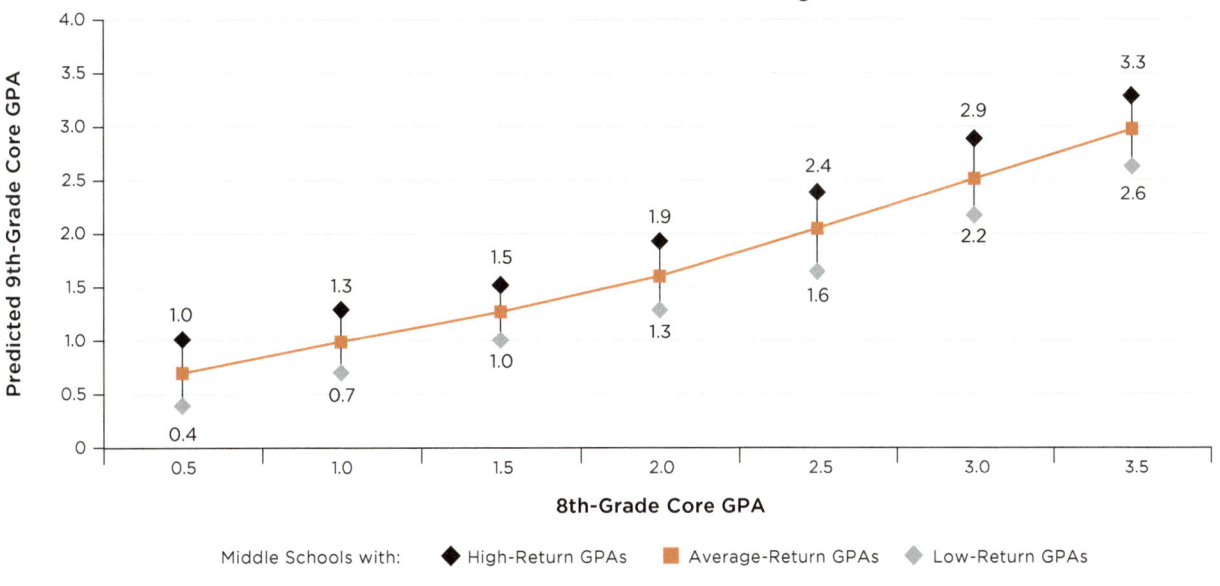

Net of Differences Attributable to High Schools

Middle Schools with: ◆ High-Return GPAs ■ Average-Return GPAs ◆ Low-Return GPAs

Note: The "average-return" line represents the average relationship between eighth-grade core GPA and ninth-grade core GPA. For example, students with a 2.5 GPA in eighth grade earn a 2.0 GPA in ninth grade, on average. Students with the same eighth grade GPA who attend the same high school earn different ninth grade GPAs, on average, depending on which middle school they attended, as represented by the triangles and diamonds. For example, eighth-graders with a 2.5 GPA from "high-return" middle schools will earn ninth grade GPAs of 2.4, on average, while eighth-graders with a 2.5 GPA from "low-return" middle schools will earn ninth grade GPAs of 1.6, on average.

To calculate these numbers, we ran models which cross-nested students simultaneously in their middle school and high school. A series of dummy variables representing each of the seven eighth-grade core GPA categories was used to predict ninth-grade core GPA, with students included in a category if their GPA was within 0.25 GPA points of the category value. The model included within-category continuous variables (one continuous variable for each dummy variable) to capture specific GPA values, calculated as the difference between the eighth-grade GPA and the midpoint of the category. This was done in order to control for non-uniform distributions of GPA within the category across schools (e.g., in case students who were at the low or high end of the distribution in the category were more likely to be in undervalued or overvalued schools). Centering at the midpoint allowed us to avoid problems with multicollinearity, and provides an estimate of the value at the specific mid-point of the category. The model did not include an intercept, and allowed the dummy variables for each group to vary across middle and high schools. This produced estimates of the variance in middle school effects and high school effects on high school GPAs for students at each eighth grade GPA point.

---

45 The middle school differences in on-track rates and probability of earning As or Bs shown in Chapter 3 appear larger than the school differences in GPAs because the charts in Chapter 3 are based on benchmarks, rather than averages (whether students are above or below a particular level of performance). The use of benchmarks to gauge effects on performance tends to amplify differences among students close to the benchmark while suppressing differences among students far from the benchmark.

Where students attend high school makes an even bigger difference for their likelihood of being on-track or earning high grades than where they attended middle school (see Figure 11, right panel; Figure 12, right panel on p.39). For example, among students with a moderate probability of passing their ninth-grade math class, based on eighth-grade indicators, their chances of being on-track varies from 75 percent in some high schools to 31 percent at other high schools, net of middle school effects (i.e., comparing similar students from similar middle schools). High school effects on the likelihood of earning high grades are comparable to those of being on-track. Among students with a moderate probability of earning high grades, the probability of doing so ranges from 40 to 77 percent.

When we look at the characteristics of the schools where students earn higher or lower grades than their qualifications would predict, we see the opposite pattern as with the middle grade schools. Students are more likely to be on-track or earn high grades if they attend high schools that serve more low-achieving, disadvantaged peers, compared to students with similar eighth-grade qualifications who attend higher-achieving high schools (see Table 4, columns B and E). This might result from lower standards at high schools serving more disadvantaged students with low incoming test scores, or from grading practices that are based on comparisons among students (e.g., grading on a curve).[46] Students might also feel less capable and withdraw effort if they attend a school with high-achieving peers where they feel everyone else is smarter than they are, or exhibit more self-efficacy and engagement if they are a strong student relative to their school peers.

Students from high-achieving middle schools are more likely to attend high-achieving high schools than are students from low-achieving middle schools. Thus, there are two contradictory effects on grades that come from attending a high-achieving middle school—students do better than their grades, attendance, and test scores would predict, compared to students from a low-achieving middle school, but they tend to send students to high schools where students have a lower likelihood of passing their classes and earning high grades. These two school effects cancel each other out. This can be seen in Table 4, columns C and F, which show middle school effects inclusive of the effects of the high schools where the middle schools' students tend to enroll. While the correlation of on-track rates with middle school average math scores is 0.21 net of high school effects, the correlation is close to zero (-0.03) when high school effects are included with middle school effects. The largest school effects would be observed among students who attend high schools that are atypical for their middle school. Students who moved from a strong middle school to a weak high school would be much more likely to pass in ninth grade than their middle grade performance would indicate, while students who moved from a weak middle school to a strong high school would be much less likely to pass than their middle grade performance would suggest.

In general, knowing which school students attend in the middle grades, and which school they attend in ninth grade, substantially improves the prediction of their risk of failure. Sophisticated indicator systems could consider these school effects when calculating students' risk of ninth-grade off-track status. As shown in Figure 7 on p.35, by considering school effects, over half of students who are off-track in ninth grade can be identified using eighth-grade indicators. Using eighth-grade GPA together with attendance and school effects identifies half of students who will be off-track in ninth grade, without falsely identifying many as at risk of being off-track when they are not.

Knowledge of school effects also improves the prediction of which students are at risk for low grades in ninth grade. As shown in Figure 10 on p.38, incorporation of school effects reduces the proportion of students falsely identified as at risk of low grades to about 50 percent. This may not be low enough to be useful for targeting students for intervention, but the information might be used to have discussions with students and families about students' risk for low grades and what they can do to reduce that risk.

Middle Grade Indicators Predict Who Will Be On-Track and Who Will Earn High Grades in Eleventh Grade

So far, this chapter has shown how eighth-grade indicators predict students' likelihood of being able to pass their classes and earn high grades in ninth grade.

Ultimately, we want to know whether eighth-grade indicators can predict whether students drop out or graduate from high school and earn the high grades they will need to succeed in college. The cohort of students used in this report had not yet reached twelfth grade at the time of these analyses, so we focus on their performance at the end of eleventh grade (the 2011-12 school year). Nearly all students who are on-track by the end of eleventh grade graduate at the end of twelfth grade (94 percent do so).[47] Those who are off-track in eleventh grade either have already dropped out or are very likely to drop out—only 37 percent of off-track eleventh-graders graduate, among those who have not yet dropped out. Moreover, their course performance by the end of eleventh grade is what matters for applications to college.

The best indicators of students' course performance by the end of eleventh grade are the same ones that are most predictive of course performance in ninth grade (see Table 5). Core GPA is the strongest single predictor of eleventh-grade on-track status. Combining attendance and eighth-grade core GPA is more predictive of being on-track at the end of eleventh grade than just eighth-grade core GPA alone; it is also more predictive than combining eighth-grade core GPA with any other eighth-grade indicators, including ISAT scores. Combining seventh-grade GPA with eighth-grade core GPA and attendance slightly improves the prediction, but the

TABLE 5

Students' Middle Grade Core GPAs Are the Strongest Predictor of Being On-Track and Earning High Grades in Eleventh Grade

Single Indicator	On-Track at the End of 11th Grade			Earning As or Bs in 11th-Grade Core Classes		
	Correlation	Pseudo-R²	% Correct	Correlation	Pseudo-R²	% Correct
8th-Grade Core GPA with Squared Term	0.43	0.18 0.18	0.71 0.71	0.41	0.17 0.18	0.79 0.79
8th-Grade Math GPA	0.38	0.14	0.69	0.35	0.13	0.78
8th-Grade English GPA	0.41	0.16	0.70	0.37	0.15	0.78
8th-Grade Core Course Failures	-0.32	0.10	0.69	-0.20	0.06	0.76
8th-Grade Attendance with Squared Term	0.37	0.15 0.15	0.71 0.71	0.18	0.04 0.05	0.76 0.76
8th-Grade Math ISAT with Squared Term	0.30	0.10 0.10	0.66 0.66	0.35	0.11 0.11	0.78 0.78
8th-Grade Reading ISAT with Squared Term	0.26	0.07 0.08	0.65 0.66	0.28	0.08 0.08	0.77 0.77
8th-Grade Suspensions	-0.25	0.07	0.68	-0.10	0.02	0.76
8th-Grade Misconduct	-0.18	0.03	0.67	-0.07	0.01	0.76
8th-Grade Grit[1]	0.07	0.01	0.68	0.03	0.00	0.74
8th-Grade Study Habits[1]	0.10	0.01	0.68	0.11	0.01	0.74
7th-Grade Core GPA	0.41	0.17	0.71	0.39	0.16	0.79
7th-Grade Attendance	0.32	0.11	0.70	0.16	0.04	0.76
7th-Grade Math ISAT	0.29	0.09	0.66	0.34	0.11	0.77
7th-Grade Reading ISAT	0.25	0.07	0.65	0.28	0.08	0.77

46 This is consistent with prior research that showed that student performance is shaped by students' ability levels relative to their classroom peers; students receive lower grades than other students with similar skill levels if they are in a classroom where they have weak skills compared to their classroom peers. See Kelly (2008); Farkas, Sheehan, and Grobe (1990); Nomi and Allensworth (2012). However, as noted in Figure 13, observed inconsistencies in grading are generally about equal to half of a GPA point, at best.

47 Students who are on-track at the end of eleventh grade have accumulated at least 17 full-year course credits required for graduation.

TABLE 5: CONTINUED

Students' Middle Grade Core GPAs Are the Strongest Predictor of Being On-Track and Earning High Grades in Eleventh Grade

Single Indicator	On-Track at the End of 11th Grade			Earning As or Bs in 11th-Grade Core Classes		
	Correlation	Pseudo-R^2	% Correct	Correlation	Pseudo-R^2	% Correct
Combining Two 8th-Grade Indicators						
8th-Grade Core GPA + Attendance		**0.23**	**0.74**		**0.18**	0.79
8th-Grade Core GPA + Math ISAT		0.19	0.72		0.18	0.80
8th-Grade Math + Reading ISAT		0.10	0.66		0.11	0.78
Combining Three or More Eighth-Grade Indicators						
8th-Grade Core GPA + Math ISAT + Reading ISAT		0.19	0.72		0.19	0.79
8th-Grade Core GPA + Attendance + Math ISAT + Reading ISAT		0.23	0.74		**0.19**	**0.80**
Background Characteristics[2]		0.07	0.67		0.09	0.77
8th-Grade Core GPA + Attendance + Math ISAT + Reading ISAT + Background Characteristics		0.23	0.74		0.20	0.80
8th-Grade Core GPA + Attendance + Math ISAT + Reading ISAT + Course Failures + Suspensions + Misconduct + Background Characteristics		0.24	0.75		0.20	**0.80**
Adding in 8th-Grade Indicators						
8th-Grade Core GPA + Attendance + Math ISAT + Reading ISAT + 7th-Grade GPA		0.24	0.75		0.20	0.80
All 7th- and 8th-Grade Indicators		0.24	0.75		**0.21**	**0.80**
Adding in School Effects						
8th-Grade GPA + Attendance + School Effects		0.30	0.75		0.26	0.81
All 7th- and 8th-Grade Indicators + School Effects		0.31	0.76		0.29	0.81

Note: 1) Grit and study habits are calculated from students' responses to items on UChicago CCSR's annual survey of CPS students. The elementary/middle grade student survey had a response rate of 59 percent in 2009. Because not all students answer the survey, the sample size for these models is smaller than the sample sizes for the other models included in this table. The percent of students who are on-track or earn high grades is slightly higher in this smaller sample resulting in a somewhat higher correct prediction rate for these two variables. 2) Background characteristics include race, gender, special education status, neighborhood poverty level, and socioeconomic status, free reduced price lunch status, and whether a student was older than 14 when entering high school. 3) The bolded numbers represent the best indicator or combination of indicators in each group.

improvement in prediction from a pseudo-R^2 of 0.23 to 0.24 may not warrant a more complicated indicator system that comes from using three indicators versus two indicators.

Core GPA is also the best single predictor of whether students earn As or Bs in eleventh grade (**see Table 5**). Combining eighth-grade core GPA with attendance, ISAT scores, or seventh-grade GPA only somewhat improves the prediction of who earns As or Bs over using eighth-grade core GPA alone, most likely because the combination of predictors only differentiates between students who have earned very high grades.

Summary

Eighth-grade core GPA is the strongest single predictor of on-track status and earning high grades in high school. Students' grades across all subjects are more predictive of their grade in a specific class (math or English) than their prior grade in the corresponding subject. Combining core GPA with attendance, or with seventh-grade GPA, gives an even better prediction of who will be on-track at the end of ninth grade, or earn high grades, than core GPA alone.

Test scores, either alone or in combination with core GPA, are not all that predictive of who is on-track at the end of ninth grade. This may seem counter-intuitive because test scores are often the primary focus in policy discussions about improving educational attainment and they often are used to identify students in need of additional academic support. Often overlooked, attendance rates and GPA in earlier grades are much better for identifying who will fail their classes and be off-track at the end of ninth grade.

Eighth-grade test scores do help predict who will get high grades in high school, but only among students who already were getting high grades in middle school. Attendance provides even more information about who will get high grades in high school, among students with high prior grades, than test scores. Neither test scores nor attendance provide much information about who will earn high grades in high school among students who had a 2.0 or below in eighth grade, in part, because it is so unlikely that students with low grades in middle school will earn high grades in high school.

Combinations of three or more indicators do not considerably improve the prediction of who is on-track or who earns high grades over predictions based on only two indicators (grades and attendance), suggesting that a complex system incorporating multiple indicators will not provide much more information than only two indicators. Knowing where students went to middle and high school, however, does substantially improve the prediction of whether students will be on-track or earn high grades.

Although middle grade indicators cannot identify all students who are at risk of being off-track, they can be used to identify a subset of students who are at high risk of ninth-grade failure. About half of students who are off-track in the ninth grade can be identified accurately with middle grade predictors—few of the students who are identified as at risk succeed. Resources devoted to intervention for these students would not be wasted on students who would succeed without any intervention. The next chapter examines what middle grade indicators tell us about who is likely to be off-track by the end of ninth grade.

CHAPTER 4

Who Is at Risk of Being Off-Track at the End of Ninth Grade?

The previous chapter showed that eighth-grade core GPA and attendance together provide the best parsimonious prediction of ninth-grade failure and being off-track for graduation, of all of the potential indicators that were examined; other metrics, such as subject-specific grades, test scores, and background characteristics, do not provide more information beyond students' core grades and attendance. The prediction is far from perfect; students' experiences in ninth grade determine whether they pass their ninth-grade classes and remain on-track for graduation. But eighth-grade indicators can identify subsets of students who are at high risk or very high risk of being off-track by the end of ninth grade. In this chapter, we used eighth-grade core GPA, eighth-grade attendance, and eighth-grade ISAT scores to identify how many students were at risk of being off-track and failing in high school. We included ISAT scores in the prediction to be sure that the risk groups include students with similar tested skill levels, as well as similar course performance and attendance.

To design intervention systems, schools need to know the magnitude of the level of risk of their students—how many students are at some risk of failing, and how many are at very high risk of failing. Students with different levels of risk may need different interventions, and there are cost constraints as to how many students can be targeted with extra resources. Students with very high risk are almost certain to fail without intervention; yet, because they are at very high risk, their outcomes may be very difficult to change unless substantial resources are allocated to them. Students with moderate or low risk may succeed without any intervention; but they may need only a modest intervention to succeed, and a sizable group will fail without any support. The decision about how to allocate resources hinges on how many students are identified as being at different levels of risk.

> This chapter shows students' risk of failing based on their middle grade records. This information could be used by school practitioners to identify students who are at high risk of failure and to discuss goals for student performance with both students and their families.

Students' Risk of Being Off-Track by Middle Grade Indicators

Eighth-grade students with less than 80 percent attendance or GPAs less than 1.0 are at *extremely high* risk of being off-track in ninth grade. In Chicago, about 5 percent of middle grade students can be identified as being at *very high* risk of being off-track in the ninth grade, based on their eighth-grade GPA and attendance (**see Figure 14**). These are students with extremely low grades and attendance in the middle grades.

Eighth-grade students with C/D averages and chronic absence in middle school are at *high* risk of being off-track in ninth grade. Around 16 percent of students can be identified as being at high risk of being off-track (**see Figure 14**). These students are more likely to be off-track than on-track in high school; they have a 50 to 75 percent likelihood of being off-track. They had very poor performance in eighth grade, with an average GPA of 1.5 (a combination of Ds and Cs). Their attendance was better than students at extremely high risk of being off-track—they came to school 91 percent of the time, on average. Many of them they were still chronically absent, however, missing more than five weeks of school

FIGURE 14

The Percent of Students at Very Low, Low, Moderate, High, and Very High Risk of Being Off-Track in Ninth Grade

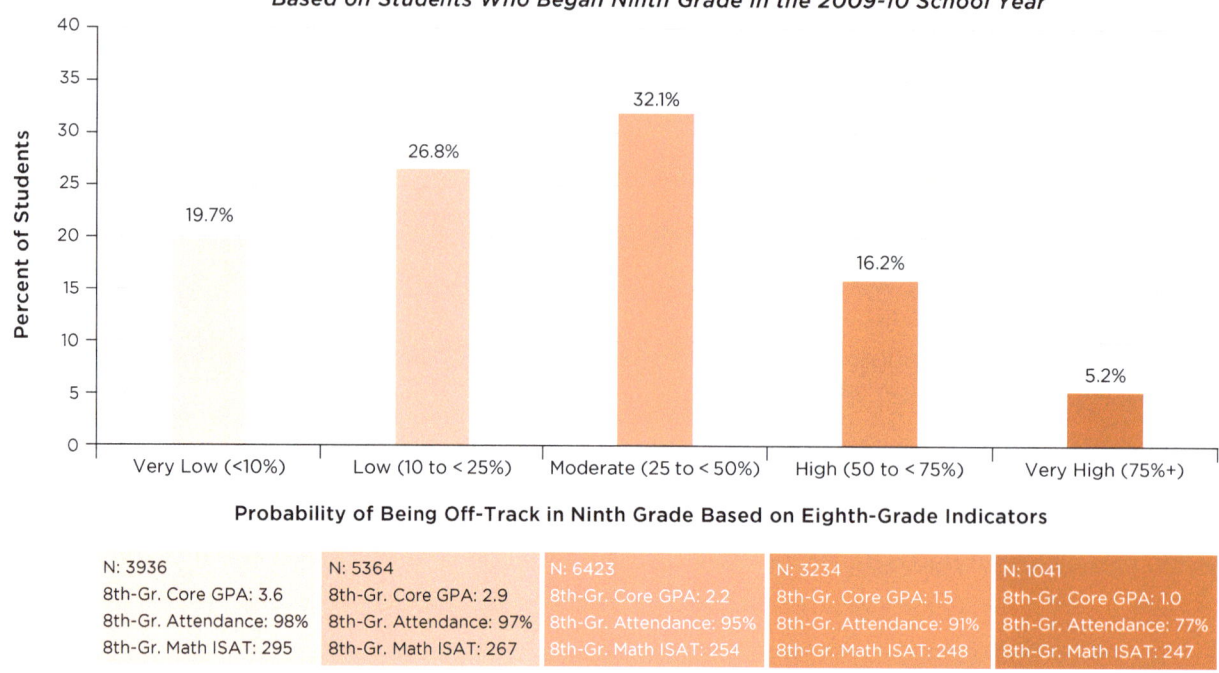

Based on Students Who Began Ninth Grade in the 2009-10 School Year

Note: The five risk groups shown in this chart were created by first running a logistic regression in which the probability of being off-track is modeled as a function of eighth-grade core GPA, attendance, ISAT math scores, and any significant interaction terms between these three indicators. Using predicted probabilities generated from the analysis, we then created the five groups, using the cut points described in the parentheses above.

FIGURE 15

Risk of Being Off-Track in Ninth Grade by Eighth-Grade Core GPA and Attendance

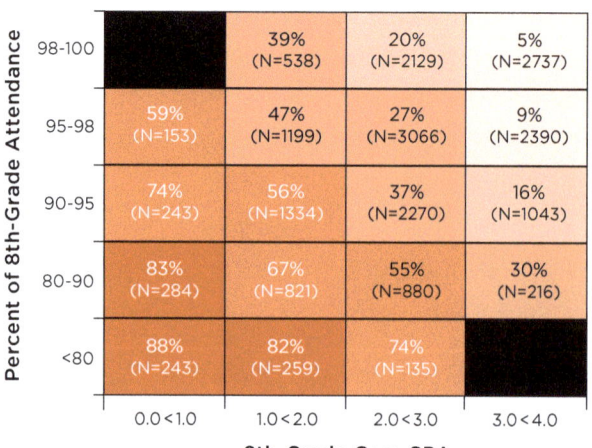

Note: Based on students who began ninth grade in the 2009-10 school year.

during their eighth-grade year. These students are also very unlikely to succeed without extra support, but they may be more responsive to intervention that is less intense than needed for students at extremely high risk. As shown in **Figure 15**, it is the combination of moderate grades with low attendance or low grades with moderate attendance that puts students at high risk of being off-track in high school. Students with moderately high attendance (between 95 and 98 percent) are at high risk if their GPA is less than 1.0, while students whose GPA is between 1.0 and 2.0 are at high risk if their attendance is less than 95 percent. Also at high risk are students whose GPA is between 2.0 and 3.0, if their attendance is less than 90 percent.

About 60 percent of eighth-grade students are at *some* risk of being off-track in ninth grade, even though their middle school performance seems satisfactory. Around one-third of first-time ninth-graders are at *moderate* risk of being off-track (between a 25 and 50 percent chance of being off-track) and another quarter at *low* risk of being off-track (between 10 and 25 percent). Students with a moderate risk of being off-track had about a C average in eighth grade and 95 percent attendance (**see Figure 14**). Students who were at low risk of being off-track had a B- GPA and 97 percent attendance, on average. While the risk of being off-track is not high for these two groups, because of their size, these two groups account for just over half of all students who were off-track at the end of ninth grade: 37 percent of all students who were off-track in ninth grade were at moderate risk, while 15 percent were at low risk based on their eighth-grade performance.

Because of the size of the moderate- and low-risk groups, costly interventions would be impractical. Even though these students are not at high risk of being off-track, they are at some risk, and modest efforts around attendance improvement could have big pay-offs in the long run because so many students are in these two groups. Such interventions might include conversations with students and parents about their risk of failing in high school, lowering risk with better attendance and effort, teaching strategies for help-seeking and support when they are in high school, and discussions about parental monitoring through the transition to high school. These students need to be closely monitored in the transition to high school; otherwise, many will show declining attendance and effort in ninth grade.

Only about one-fifth of students have *very little* risk of being off-track in ninth grade—students with a B average or higher and 95 percent or better attendance in middle school. There are some students whose risk of falling off-track to graduation is 10 percent or lower. These are students whose GPA was a 3.0 or better, and whose attendance was 95 percent or above in eighth grade. Even though being on-track for graduation is a very low bar for judging high school performance, few students leave middle school assured of being ready to meet this basic expectation.

The signals for students' risk of failing either ninth-grade English or math are the same as those for being off-track. English and math are subjects of primary concern to educators, as reading and math skills provide a base for learning in other subjects. The previous chapter showed that students' prior grades in English or math, or their test scores in reading or math, were not any more predictive of their ninth-grade grades in either specific subject than their overall GPA and attendance rate. Based on eighth-grade performance, around 11 percent of ninth-grade students are at high or very high risk of failing math, and 12 percent are at high or very high risk for failing English (**see Figures 16 and 17**). Students who are at *high or very high* risk of failing math or English had about a 1.2 GPA in eighth grade and 85 percent attendance, on average.

Students' Risk of Being Off-Track in Ninth Grade Carries On to Eleventh Grade

The same middle grade indicators that predict ninth-grade on-track status also predict whether students are on-track to graduate by the end of eleventh grade, where on-track in eleventh grade is defined as having sufficient credits to be a twelfth-grader the following year and still enrolled in school. Thus, middle grade indicators can be used to identify students who are at great risk of dropping out before they start high school. In fact, students' likelihood of being on-track in eleventh grade is similar to their likelihood of being on-track in ninth grade, based on their eighth-grade records.

Low grades and poor attendance in middle grades indicate students are unlikely to graduate. Students with less than a 1.0 eighth-grade GPA are at high risk of being off-track when they finish ninth grade, and also at the end of eleventh grade (**see Figure 18**). Only about a quarter (26 percent) of students with an eighth-grade GPA that is less than 1.0 are on-track when they finish ninth grade and about a quarter (22 percent) are still on-track at the end of eleventh grade. Students with higher eighth-grade GPAs have higher likelihoods of being on-track in both ninth and eleventh grades, and the probability is similar in both years because ninth-grade performance is very indicative of performance through the remaining high school years.

The same general pattern can be seen in **Figure 19**, which shows ninth- and eleventh-grade on-track rates by eighth-grade attendance. Students with less than 80 percent attendance are extremely likely to be off-track for graduation in both ninth grade and eleventh grade;

FIGURE 16

The Percent of Students at Very Low, Low, Moderate, High, and Very High Risk of Failing Math

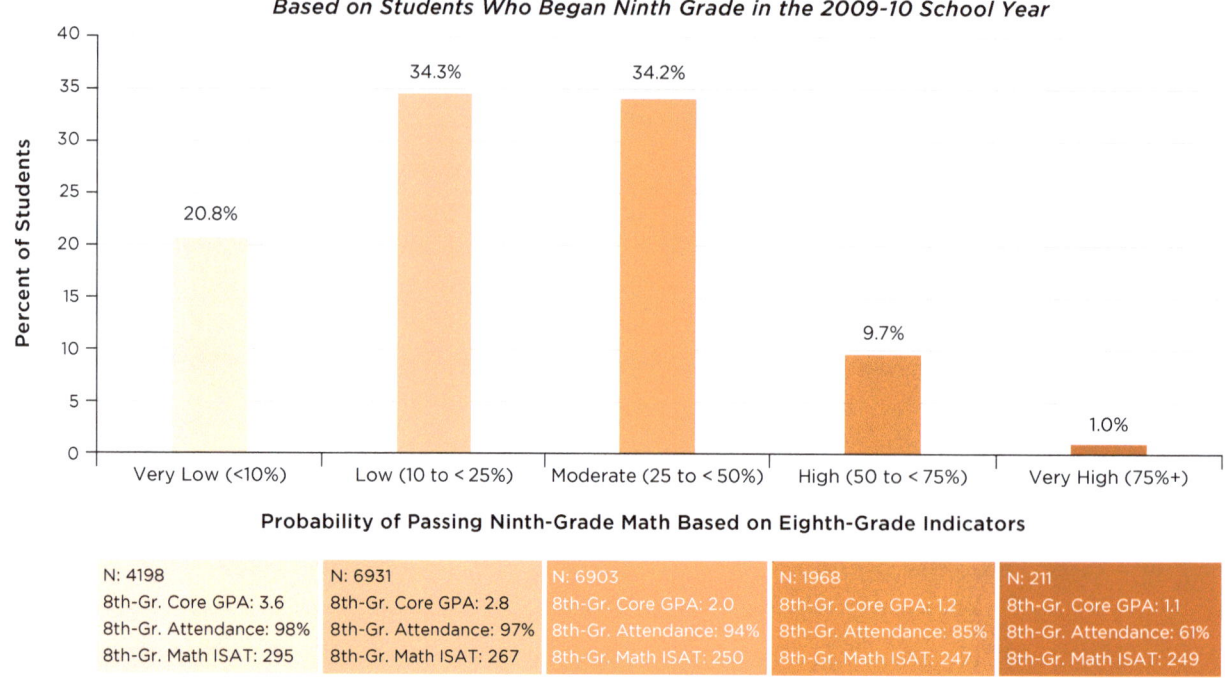

Based on Students Who Began Ninth Grade in the 2009-10 School Year

Note: The five probability groups shown in this chart were created by first running a logistic regression in which the probability of passing ninth-grade math was regressed on eighth-grade core GPA, attendance, ISAT math scores, and any significant interaction terms between these three indicators. Using predicted probabilities generated from the analysis, we then created the five groups, using the cut points described in the parentheses above.

FIGURE 17

The Percent of Students at Very Low, Low, Moderate, High, and Very High Risk of Failing English

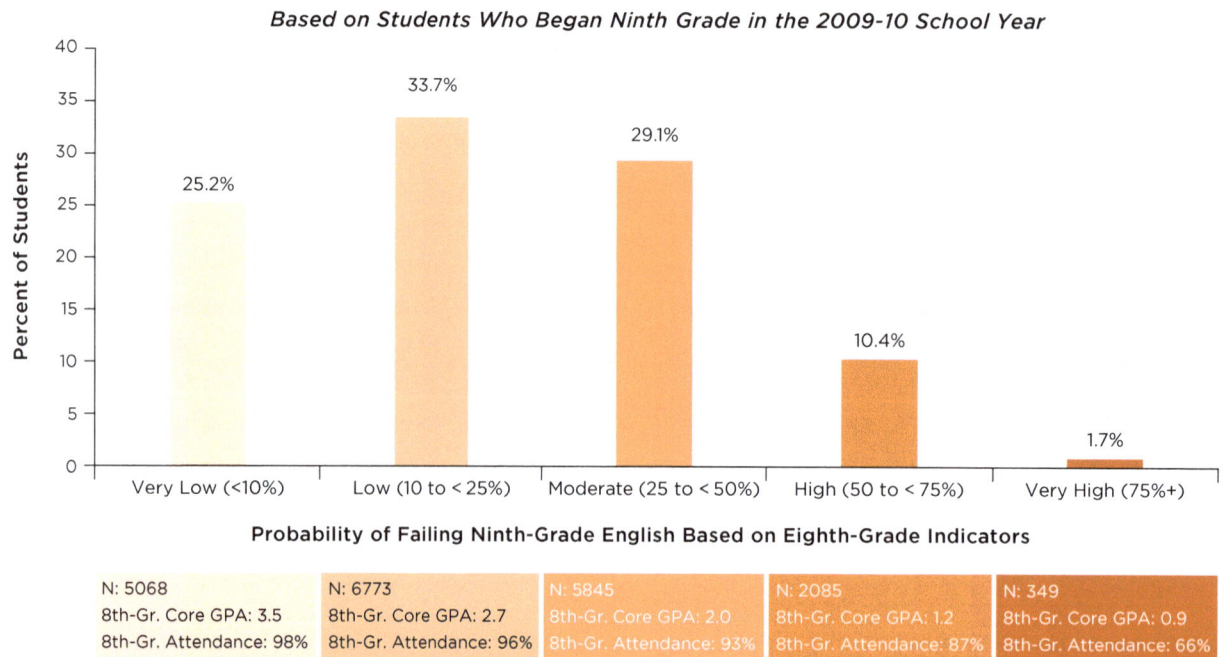

Based on Students Who Began Ninth Grade in the 2009-10 School Year

Note: The five probability groups shown in this chart were created by first running a logistic regression in which the probability of passing ninth-grade math was regressed on eighth-grade core GPA, attendance, ISAT math scores, and any significant interaction terms between these three indicators. Using predicted probabilities generated from the analysis, we then created the five groups, using the cut points described in the parentheses above.

UCHICAGO CCSR Research Report | Middle Grade Indicators of Readiness in Chicago Public Schools

FIGURE 18

The Percent of Students Who Are On-Track, Off-Track, or Dropouts at the End of Ninth Grade and Eleventh Grade on Eighth-Grade Core GPA

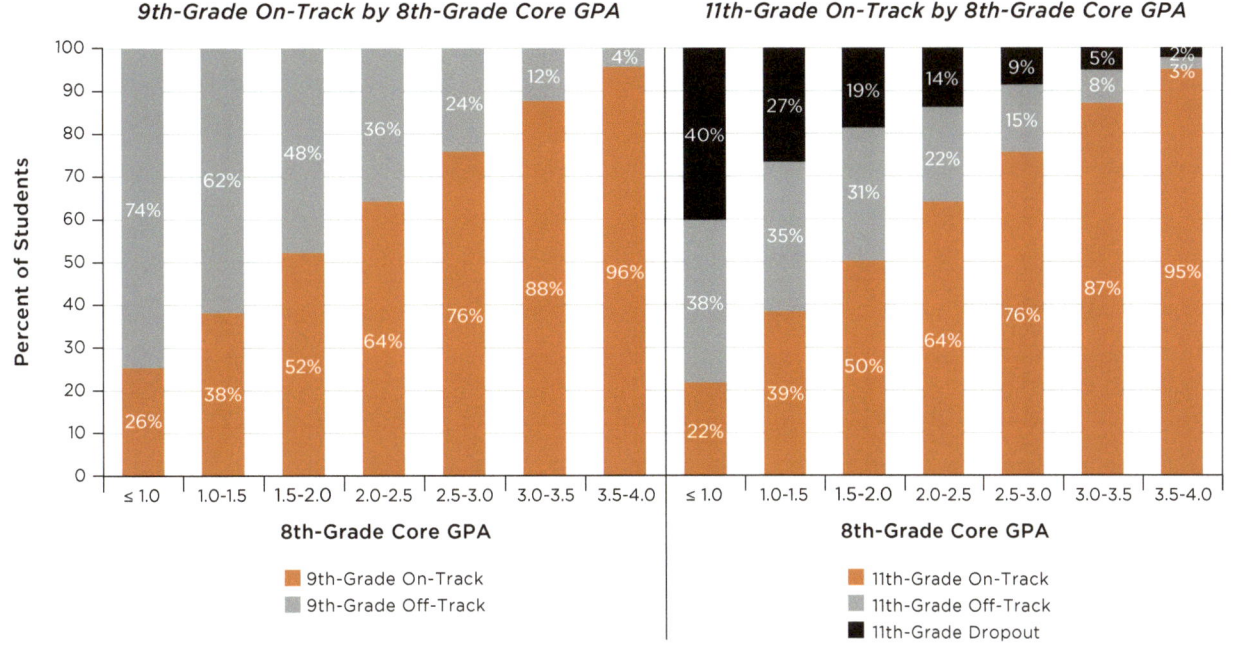

Note: Based on students who began ninth grade in the 2009-10 school year.

FIGURE 19

The Percent of Students Who Are On-Track, Off-Track, or Dropouts at the End of Ninth Grade and Eleventh Grade, Based on Eighth-Grade Attendance

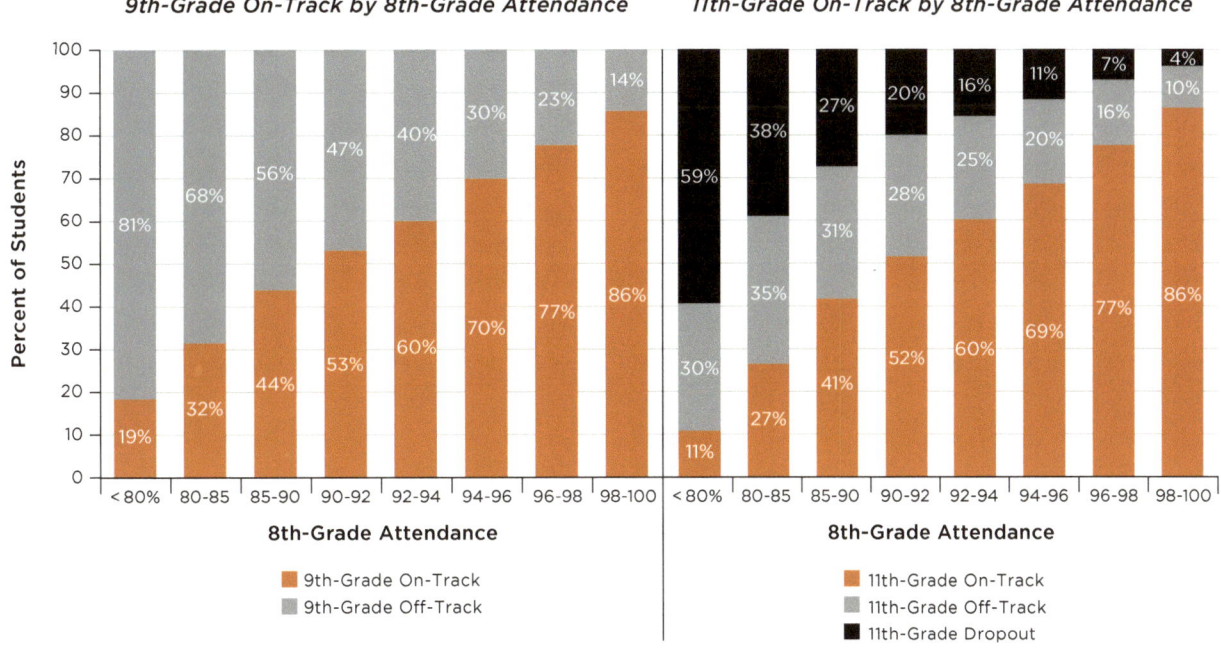

Note: Based on students entering ninth grade in the 2009-10 school year, followed through the 2011-12 school year.

FIGURE 20

The Percent of Students Who Are On-Track, Off-Track, or Dropouts at the End of Eleventh Grade Based on the Number of Course Failures in Eighth-Grade Math and English Classes

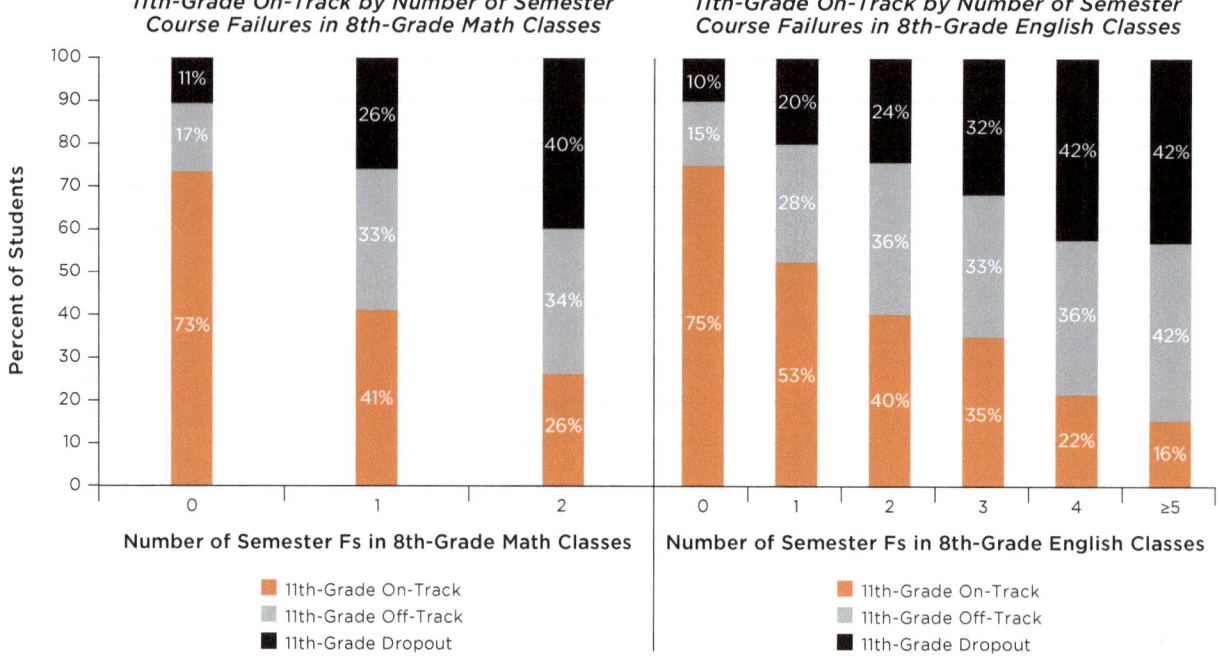

Note: Based on students entering ninth grade in the 2009-10 school year, followed through the 2011-12 school year.

their risk is greater than 75 percent. This corresponds closely to the work of Neild and Balfanz (2006) who looked for high-yield middle school indicators of dropout in Philadelphia schools. High-yield indicators were defined as those that identified students with a dropout risk of 75 percent or higher. They found that attendance less than 80 percent in middle school was a high-yield indicator of dropping out of high school. They also found that failing eighth-grade English or math was a high-yield indicator of dropout (a 75 percent or greater probability).[48] The same pattern occurs in Chicago. As shown in **Figure 20**, students who fail both semesters of eighth-grade math, or all four sections of eighth-grade language arts (reading and writing), have less than a 25 percent chance of being on-track for graduation in eleventh grade.

Throughout Middle Grades, GPAs Are Better Indicators of Risk for High School Failure Than Other Factors

Middle grade practitioners may wonder if there are some levels of performance earlier in the middle grades that indicate students are at high risk of failing when they get to high school. For simplicity, we focus on single indicators for this comparison—even though they are less predictive than combinations. We wondered if there were points at which warning bells should go off for middle grade practitioners if they see a student is performing below a particular level.

Students with D averages at any grade are at high risk of failure in high school. As shown in **Table 6**, a very low GPA, less than a 1.5, prior to eighth grade is

---

[48] Course failures were predictive of on-track in Chicago, but did not add to the prediction, once we considered students' overall GPAs and attendance.

TABLE 6

Single Indicator Thresholds for Identifying Students at High Risk of Being Off-Track in Grades Five through Eight, Where the Risk of Being Off-Track Is Greater Than 50 Percent.

		5th Grade	6th Grade	7th Grade	8th Grade
Attendance	Threshhold	84.1%	85.5%	87.8%	87.5%
	% of Off-Track Students Identified	6.7%	9.4%	16.9%	19.4%
GPA	Threshhold	1.4	1.3	1.4	1.7
	% of Off-Track Students Identified	15.3%	21.0%	30.0%	30.8%
Math ISAT Scores	Threshhold	176	196	204	227
	% of Off-Track Students Identified	1.2%	3.2%	3.8%	3.7%
Reading ISAT Scores	Threshhold	159	176	182	204
	% of Off-Track Students Identified	1.6%	2.9%	3.9%	5.0%
Number of Days Suspended	Threshhold	6	7	6	6
	% of Off-Track Students Identified	3.7%	4.8%	8.9%	9.9%

Note: Based on students who began ninth grade in the 2011-12 school year.

the clearest signal that a student is at high risk of being off-track in high school. The GPA cut-off for identifying students at high risk of being off-track is similar in fifth through seventh grade, but the percent of off-track students who are identified increases as eighth grade approaches. The district could use this threshold to identify students very early on who are almost certain not to graduate without intervention. Students with a history of very low grades in the middle grades likely need very intensive interventions if they are to eventually graduate.

Attendance is the next best indicator in grades five through seven for identifying students who are at high risk of being off-track. Students who attend less than 85 percent of days in any of the middle grades are very likely to fail classes when they arrive in high school and fall off-track for graduation. They already are chronically absent in the middle grades, and they are likely to miss school at even higher rates when they enter high school.

Math and reading ISAT scores and the number of days a student is suspended are less predictive for identifying who is at high risk to fail in high school than attendance or grades. However, there are small numbers of students whose test scores are so low, or suspension rates are so high, that they can be identified as at high risk of high school failure based on these single indicators. These are students who are at academic warning levels on the ISAT, or who are suspended for more than a week during the middle grades.

Summary

Many students who perform well in middle school fail classes in ninth grade and are off-track by the end of the year. The transition to high school brings students into a very new context, with different peers and different relationships with teachers and other adults. For almost all students, it is important to monitor their performance in the first year of high school and reach out to students who start to show signs of withdrawal. Subgroups of students enter high school already at high risk, based on their academic performance in the middle grades.

About 5 percent of students can be identified as being at extremely high risk of being off-track. These same students are also at extremely high risk of still being off-track in eleventh grade and eventually not graduating from high school. Failing classes in ninth grade means that they are not accumulating the credits they need. Unfortunately, it would take substantial support to turn around the very low grades and very poor attendance of students at such high risk of failure.

There are many other students, around 16 percent of first-time ninth-graders, who are at high risk of being off-track at the end of ninth grade. These students could go either way, based on their individual experiences. This is a group for whom interventions may be more effective. Middle school practitioners, students, and their families need to be aware that students with attendance less than 90 percent are at high risk of not graduating. Middle school and high school staff do not need to wait until these students are failing their ninth-grade classes to intervene. Mentorship programs, such as Check and Connect,[49] may be helpful in improving their grades and attendance. They could also be identified for support from the start of high school to improve their likelihood of passing ninth-grade classes.

While passing ninth-grade classes is an important step toward graduating from high school, it is not sufficient for ensuring that students are prepared to engage in college level work. To be ready for college, high school students need to be working hard at a very high level of performance so that they are learning the skills and knowledge they need to succeed in college; this means earning As or Bs in high school classes. In the next chapter, we show which students are likely to earn As or Bs in high school and how many students have little chance of doing so.

---

[49] Sinclair et al. (2005); Lehr et al. (2004).

CHAPTER 5

Who Is at Risk of Earning Less Than As or Bs in High School?

Passing courses is essential for graduating from high school, but simply passing is not enough if students are to have a good chance of succeeding in college; they need to be engaged in their classes and earning As or Bs. Students who earn Cs or Ds in high school are unlikely to graduate from college, while those with a B average (a 3.0 GPA) have about a 50/50 chance of earning a four-year college degree (**see Appendix A**). Unfortunately, few students actually achieve a GPA of at least 3.0 in ninth grade. In 2009, for example, only 23 percent of first-time freshmen earned A or B averages in their core classes. This sets the stage for poor course performance throughout high school.[50]

This chapter identifies which students are likely to earn As or Bs in high school. While the indicators that are predictive of As or Bs are similar to those for passing classes in high school, the competencies and behaviors students must demonstrate in order to earn As or Bs are much higher—and their probability of success is much lower. Eighth-graders who plan to eventually attend college need to excel in their courses in order to have a chance of earning sufficiently strong grades in high school that put them on the path to college readiness.

Eighth-Graders with Good Grades, Attendance, and Test Scores Have Only a Moderate Chance of Earning As or Bs in Ninth Grade

Chapter 3 showed that students' eighth-grade core GPAs are the best predictors of earning high grades in high school. For students with strong eighth-grade GPAs, considering their attendance rates or ISAT scores, along with GPA, improves the accuracy of the prediction. Students' probability of success based on

> This chapter shows which students are likely to earn high grades in high school—grades that make them eligible for college and likely to succeed, once there. The information in this chapter can be used to discuss goals for student performance with students and their families.

these factors can be seen in **Figure 21**. The left-hand portion of the figure shows that eighth-graders must have very strong attendance or very strong test scores, in addition to high grades, in order to have even a 50 percent chance of earning As or Bs in ninth grade. Because only students with at least a 3.0 eighth-grade GPA have at least a 22 percent chance of earning As or Bs in high school, the right-hand portion of the figure takes a finer-grained look at students with high grades by subdividing the 3.0 to 4.0 GPA category. It shows only students with the highest grades (GPAs above 3.7) have at least a 50 percent chance of earning As or Bs in ninth grade. Moreover, of the students with a GPA greater than 3.7, only those with attendance rates greater than 98 percent or ISAT math scores above 310 have more than a 75 percent chance of earning As or Bs. To put this in context, students with attendance rates of 98 percent or higher are missing less than a week of school, and those scoring at a 310 or above are in the "exceeds" range on the ISAT.

---

50 While grades are higher, on average, in eleventh and twelfth grades than grades nine and 10, this is because students with low grades tend to drop out. When we compare the same students over time, we see that grades do not improve through high school, on average.

FIGURE 21

Students' Probability of Earning As or Bs in Ninth Grade by Core Eighth-Grade GPA and Eighth-Grade Attendance or ISAT Math Score

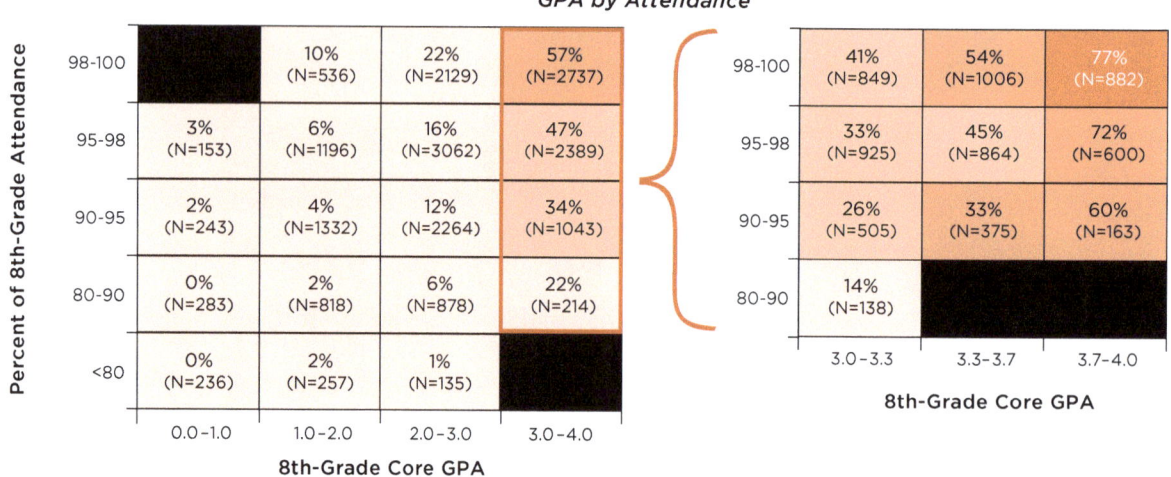

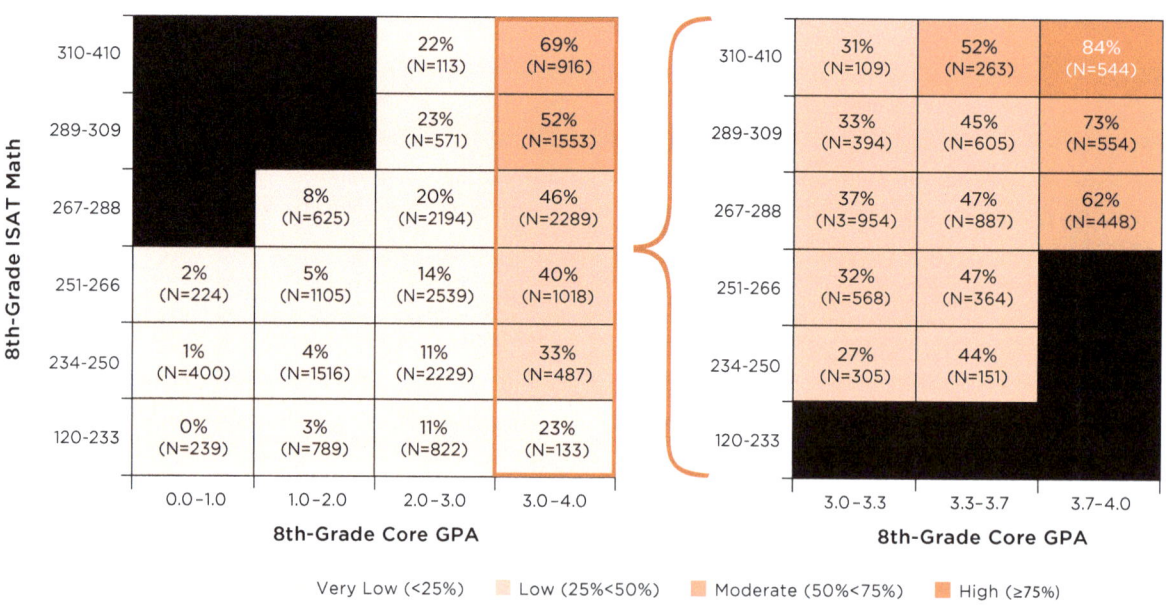

Note: Probabilities are only shown if there are at least 100 students with a specific GPA and attendance rate/ISAT score combination. The percentages are based on students entering ninth grade in the 2009-10 school year.

Two-Thirds of Students Leave Middle School with Little Chance of Earning As or Bs in High School

Few students finish eighth grade with the academic records necessary to have a good chance of earning As or Bs in ninth grade. In fact, as shown in **Figure 22**, only 2 percent of students have a *high* probability of doing so (greater than a 75 percent chance). These are exceptional students; on average, they have a core GPA of 3.93 in eighth grade, an attendance rate of 99.3 percent, and a score of 324 on the math portion of the eighth-grade ISAT—which is higher than the *"exceeds"* benchmark of 310.

Students with a *moderate* chance of earning As or Bs in ninth grade (12 percent of students), who are more likely than not to earn high grades, also have strong eighth-grade records, with an average core GPA of 3.66, attendance rate of 98 percent, and an average ISAT math score of 294. Combined with the students who have a *high* probability, a total of only 15 percent of students have more than just a 50/50 chance of earning As or Bs as ninth-graders. Despite their particularly strong eighth-grade academic records, however, none are certain to be successful in high school. Practitioners should be eager to understand why the grades of some of these students decline in high school.

The vast majority of students have less than a 50 percent probability of earning As or Bs in ninth-grade core classes. One-fifth of the cohort has between a 25 and 50 percent chance; on average, students in this group have an eighth-grade core GPA of 3.13, an attendance rate of 96.8 percent, and an ISAT math score of 275. These students also have strong academic records; yet, this group is unlikely to earn As or Bs in high school (less than a 50 percent chance). Nearly two-thirds of students leaving CPS middle schools (65 percent of students) have less than a 25 percent chance of earning a GPA of at least 3.0 in ninth grade. Although close to 80 percent of CPS students enter high school aspiring to earn a four-year-college degree, the majority are simply unprepared to do so. Students' performance does not align with their aspirations, but neither they nor their teachers may realize it. In order to be on-track for college readiness, students need to be highly engaged in their classes, so much so that they are earning As or Bs. If this is not happening in middle school, it is unlikely to begin in high school when students tend to have less support and monitoring.

FIGURE 22

Students' Probability of Earning As or Bs in Ninth-Grade Core Classes Based on Eighth-Grade Outcomes

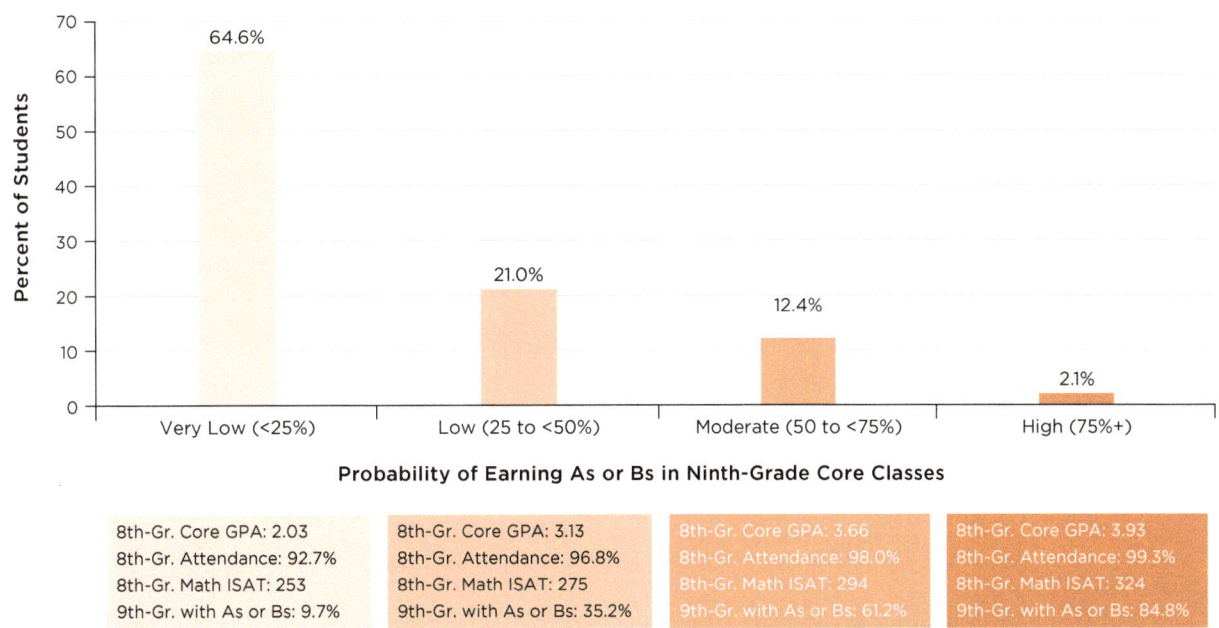

Note: The percentages are based on students entering ninth grade in the 2009-10 school year. The four probability groups shown in this chart were created by first running a logistic regression in which the probability of passing ninth-grade math was regressed on eighth-grade core GPA, attendance, ISAT math scores, and any significant interaction terms between these three indicators. Using predicted probabilities generated from the analysis, we then created the four groups using the cut points described in the parentheses above.

The Likelihood of Earning As or Bs in Subject-Specific Classes Is Similar to That Across All Core Classes

Educators may wonder whether different indicators are predictive of high grades in particular classes, such as English versus math. We found almost no differences in which indicators of performance predicted high grades in math versus English. Subject-specific indicators, such as grades or test scores in English or math, were less predictive of grades in ninth-grade English and math than students' core GPA and combined test scores across subjects. Most students have low probabilities of earning As or Bs in ninth-grade English and math, although their chances are slightly better in English than in math (**see Figures 23 and 24**). About three-fourths of Chicago students leave middle school with less than a 50/50 chance of earning As or Bs in ninth-grade English; 84 percent of students have less than a 50/50 chance of earning As or Bs in ninth-grade math, based on their eighth-grade records. Less than 5 percent of students leave eighth grade with a very high likelihood of earning As or Bs in ninth-grade English (with at least a 75 percent chance of doing so). Less than 2 percent have a very high likelihood of earning As or Bs in math in ninth grade, based on their eighth-grade records.

By Eleventh Grade, Even Fewer Students Earn Bs or Better

If students are followed an additional two years—to eleventh grade—the patterns look similar to those seen in ninth grade, although grades are somewhat lower in eleventh grade and some students have dropped out of school. Grade point averages generally do not improve as students progress through high school, so low likelihoods for earning As or Bs in ninth grade foretell low GPAs in eleventh grade when students are applying to college. Put another way, students' course performance in eighth grade has implications for their grades not only in the following year but also for the entirety of their high school careers.

Figure 25 shows students' ninth-grade GPAs and eleventh-grade GPAs, based on their eighth-grade GPAs. Eleventh-grade GPAs are divided into groups, based on prior research that ties high school grades to college outcomes: students with a GPA below 2.0 are not likely to graduate from college and only have access to college if they have ACT scores of 21 or higher, which is rare. Those with a GPA between 2.0 and 3.0 are qualified for a non-selective or somewhat selective college, if they also have an ACT score of at least 18. However, while they can enroll in college, their chances of graduating from college are slim. In order to be qualified for a selective college, and to have at least a 50/50 chance of graduating, students need a GPA above 3.0 and an ACT score of at least 18.[51] (**See Appendix A** for a summary table that ties college access to students' high school GPAs and ACT scores.)

Students leaving eighth grade with very high grades—an A average of 3.5 or higher—have fairly even odds of leaving high school with a B average or better (3.0 or above). Sixty-one percent of the students with an eighth-grade GPA of at least 3.5 earn As or Bs in ninth grade; that proportion drops to 54 percent in eleventh grade. These students have access to selective colleges, if they have an ACT score of at least 18. Another one-third of the students with the top eighth-grade grades earn a GPA between 2.0 and 3.0 in ninth and eleventh grade. While these students have access to somewhat selective colleges, their chances of graduating from college are less than 40 percent (**see Appendix A**).

Among students who earned a mix of As and Bs in eighth grade (with a GPA between 3.0 and 3.5), less than a third (29 percent) finish eleventh grade with a GPA that signals they are likely to succeed in college (at least a 3.0). Another 24 percent finish with grades so low they are not even qualified for college (less than a 2.0).

Eighth-graders who earn low grades have almost no chance of graduating from college. More than half of the students with an eighth-grade GPA between 1.5 and 2.0 are not qualified for college, and 20 percent drop out by eleventh grade. Students who earn an eighth-grade GPA of less than 1.0 are nearly as likely to drop out (44 percent) by eleventh grade as not, and the vast majority who do stay in school perform at levels that leave them unqualified for college.

---

[51] Roderick et al. (2006)

FIGURE 23

The Percent of Students at Very Low, Low, Moderate, and High Probability of Earning As or Bs in Ninth-Grade English Classes

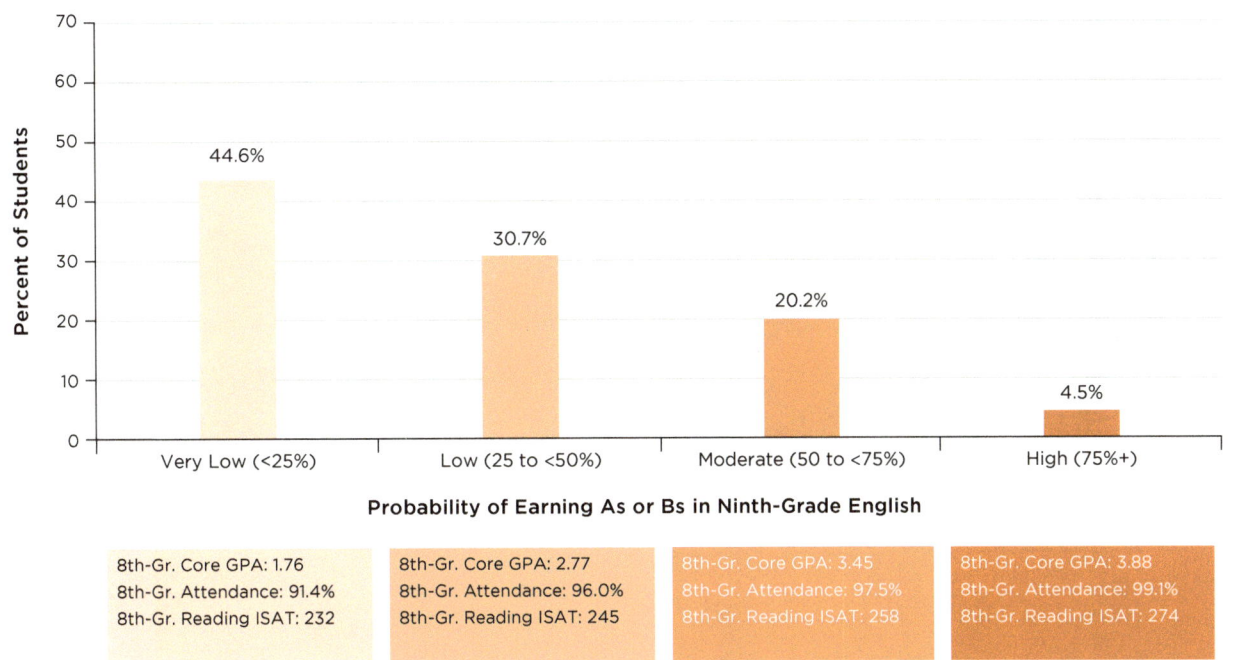

FIGURE 24

The Percent of Students at Very Low, Low, Moderate, and High Probability of Earning As or Bs in Ninth-Grade Math Classes

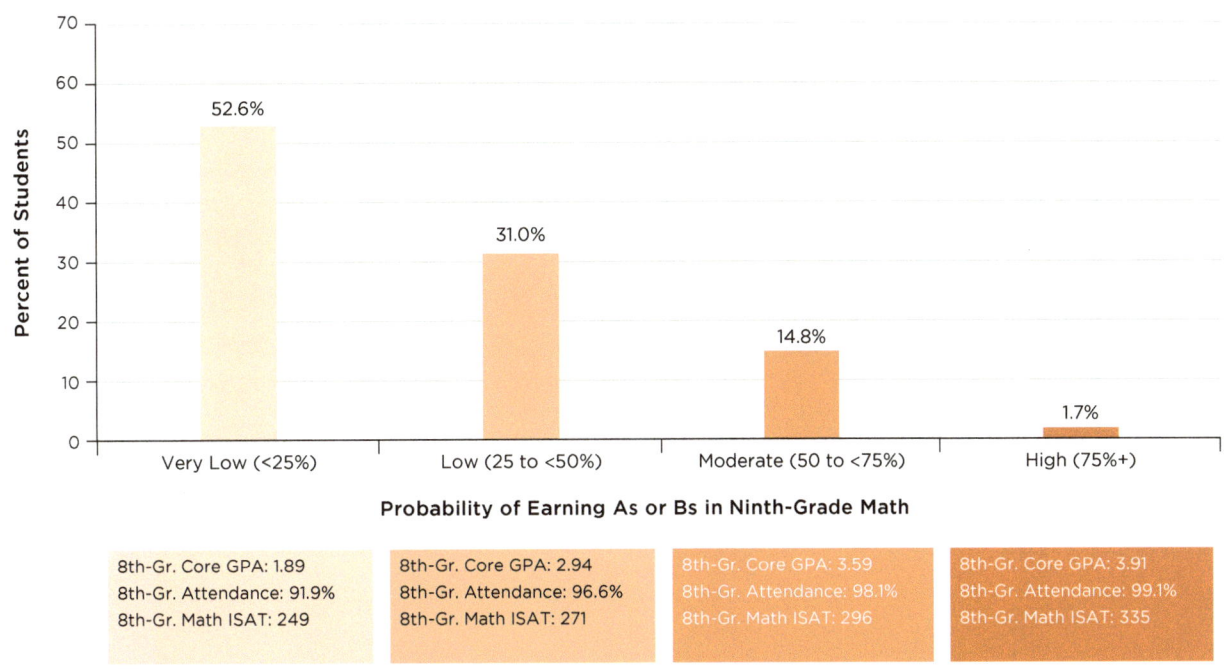

Note for Figures 23 and 24: The percentages are based on students entering ninth grade in the 2009-10 school year. The four probability groups shown in this chart were created by first running a logistic regression in which the probability of passing ninth-grade math was regressed on eighth-grade core GPA, attendance, ISAT math scores, and any significant interaction terms between these three indicators. Using predicted probabilities generated from the analysis, we then created the four groups using the cut points described in the parentheses above.

FIGURE 25

Course Performance in Eighth Grade Is Associated with Eleventh-Grade GPA in the Same Way as Ninth-Grade GPA

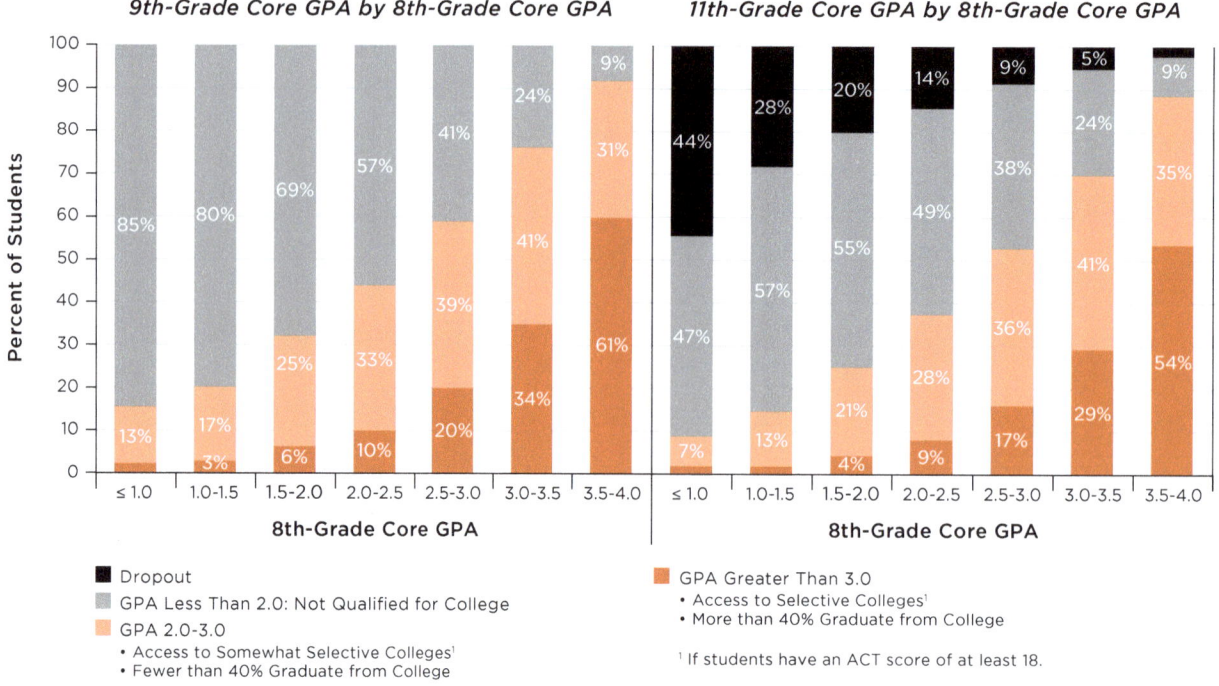

Dropout
GPA Less Than 2.0: Not Qualified for College
GPA 2.0-3.0
 • Access to Somewhat Selective Colleges[1]
 • Fewer than 40% Graduate from College

GPA Greater Than 3.0
 • Access to Selective Colleges[1]
 • More than 40% Graduate from College

[1] If students have an ACT score of at least 18.

Note: Based on students entering ninth grade in the 2009-10 school year, followed through the 2011-12 school year.

Strong Test Scores Do Not Inoculate Students Against Poor High School Outcomes

One of the most common strategies for improving students' educational attainment is to try to increase their skills in reading and math. However, even students with very strong test scores can struggle in high school.

Among students with strong test[C] scores in eighth grade:

- About a third (35 percent) had an average of B or better in their ninth-grade core classes.
- One-fifth (17 percent) had an average lower than C, making them very unlikely to even enroll in college and almost certain not to graduate.
- Over a fifth (22 percent) missed more than 20 days of school in ninth grade.

C Strong test scores are defined as meeting the eighth-grade 2013 Illinois State Standards in both reading and math. The 2013 standards were raised to be aligned with college readiness benchmarks. These numbers are based on the 2009 ninth-grade cohort, applying the 2013 state standards to define the group of high-scoring students in 2009.

Summary

While a student's eighth-grade record can give some idea of his likelihood to succeed in ninth grade, many Chicago students experience a large decline in performance that is not evident until the transition to high school. Even students with exemplary eighth-grade records suffer some decline and are unlikely to maintain their eighth-grade levels of performance during high school. Only those eighth-graders with GPAs greater than 3.0 have even a moderate chance of earning As or Bs in ninth grade. Students with a good chance of high grades in high school tend to have eighth-grade GPAs of 3.5 or higher, along with strong attendance or test scores.

This suggests that course performance in the middle grades needs to be very strong if students are to be to be ready for college at the end of high school. Earning a mix of Bs and Cs in eighth grade is simply not good enough. Many students with an eighth-grade GPA less than 3.0 drop out by eleventh grade, and the grades of all but a few students who are still enrolled are so low that they will be unqualified for any four-year college (less than a 2.0). At the same time, nine out of 10 students with an eighth-grade GPA greater than 3.5 go on to finish eleventh grade with a GPA that provides access to at least a somewhat selective college (greater than a 2.0). Students who aspire to college must be engaged in their courses and performing at a high level even prior to ninth grade.

Most students are unlikely to earn As or Bs in ninth grade, despite the fact they may be doing so in eighth grade. High schools may want to investigate why it is so difficult for students with strong middle grade records to be successful in ninth grade. If high schools could monitor the performance of their students, they might discover what types of supports are needed to keep grades from dropping. To help students at least maintain their levels of performance from the previous year would yield significant improvements in academic records and their likelihood of succeeding in college.

CHAPTER 6

Indicators of Whether Students Will Meet Test Benchmarks

ACT scores, along with students' GPA and other factors, determine the type of college students have access to after high school graduation. Students with ACT scores of 24 or higher, in combination with GPAs of 3.0 or higher, are likely to have access to very selective colleges. (**Table A1 in Appendix A** shows the relationships of students' eleventh-grade GPA, ACT scores, and the kind of colleges students have access to given their qualifications.) Students with the same test scores who attend colleges with different levels of selectivity have different earnings over their career. This is especially true for minority students, and these differences in earnings based on college selectivity increase over time.[52] Besides being important for college access, ACT scores are also important when applying for scholarships and loans to pay for college.

In Chicago, students take three tests as part of the Educational Planning and Assessment System (EPAS): the EXPLORE in the fall of eighth and ninth grade, PLAN in the fall of tenth grade, and ACT in the spring of eleventh grade.[53] These tests measure student achievement in English, reading, mathematics, and science. The four subject-area scores are averaged together to calculate a composite score. This portion of our analysis focuses on students' PLAN scores, because the PLAN is taken after the ninth-grade year. At the end of the chapter, the focus shifts to ACT scores, which are reported to colleges as part of the application process.

The PLAN test scores range from 1 to 32. For each subject, ACT has defined a college readiness benchmark; this is the score at which ACT has determined that students have a 50 percent chance of earning a B or

> This chapter evaluates potential middle grade indicators of performance on high school tests (EPAS) and which combinations of indicators provide the best prediction. This chapter focuses on composite scores first, and then on subject-specific EPAS tests.

better and a 75 percent chance of earning a C or better in corresponding college courses.[54] The PLAN college readiness benchmarks are 15 for English, 17 for reading, 19 for math, and 21 for science; the composite value is 18. This chapter examines students' average test scores, whether students reach the benchmarks in the different subjects, and whether students score a PLAN composite of 18 or above.

Many Chicago students do not meet the college readiness benchmarks on the PLAN; 48 percent of first-time freshmen in the fall of 2010, who took PLAN in the fall of 2011, reached the benchmark in English, 30 percent did in reading, 16 percent in math, and only 6 percent in science. These subject-specific patterns are similar to the results of the ACT taken in eleventh grade. While these percentages are lower than the national numbers, the subject-specific trends mirror the trends nationwide. Seventy percent of the 2011-12 PLAN-tested tenth-graders, nationally, met the benchmark in

---

52 Dale and Krueger (2012); Hoxby (2001).
53 In the past, CPS students also took the PLAN test in the fall of their eleventh grade. Some students might also take the ACT in the fall of their twelfth grade to improve their ACT score before applying to college.
54 Those are English composition, social science, college algebra, and biology. Social science college courses included history, psychology, sociology, political science, and economics classes (Allen and Sconing, 2005). In September 2013, ACT revised the ACT college-readiness benchmarks with more recent data (Allen, 2013). This has resulted in changes to the reading and science benchmarks; the reading benchmark went up a point, and the science benchmark went down a point for all tests in the EPAS series. For tests taken in 2013 and later, ACT will apply these revised benchmarks.

English, 52 percent in reading, 36 percent in math, and 27 percent in science.[55]

Given the low percentages of students reaching the benchmarks, many practitioners are looking for ways to help students meet these benchmarks through early intervention. Because the EPAS system is not available prior to eighth grade, it is difficult for school practitioners, students, and parents to know whether middle grade students are on a trajectory that makes it likely they will meet the benchmarks in high school and what the goals should be on tests given in the middle grade years in order to be aligned with later high school tests. Therefore, this chapter shows how middle grade indicators are related to PLAN test scores and the degree to which they can predict whether students will reach the college-readiness benchmarks on the PLAN and ACT.

ACT Benchmarks

ACT's college-readiness benchmarks are described in a report by Allen and Sconing (2005) and then revised in Allen (2013).

The benchmarks were calculated based on data that came from colleges that participated in ACT's Course Placement Service. In the 2005 report, the English benchmark analysis was based on 46 two-year colleges and 46 four-year colleges with 76,122 students, while the science benchmark analysis was based on 17 two-year colleges and 14 four-year colleges with 14,136 students.[D] Benchmarks were chosen to be the median value of ACT scores across colleges that give a 50/50 chance to students to earn a B or better in a college course. These cut-off scores varied from college to college. For example, in half of colleges, students with an ACT score of 18 have a 50/50 chance of getting a B or better in English Composition; in another quarter students only need a 14 to have a 50/50 chance of earning a B or better, while in 25 percent of colleges students need a score of 20 in English ACT to have a 50/50 chance at a B or higher. The variability is lower for algebra and science, and fewer students were part of those analyses.

ACT benchmarks provide a context from which one can make meaning out of a score. For example, on its own, a score of 20 has no meaning. Knowing, however, that the benchmark score on the math portion of the ACT represents the point at which a student has a 50/50 chance of getting a B or higher in a college algebra class puts a score of 20 in context as one that is not too far behind the benchmark.

Yet, while they provide meaning to a specific score, differences in the preparation and later success of students who meet the benchmark versus those who do not are not necessarily meaningful. There are many factors other than students' ACT scores that are more strongly associated with their college success than their test score. These factors include attributes of the college a student attends and the classes in which the student enrolls at that college—the quality of instruction, institutional setting, and fit between student and college. They also include other academic skills and noncognitive factors that are not measured on the ACT—such as students' ability to show up to class and put forth their best effort and creativity, as well as the supports they receive from family and peers.

Just because students make a benchmark does not mean that they will do well in their college classes; students who meet the ACT benchmarks have a 50 percent chance of scoring Bs or better in their college classes. That means that half of the students who score just at or above the benchmark do not receive at least a B. At the same time, many students who score below the benchmark do perform well. With ACT's reading benchmark, for example, a score of 21 gives a student a 50 percent chance of a B in a college social science class, but a score of 16—one that is 4 points lower and equivalent to about three to four years of growth in high school—gives a student a 40 percent chance of earning a B or better.[E] Thus, a large difference in scores results in only a slight difference in the probability of success.

D The 2013 report replicates the same analysis with more recent data. The number of students varied from 131,000 for social science to 42,000 for biology, while the number of colleges varied from 136 in the English Composition I analysis to 90 for biology analysis.

E Based on graph of the relationship between ACT scores and grades at a "typical" college in Allen and Sconing (2005).

---

55 ACT, Inc. (2012).

PLAN Composite Scores Are Strongly Predicted by Eighth-Grade State Test Scores (ISAT Scores)

Eighth-grade test scores on the ISAT are the strongest single predictor of tenth-grade PLAN test scores, compared to all other indicators of middle school performance. This is not surprising—just as grades are the best predictor of future grades, test scores are the best predictor of future test scores. The relationship of past test scores to future test scores is much stronger, however, than the relationship of past grades to future grades. Students' scores on ACT's PLAN are strongly tied to their incoming performance on the State ISAT tests. The tenth-grade PLAN composite score is correlated with students' eighth-grade ISAT math score at 0.79 and with their eighth-grade ISAT reading score at 0.74. In general, correlations of 0.80 or higher tend to be measuring the same underlying construct. Note that these are correlations between two different tests, which are not on the same scale, taken more than a year apart, and are testing *different subjects*. Despite all this, the relationship of past test scores with future test scores is very strong.

Higher math test scores in eighth grade correspond to higher scores on PLAN (**see Figure 26**). Students exceeding standards in eighth-grade math have a very good chance of scoring 18 or higher on the PLAN composite; more than 94 percent do so. Students at the high end of the "meets" range have a very high chance as well; 3 out of 4 students do so. Those students in the lower part of the "meets" range have about a one in four chance of attaining an 18 (28 percent). Students who do not meet standards in eighth grade have almost no chance of scoring 18 or above in PLAN composite. Among students who take the PLAN in tenth grade, those not meeting state standards in eighth grade are almost certain to score *"at chance"* on the PLAN (below 13). Their skills are not well measured by the test.

Students with low scores in eighth grade are also less likely to actually take the PLAN test in the fall of their tenth-grade year. A quarter of students who did not take the PLAN test left the district before the test took place

FIGURE 26

Percent of Students Not Taking PLAN Tests, Percent of Students Scoring 18 or Above on PLAN Composite, and the Average PLAN Composite Scores by Eighth-Grade Math ISAT Scores

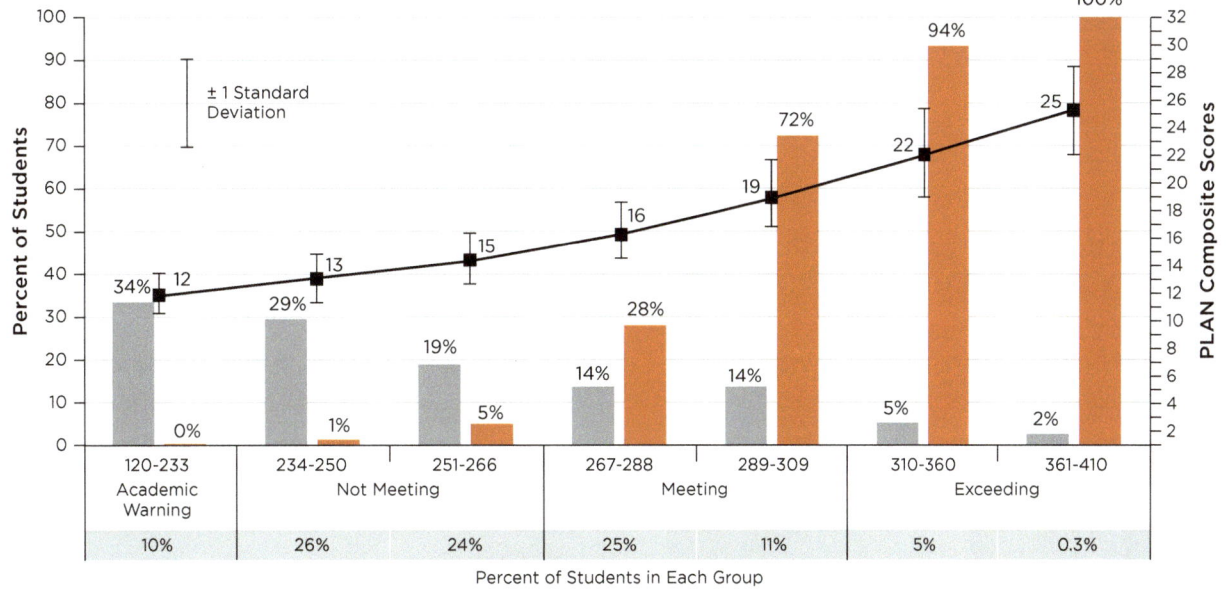

Note: This figure shows the relationship between eighth-grade ISAT math scores and the percent of students not taking PLAN in tenth grade (gray bars), the percent of students scoring 18 or above in PLAN composite scores (orange bars), and the average composite score with a ±1 standard deviation to show the variability in scores (the squares represent the average PLAN composite score and the whiskers represent the ±1 standard deviation around the mean). This chart shows the performance of students who entered ninth grade in the 2009-10 school year, and took the PLAN in fall 2010. Eighth-grade test scores are represented using state standards in 2013.

Chapter 6 | Indicators of Whether Students Will Meet Test Benchmarks

and 7 percent dropped out of school. The rest (66 percent) were still in school—some of them were in ninth grade (25 percent), but a large proportion (41 percent) was enrolled in tenth grade and did not take the test. The analyses presented in this chapter are based on students who took the PLAN tests their second year of high school. Because they represent only those students with test scores who were enrolled in the tenth grade, the average PLAN scores and percent meeting the benchmark at each level of the ISAT are somewhat biased upward—they would likely be lower if all students who took the eighth-grade ISAT were tested on the PLAN in tenth grade. Even with this upward bias, the probability of scoring 18 or above on the PLAN composite for students at the most typical ISAT score levels is very low.

Test scores in earlier grades are almost as predictive of PLAN scores as eighth-grade test scores, and much more predictive than background characteristics, grades, or attendance. Table 7 shows the degree to which middle grade indicators predict students' performance on the PLAN—both the prediction of the composite score and the probability of scoring 18 on the composite. Not only are tests taken in eighth grade highly correlated with PLAN composite scores, but tests taken in years prior to eighth grade are almost as predictive. The correlations between PLAN composite scores and ISAT scores in eighth, seventh, and even sixth grade are nearly identical. The correlation between the ISAT scores in two consecutive years is also high: in reading it is 0.81 and in math it is 0.88. This implies that students who score high one year will tend to score high the following year and the data from either year—eighth or seventh grade—can predict how students will do on the PLAN. Even sixth-grade test scores are very good predictors of PLAN composite scores and better predictors than other eighth-grade indicators that are not based on tests. Chapter 8 shows students' test trajectories in the middle grades and what these correlations mean for differences in students' test score growth over the middle grade years.

Eighth-grade course performance, other middle grade indicators, and background variables are weaker predictors of PLAN composite scores than middle grade test data. While eighth-grade core GPA is correlated with tenth-grade test scores, the correlation is much weaker than with prior test scores—around 0.56 (**see Table 7**). Combined, students' background characteristics (e.g., race, gender, special education status, free and reduced-priced status, neighborhood poverty and socioeconomic status, and whether students are old for grade) explain a third of the variation in test scores, similar to core grades (see adjusted-R^2 in **Table 7**). Special education, whether students are old for grade, free and reduced-priced lunch, and race data are the background variables most strongly associated with test scores. Attendance, misconducts, suspensions, grit, and study habits have very weak relationships with tenth-grade test scores, explaining a meager proportion of the variation in test scores.

PLAN scores are better predicted by using more than one prior test score, from multiple subjects or grades. Two middle grade test scores combined from different subjects (reading and math) or from different grades (seventh and eighth grade) are slightly more predictive of PLAN scores in any subject than just one test by itself. For example, the adjusted-R^2 from a model in which eighth-grade math and reading ISAT scores are combined to predict PLAN math scores in tenth grade improves from 0.63 to 0.68, compared to a model with only eighth-grade math ISAT scores (**see Table 7 and Table E.2 in Appendix E**). This is because any one score is likely to have measurement error; students have good days and bad days, and multiple measures provide a more precise estimate of their true ability than one score by itself. This also suggests that each test measures underlying general skills as much as subject-specific learning. The addition of the information of one more test score helps with the prediction of the PLAN scores mainly for students close to exceeding or exceeding in math in eighth grade, where there is more variation in their scores. This could be an indication of a lack of precision in scoring at the high end of the ISAT or that school effects are more important for these students, as discussed later in the chapter.

Once we know students' reading and math test scores in eighth grade, adding other information does not help much with the prediction of high school test scores, with the exception of adding school information

TABLE 7

Eighth-Grade ISAT Scores Are Strong Predictors of Tenth-Grade PLAN Composite Scores; Other Middle Grade Indicators Add Little to the Prediction

Middle Grade Indicators	PLAN Composite Scores		Scoring 18 or Above in PLAN Composite	
Single Indicator	Correlation	Adjusted-R^2	Pseudo-R^2	Percent Correct*
8th-Grade Reading ISAT				
Linear Term	0.74	0.56	0.38	86.5%
Linear & Squared Terms	—	0.58	0.38	86.5%
8th-Grade Math ISAT				
Linear Term	0.79	0.63	0.39	87.3%
Linear & Squared Terms	—	0.63	0.39	87.4%
7th-Grade Reading ISAT	0.74	0.55	0.35	85.8%
7th-Grade Math ISAT	0.76	0.61	0.38	87.0%
6th-Grade Reading ISAT	0.74	0.54	0.35	84.8%
6th-Grade Math ISAT	0.76	0.58	0.36	85.4%
8th-Grade Core GPA	0.56	0.31	0.22	82.5%
8th-Grade Attendance	0.22	0.05	0.03	77.2%
8th-Grade Suspensions	-0.16	0.02	0.02	77.2%
8th-Grade Misconducts	-0.11	0.01	0.01	77.2%
8th-Grade Grit	0.04	0.00	0.00	74.7%
8th-Grade Study Habits	0.02	0.00	0.00	74.8%
8th-Grade Background Characteristics	—	0.32	0.18	80.4%
Combining Two or More 8th-Grade Indicators				
8th-Grade Reading and Math ISAT Tests		0.68	0.44	89.0%
8th-Grade Reading and Math ISAT Tests + Core GPA		0.69	0.45	89.3%
8th-Grade Reading and Math ISAT Tests + Background Characteristics		0.70	0.44	89.2%
All 8th-Grade Student-Level Indicators		0.71	0.45	89.6%
Adding Seventh-Grade Indicators				
8th- and 7th-Grade Reading and Math ISAT Tests		0.72	0.46	89.8%
Adding School Effects				
School Effects Alone (Middle and High School Effects)		0.50	†	†
All 8th-Grade Student-Level Indicators + School Effects		0.75	†	†

Note: See Table E2 in Appendix E for a complete analysis of all middle grade indicators, including gains and growth in test scores. Sample size was kept the same for most analyses to make comparisons easier, except when data from surveys were analyzed. In those cases the sample sizes get smaller. That is the case when grit and study habits are part of the analysis. * Given the data for this cohort and analyses, a model with no explanatory variables would be able to correctly predict 77.2 percent of students whether they score 18 and above versus lower than 18. † Given the low variability in the percent of students scoring 18 or above in the PLAN composite by middle and high school, these models could not be run.

or test scores from prior years. Adding core GPA, for example, to eighth-grade reading and math test scores improves the adjusted-R^2 from 0.68 to 0.69, and adding all eighth-grade variables gives an adjusted-R^2 of 0.71. Adding seventh-grade ISAT scores in reading and math increases the adjusted-R^2 to 0.72. Given the small improvements of including extra variables, it may not be worth including more than two test scores in an indicator system to predict test scores in high school.

An indicator system based on reading and math eighth-grade scores correctly identifies 95 percent of the students at risk of not meeting the benchmark on the PLAN composite (see Figure 27). At the same time, 30 percent of the students who are identified as at risk will actually have a score of 18 or above. (The y-axis of Figure 27 shows the proportion of students correctly classified as scoring below 18, and the x-axis shows the proportion of students incorrectly classified as scoring below 18. The different points represent various models for predicting whether students meet a PLAN composite score of 18.) A model using attendance, suspensions, misconducts, grit, or study habits to predict which students score below 18 is no better than making a random guess, as indicated by the location of those model statistics on the dotted diagonal line. Other indicators (e.g., background characteristics, core GPA, or middle grade test scores) provide increasingly more accurate predictions, as indicated by the movement of the dots further to the upper-left of the figure. In particular, using students' scores from multiple tests (reading and math, seventh and eighth grade) improves the accuracy of the prediction.

Students' test scores in high school depend on where students attend middle school and high school. Middle school and high school effects explain part of the variation we see in PLAN scores for students with similar middle grade test scores (see Table 7). Figure 28 shows the degree to which students' PLAN scores are systematically different, depending on which middle school and which high school they attend (see panel A for the impact of attending different middle schools and panel B for high schools, net of the effects of the other). Students with the same predicted PLAN scores, based on ISAT scores in the middle grades, can have PLAN scores that differ by as much as two points,

FIGURE 27

Correct versus Incorrect Classification of Students Not Scoring 18 on the PLAN Composite

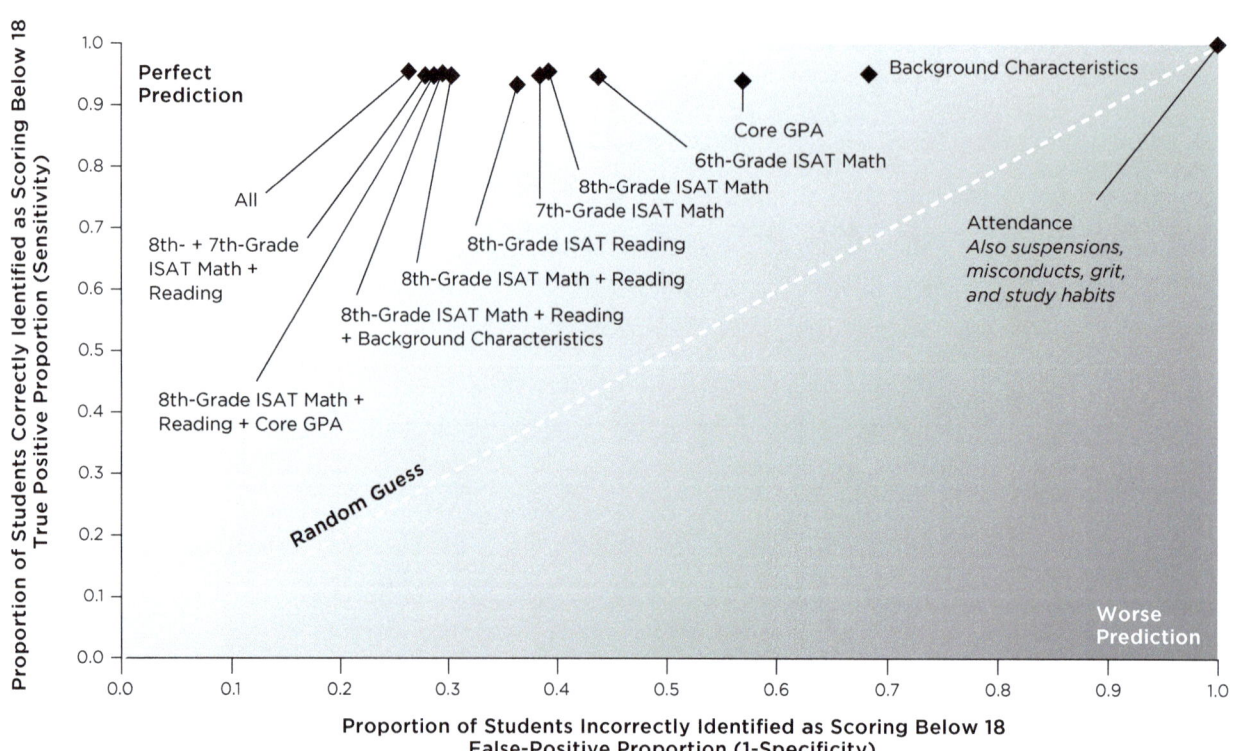

FIGURE 28

Variation in Predicted PLAN Scores by Predicted PLAN Based on Middle Grade Indicators

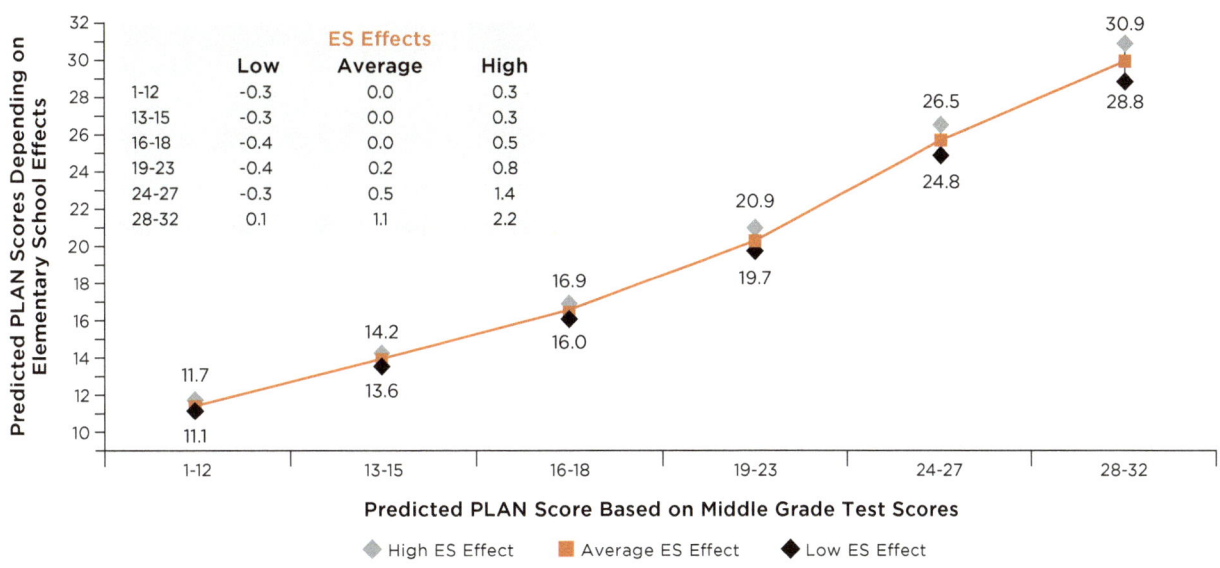

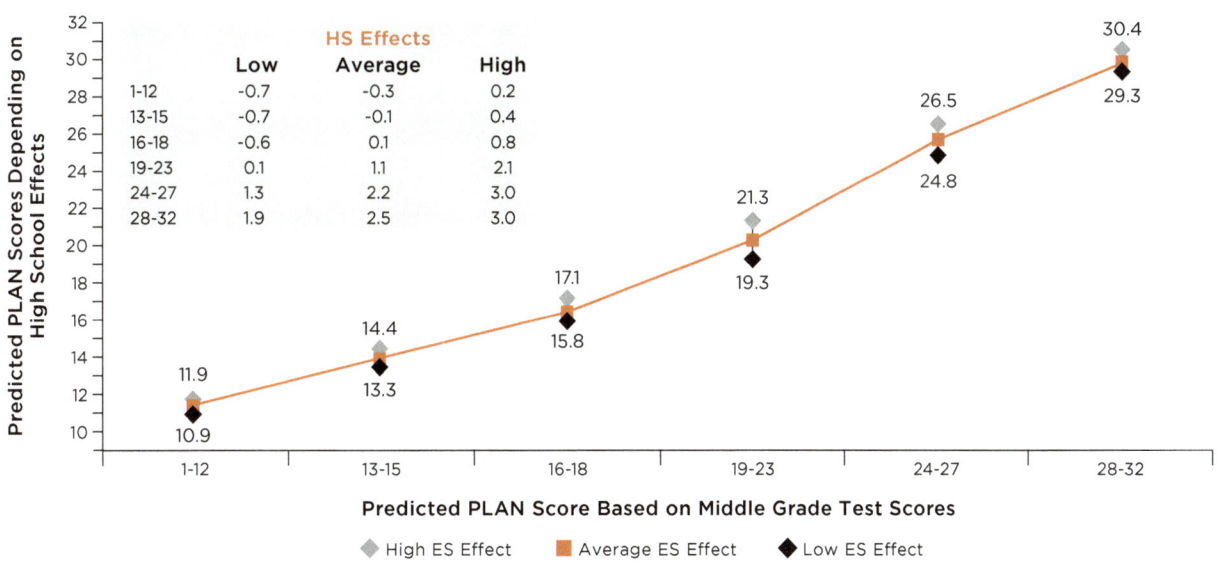

Note: These graphs show the variability of students' predicted PLAN composite scores depending on which elementary/middle school (panel A) or high school (panel B) students attend. The graphs are based on cross-nested models in which students are simultaneously nested in their elementary/middle school and also in their high school. School effects are determined from the variation in school residuals, after controlling for students' eighth-grade reading and math ISAT scores; see Appendix C for additional details on the models. The black squares in each graph represent the average PLAN composite score based on students' eighth-grade reading and math ISAT scores. The diamonds above and below the black squares represent the predicted PLAN scores for students with similar eighth-grade ISAT scores attending elementary/middle schools with high and low effects (panel A) and attending high schools with high and low value effects (panel B); high and low school effects are defined as one standard deviation above or below the mean, respectively. The table on each graph shows the value of these school effects as well (i.e., how many PLAN points the model predicts that a student score based on whether they attend a school where students score higher or lower than typical). Each row represents the range of school effects for students with similar eighth-grade records; values by columns can be compared to see how different school effects are for students with different performance in eighth grade.

depending on which middle school they attended, after removing any effects of where they attend high school. Among students with high scores, middle school effects are particularly strong. These differences might be due to variation in the types of skills students learned in the middle grades—students at schools that taught specifically to the types of questions on the ISAT, at the expense of the types of skills and questions asked on ACT's EPAS system (PLAN test), might not score as well on the PLAN as their ISAT scores would suggest. Some middle schools may have better prepared their students for the type of work that prepares them to score well on the EPAS. Schools at which students perform better on high school tests than their middle grade tests would predict also tend to have students that get better high school grades than their middle school grades would predict; the correlation between middle school effects on grades and tests scores is 0.34, net of high school effects and students' eighth-grade achievement.

Variation in PLAN scores for students with the same ISAT scores also depend on the high school they attend. These differences could represent different rates of learning in high school or alignment of high school instruction with the PLAN. High school effects tend to be larger for students scoring in the middle of the distribution, not the extremes. Two students with same middle grade ISAT score, who came from the same elementary school, can vary in their PLAN math score by as much as 2 points, depending on which high school they attend. Students gain about a point a year on average, which suggests that students gain about twice as much each year on their math scores at some schools than at others.

High ISAT scores not only increase students' likelihood of scoring well on the PLAN but also give them access to high schools where students show higher-than-average gains. Students with low scores in the middle grades generally attend high schools where students make smaller-than-average gains. As shown in the table within **panel B of Figure 28**, among students with low test scores, some attend high schools where the average school effect is 0.7 points below average, while others attend schools where the average effect is about 0.2 above expected; while there is a range among the school effects, none are particularly high and some are quite low. On the other hand, high-scoring students generally attend high schools that contribute to their scores by almost two points or more on average. These estimates come from models that compare gains among students with the same incoming scores, suggesting that students with high skills leaving the middle grades tend to go to high schools with above-average gains.

Students who attend middle schools with high-achieving, more advantaged peers are more likely to score higher on their PLAN math test than their ISAT scores would predict, compared to students with the same eighth-grade test scores who attended middle schools with lower-achieving, less advantaged peers. **Table 8** shows the relationships of middle school characteristics with middle school effects on test scores—effects that are not reflected in students' ISAT scores, and net of any effects that result from where their students attend high school. The second column shows high school effects, net of any effects of where students attend middle school, and controlling for their eighth-grade ISAT scores. The final column shows middle school effects without controlling for high school effects, allowing for the fact that middle schools tend to send their students to particular high schools. Students' high school PLAN scores are better than their ISAT scores at predicting if they come from middle schools serving students who come from neighborhoods with lower levels of poverty (r=-0.34), fewer students who are over-age for their grade (r=-0.34), and more students who are white (r=0.32).

Students are also more likely to have higher PLAN composite scores if they attend high schools with higher-achieving and more advantaged peers (**see the second column of Table 8**), even after removing any effects of their middle school. The absolute size of these correlations is always larger for high schools than for middle schools, but these correlations only reflect school effects that are not reflected in students' eighth-grade ISAT scores. Attending high schools with high-scoring students is particularly strongly associated with students scoring higher on the PLAN than their ISAT scores would predict (r=0.77). This is consistent with prior research that suggests students learn more in classes with higher-achieving peers.[56] Their scores are also higher if they attend high schools serving students who come from neighborhoods with lower levels of poverty (r=-0.42), fewer students who are over-age for their grade

TABLE 8

Relationships of School Characteristics with School Effects on Math PLAN Test Scores

	Correlation of Middle School Effects with School Variables, Controlling for High School Attended	Correlations of High School Effects with School Variables, Controlling for Middle School Attended	Correlation of Middle School Effects with School Variables, Not Removing High School Effects
ISAT Math	0.21***	0.77***	0.40***
% Latino	0.12**	0.09	0.08-
% African American	-0.27***	-0.26**	-0.29***
% White	0.32***	0.46***	0.44***
% Over Age	-0.34***	-0.48***	-0.43***
% Special Education	-0.17**	-0.34***	-0.14***
Average Concentration of Poverty	-0.34***	-0.42***	-0.43***
Average Social Capital	0.15**	0.29**	0.30***
General	-0.13**	-0.43***	-0.28***
Magnet	0.18***	0.58***	0.32***
Vocational	NA	-0.12	NA
APC	NA	-0.18*	NA

Note: Residuals result from 1) a 2-level model where students are nested with in elementary schools and 2) a 2-level cross-nested model where students are nested with in elementary and high schools. Each model was used to predict the PLAN composite scores based on eighth-grade ISAT reading and math scores at the student level. No predictors were included at the school level.

(r=-0.48), and more students who are white (r=0.46).

Because students from high-performing, more socially advantaged middle schools are also likely to attend more advantaged high schools, the relationships of middle school characteristics with middle school effects are larger if we do not control for high school effects when gauging middle school effects (**see column three of Table 8**). Students from socially advantaged middle schools (those with fewer students in high-poverty neighborhoods, fewer students old for grade, and serving more white students) have higher high school test scores than their ISAT scores would predict, not only because their middle schools provide direct advantages, but also because these students are more likely to attend high schools where students score higher than expected.

Any subject-specific ISAT test is strongly predictive of any subject-specific PLAN score. Improving PLAN composite scores requires improving ISAT scores in any or all of the subject-specific tests. **Table 9** shows the correlations of the PLAN subject-specific scores with middle grade test scores and grades. More detailed information on other middle grade predictors can be found in **Appendix E**. The correlations between the reading and math ISAT tests are lower with the PLAN subject-specific scores than with the composite scores. The ISAT math test by itself is correlated at 0.79 with the PLAN composite score, which is higher than the correlation with the PLAN math test (0.77). Such high correlations suggest that the tests may be measuring general academic skills and the ability to take tests, at least as much as they measure skills in specific subjects. The correlations between the ISAT scores and the PLAN composite are higher than the correlations with the subject-specific tests because there is less measurement error when multiple scores are combined (random errors on one test tend to cancel each other out). The reading and math ISAT tests together are more predictive of any subject test than the subject-specific tests are of later tests of the same

---

56 Nomi and Allensworth (2013); Ballou (2007); Gamoran (1996).

TABLE 9

Correlations of Test Scores and GPA in Eighth Grade with Tenth-Grade Test Scores

	Tenth-Grade PLAN				
	English	Reading	Math	Science	Composite
8th-Grade ISAT Reading	0.70	0.66	0.64	0.60	0.75
8th-Grade ISAT Math	0.71	0.62	0.77	0.66	0.79
ISAT Reading & Math Combined	0.76	0.68	0.76	0.67	0.83
8th-Grade English GPA	0.49	0.44	0.46	0.41	0.52
8th-Grade Math GPA	0.42	0.37	0.45	0.39	0.47
8th-Grade Core GPA	0.51	0.46	0.50	0.45	0.56

subject (except in the case of math). Likewise, combining seventh- and eighth-grade scores provides a better prediction than scores from just one grade level.

Eleventh-Grade ACT Scores Are Highly Correlated with Scores in Sixth, Seventh, and Eighth Grade

In eleventh grade, students take the ACT tests. The scores from these subject tests, along with the composite score, are part of the information that colleges use for determining admissions. Not surprisingly, the best indicators of ACT composite scores and whether students will score 21 or above are the same indicators that are most predictive of PLAN scores (see Table 10). Test scores in eighth grade or seventh grade, or even sixth grade, are highly correlated with ACT scores, just as they are highly correlated with PLAN scores. The correlation between the PLAN and ACT composite scores is very high (0.89), but still the correlations between middle grade ISAT tests and the ACT tests taken three years later are also very strong (between 0.75 and 0.80, depending on grade level and subject). Other information, such as GPA, attendance, suspensions, and grit, does not add much to the prediction of ACT, once we know students' eighth-grade scores.

Summary

Students' middle grade ISAT scores are highly predictive of their future scores on the EPAS system. Reading and math ISAT tests strongly predict performance on any of the high school tests, regardless of the subject or grade level of the prior or subsequent test. Two test scores provide a better prediction than one score—either by combining the scores across subjects or across grades, since both reduce the measurement error associated with one score. There is no need to develop a complicated prediction system that includes information about students' backgrounds or course performance, since this provides little additional accuracy to the prediction of later test scores.

Students from particular middle schools perform better on the high school tests than expected—given their ISAT scores—regardless of the high school they attend. This suggests that some middle schools may be preparing their students in ways that are more aligned with the types of skills tested on the EPAS than other schools, while other schools are preparing students to do well on the ISAT in ways that do not translate to the EPAS. There are also high school effects; students make higher gains on tests at some high schools than others. In general, students with higher scores in the middle grades enroll in high schools with higher average gains. They might have more options available to them than lower-scoring students.

Most CPS students are at risk of not reaching the benchmarks on the PLAN or the ACT. Thus, targeted interventions would be impractical, even though students can be accurately identified. Also, because the prediction of reaching EPAS benchmarks is so precise, it suggests that it is difficult to change students' test score trajectories, as few students achieve outcomes other than those that were expected. This is discussed more thoroughly in Chapters 7 and 8.

TABLE 10

Relationships of Middle Grade Indicators with ACT Composite Scores

Middle Grade Indicators	ACT Composite Scores		Scoring 21 or Above in ACT Composite	
Single Indicator	Correlation	Adjusted-R^2	Pseudo-R^2	Percent Correct*
8th-Grade Reading ISAT				
Linear	0.76	0.58	0.39	84.1%
Linear & Squared Terms		0.58	0.39	84.1%
8th-Grade Math ISAT				
Linear	0.80	0.64	0.41	85.7%
Linear & Squared Terms	—	0.64	0.41	85.7%
7th-Grade Reading ISAT	0.75	0.57	0.36	83.5%
7th-Grade Math ISAT	0.80	0.63	0.40	84.9%
6th-Grade Reading ISAT	0.75	0.56	0.36	83.1%
6th-Grade Math ISAT	0.77	0.59	0.37	83.6%
8th-Grade Core GPA	0.56	0.31	0.22	78.9%
8th-Grade Attendance	0.18	0.03	0.02	72.0%
8th-Grade Suspensions	-0.13	0.01	0.02	72.0%
8th-Grade Misconducts	-0.08	0.01	0.01	72.0%
8th-Grade Grit	0.01	0.00	0.00	69.7%
8th-Grade Study Habits	-0.01	0.00	0.00	69.7%
8th-Grade Background Characteristics	—	0.33	0.20	77.1%
Combining Two or More 8th-Grade Indicators				
8th-Grade Reading and Math ISAT Tests		0.70	0.46	87.3%
8th-Grade Reading and Math ISAT Tests + Core GPA		0.71	0.46	87.6%
8th-Grade Reading and Math ISAT Tests + Background Characteristics		0.73	0.47	88.0%
All 8th-Grade Student-Level Indicators		0.74	0.47	88.0%
Adding Seventh-Grade Indicators				
8th- and 7th-Grade Reading and Math ISAT Tests		0.73	0.48	88.2%
Adding School Effects				
School Effects Alone (Middle and High School Effects)		0.51	†	†
All 8th-Grade Student-Level Indicators + School Effects		0.79	†	†

Note: There are 14,928 students included in these analyses. A model with no explanatory variables would be able to predict correctly 72.0 percent of students whether they score 21 and above versus lower than 21. †Given the low variability in the percent of students scoring 21 or above in ACT composite by middle and high school, these models could not be run.

CHAPTER 7

Who Is at Risk of Not Reaching the PLAN and ACT Benchmarks?

In the previous chapter, we showed that middle grade test scores strongly predict how students will score on their tenth- and eleventh-grade tests. In this chapter, we show who is at risk of not reaching benchmarks and how middle grade ISAT scores are related to PLAN scores. Only students with very high test scores in the middle grades (close to exceeding standards in math and in reading) have a good chance to reach the benchmarks in tenth grade. Unfortunately, most students are scoring far from the high scores (high *"meets"* range or *"exceeds standards"*) and have an extremely small chance of reaching those benchmarks. The strong relationship between ISAT and EPAS scores allows middle grade practitioners, parents, and students to identify students' likely scores on the PLAN—which could help them set challenging, but attainable, learning goals that are appropriate for individual students, as opposed to benchmarks that are universally applied even if unattainable by currently known practices.

The Vast Majority of Students Are at Very High Risk of Not Reaching the Tenth-Grade PLAN Benchmarks

More than half of CPS students are not meeting standards, and one-quarter just barely meet standards (low range of the *"meets"* range) in eighth-grade math. A student who is just meeting standards or is just below standards is likely to score below the benchmark in all four subjects tested in PLAN—from two points below in English to six points below in science. In order to meet the ACT benchmarks at the end of eleventh grade, students who are one point behind on the PLAN will need to make gains that are twice what is typical over the tenth- and eleventh-grade years, while students that are two points behind would need to grow three times the average rate.[57]

> This chapter shows the levels of performance in the middle grades that give students a chance of meeting PLAN and ACT benchmarks in the tenth and eleventh grades.

Students are less likely to meet the math and science benchmarks than the reading and English benchmarks. This occurs not because students have lower performance in math and science but because the benchmarks are set higher. Based on their middle grade test scores, about one-third of students are at very high risk (less than a 1-in-4 chance) of scoring below the English benchmark, and over half of students are at very high risk of scoring below the reading benchmark (**see Figure 29**). Over three-fourths of students are at very high risk of missing the math benchmark, and over 90 percent of students are at very high risk of missing the science benchmark. Nationally, in 2011-12, only about one-fifth of PLAN takers pass all four benchmarks; 70 percent pass English, 52 percent pass reading, 36 percent pass math, and 27 percent pass science.[58]

While many students have extremely low probabilities of reaching any of the ACT benchmarks, there are some groups of students who have a fairly good chance of reaching some of the benchmarks. Almost half of students have a good chance (greater than 50 percent) of meeting the benchmarks in English, and almost a quarter of students have a good chance of meeting the benchmarks in reading. On average, these students have scores that are at the high end of the "meets" range on their reading tests in the middle grades. Fourteen

---

[57] Based on a typical growth of just over one point per year.

[58] ACT, Inc. (2012).

FIGURE 29

Percent of Students at Different Risks for Not Reaching Benchmarks on the PLAN English, Reading, Math, and Science Tests

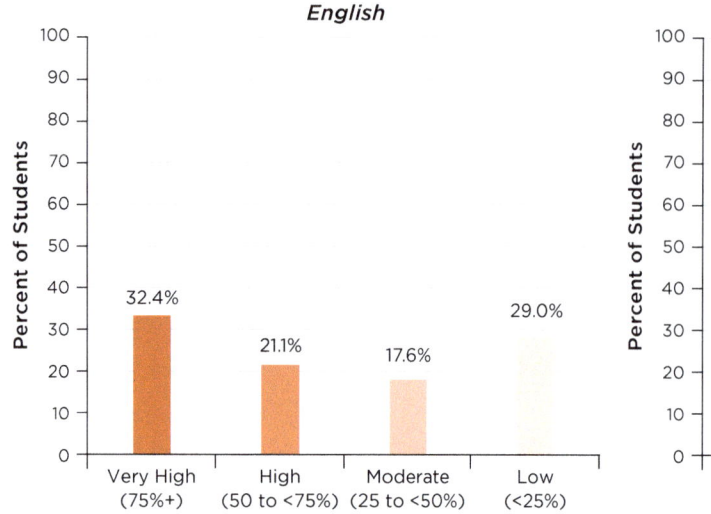

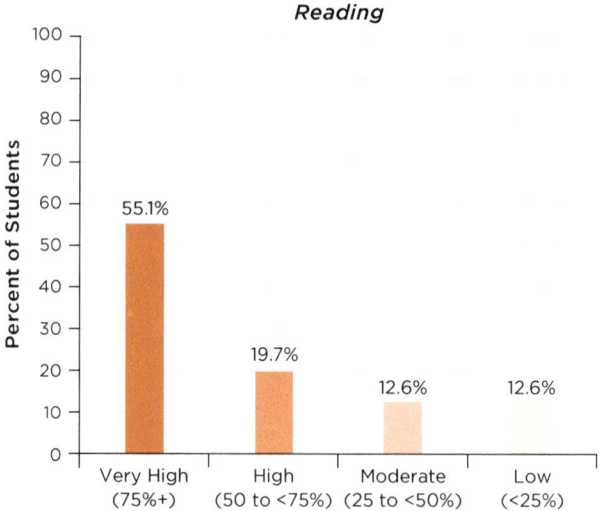

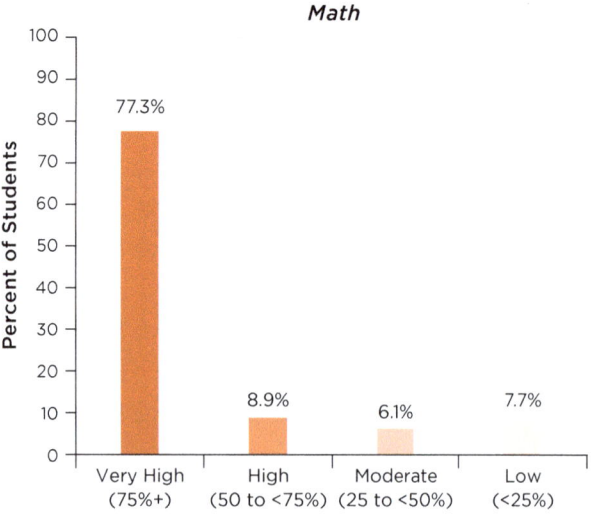

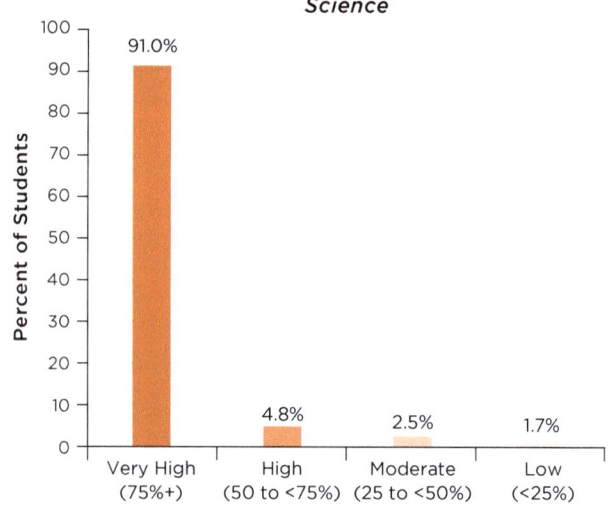

Note: The first bar on the left of each graph shows the percent of students who are at very high risk of not reaching the benchmark (greater than 75 percent chance). The next bar represents the group of students at high risk: students with a probability between 50 and 75 percent of not reaching the benchmark. The third bar shows students with probabilities between 25 and 50 percent, who are at moderate risk. And the last column shows the percent of low-risk students, with probabilities less than 25 percent of not reaching the benchmark. Each chart is created based on a model with the best two predictors. In the case of English and science, those two predictors are the eighth-grade ISAT reading and math scores; in the case of reading the two best predictors were the eighth- and seventh-grade ISAT reading and the in the case of math they were the eighth- and seventh-grade ISAT math. The letters in parenthesis next to the average ISAT scores denotes the 2013 student performance level.

percent of students have at least a 50 percent chance of meeting the PLAN math benchmark based on their middle school math scores, and less than 5 percent do on the science test. These students were exceeding standards, or close to exceeding standards, on the math tests in the middle grade years. Only students who are exceeding, or close to exceeding, standards on both the math and reading ISAT in eighth grade have a good chance of scoring at least an 18 on the PLAN composite (see Table 11). Students who just meet state standards on both the math and reading tests in eighth grade have just a 28 percent chance. Students who are not meeting state standards on either test have close to a zero probability of reaching an 18 on the PLAN composite.

The Benchmarks Are Not Meaningful for Many Students

The reality is that most students in CPS come to high school with skills that make them very unlikely to reach the ACT benchmarks. However, that does not mean that they will be unprepared for college. The benchmarks provide a context for understanding the scores, but they are not deterministic in terms of students' actual performance in college (see *ACT Benchmarks*, p.64). It is more important that students score as high as possible so that they can access a wider range of colleges.

Students with the same ISAT scores can end up with very different PLAN scores, although it is unlikely for them to move out of a particular range of scores. For example, of the students scoring 241-245 in math in eighth grade, none reach an 18 on the PLAN; but 20 percent score 15 or higher, 20 percent score 14, 25 percent score 13, and 34 percent score 12 or below (see Figure 30). A PLAN score of 15 gives students a shot at attaining ACT scores that make them eligible to enter a four-year college. For these students, a challenging, yet attainable, goal would be to aim for 15 in the PLAN composite. This has implications for the type of instruction that will lead them to make the largest gains.

Students with ISAT math scores in the *"meets"* range of 286-290 have a 50/50 chance of scoring 18 or above on the PLAN and end up with scores that range from about 13 to 24. These are students with a good shot at making ACT's benchmarks and being eligible for selective colleges and scholarships, but their prospects are uncertain. Their experiences in high school will shape whether they attain the benchmark goal. High schools

TABLE 11

Percent of Students Scoring 18 or Higher in PLAN Composite by Eighth-Grade Scores

		Eighth-Grade Reading ISAT (2013 Student Performance Levels)						
		Academic Warning	Below Standards	Meets Standards		Exceeds Standards		
Eighth-Grade Math ISAT (2013 Student Performance Levels)		120-217	218-232	233-247	248-259	260-270	271-319	320-364
Academic Warning	120-233	0% n=787	0% n=609	0% n=293				
Below Standards	234-250	0% n=682	0% n=1,901	1% n=1,841	4% n=367			
	251-266	0% n=128	1% n=870	2% n=2,526	11% n=1,273	23% n=212		
Meets Standards	267-288			4% n=224	9% n=1,793	28% n=2,292	53% n=949	72% n=358
	289-309				34% n=206	62% n=814	79% n=729	90% n=681
Exceeds Standards	310-360					81% n=154	95% n=287	99% n=597
	361-410							

Note: Based on students who entered ninth grade in the 2009-10 school year.

should pay particular attention to students in this group in order to help them earn eligibility to selective enrollment colleges.

Students who are exceeding ISAT standards are likely to score at least an 18 on the PLAN, but in order to have access to highly selective colleges, which often have higher graduation rates and more financial aid than less selective colleges, they will need much higher scores. This is a group of students who should aim for test scores in the 20s.

FIGURE 30

Distribution of PLAN Composite Scores by Eighth-Grade Math and Reading Test Scores

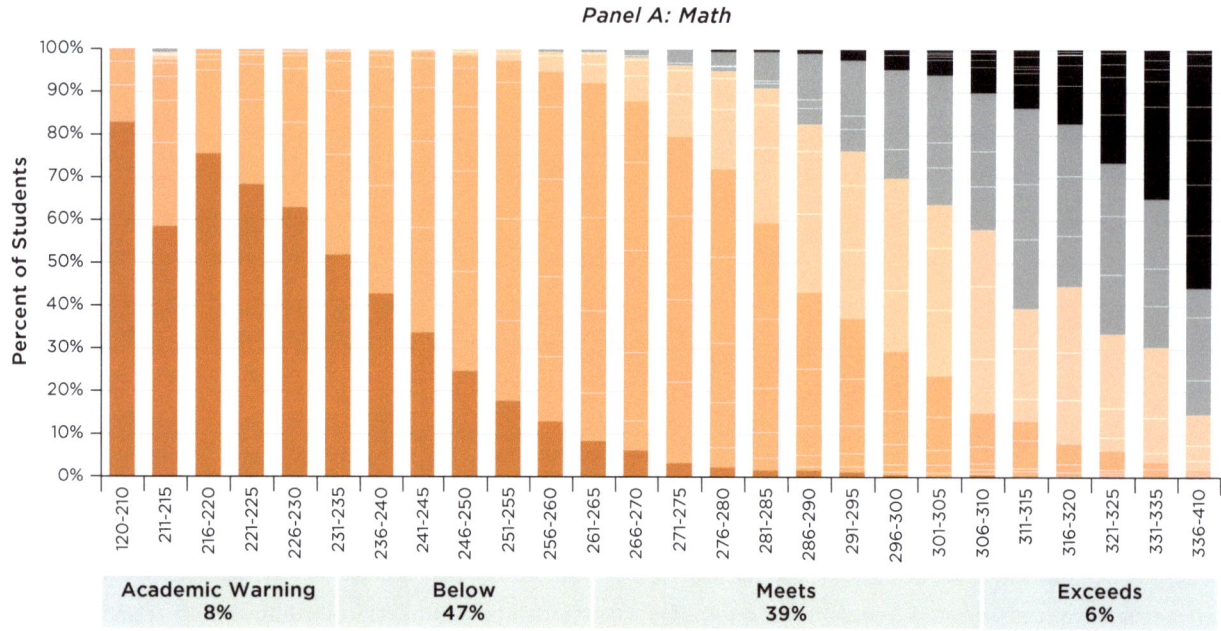

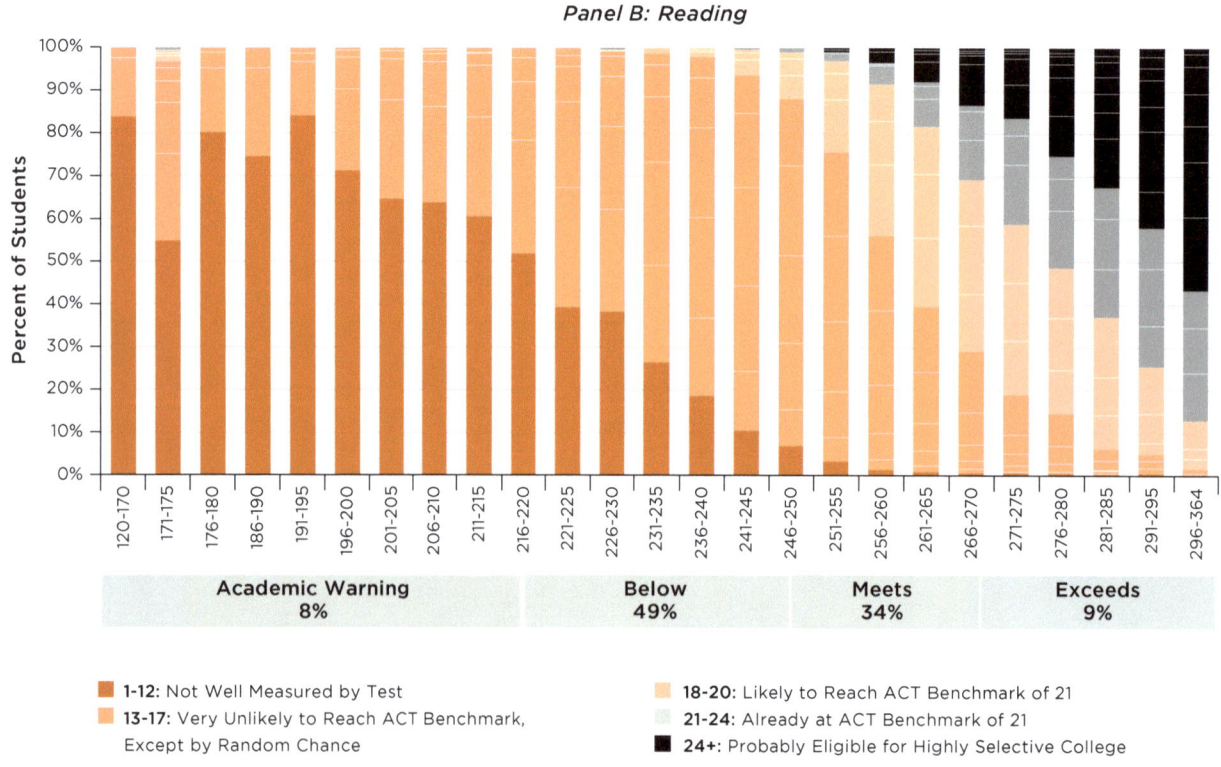

Note: Each horizontal white line in the vertical bars indicates a particular score point.

Low Test Scores Mean Most Students Will Have Access to College Only if They Have High GPAs

When we follow students to the end of the eleventh grade, we can see that only students exceeding standards, or in the high end of the "meets" range, on the ISAT have a good chance of meeting a score of 21 on the ACT (see **Figure 31**). A score of 21 on the ACT composite is considered by many to be *"college-ready,"* as it is the average of the subject-specific benchmarks. Many of the students exceeding standards in math or in reading in eighth grade score a 24 or higher on their ACT, and most score at least a 21. Almost half have a core GPA greater than 3.0, which provides them with access to very selective colleges. The other half of students with the top test scores, however, do not have a GPA of at least 3.0, and this will limit their access to college despite their high test scores.

Students who just meet standards on the ISAT math (in the 267-288 range) are extremely unlikely to score above 21 on the ACT; this represents the largest group of CPS students. Furthermore, on average, their core GPA in eleventh grade is 2.3, which will provide them with access only to two-year colleges, where the likelihood of eventually obtaining a four-year degree is extremely small. These students need to have GPAs of at least 2.5 in order to have access to somewhat selective colleges.

Of students not meeting the old standards in eighth grade (234-266), hardly any score higher than an 18 on the ACT. With an average eleventh-grade core GPA of 1.8, these students have access to few colleges. If students not meeting ISAT standards enter high school with plans to go to college, they need support and motivation to ensure their grades are as high as possible, earning at least as many As and Bs as Cs. Strong effort in their classes should also pay off for improving their test scores.[59] Pushing these students to get higher GPAs and improve their academic skills could improve their chances to attend a four-year college.

FIGURE 31

Eleventh-Grade ACT Composite Scores by Eighth-Grade ISAT Math and Reading Scores

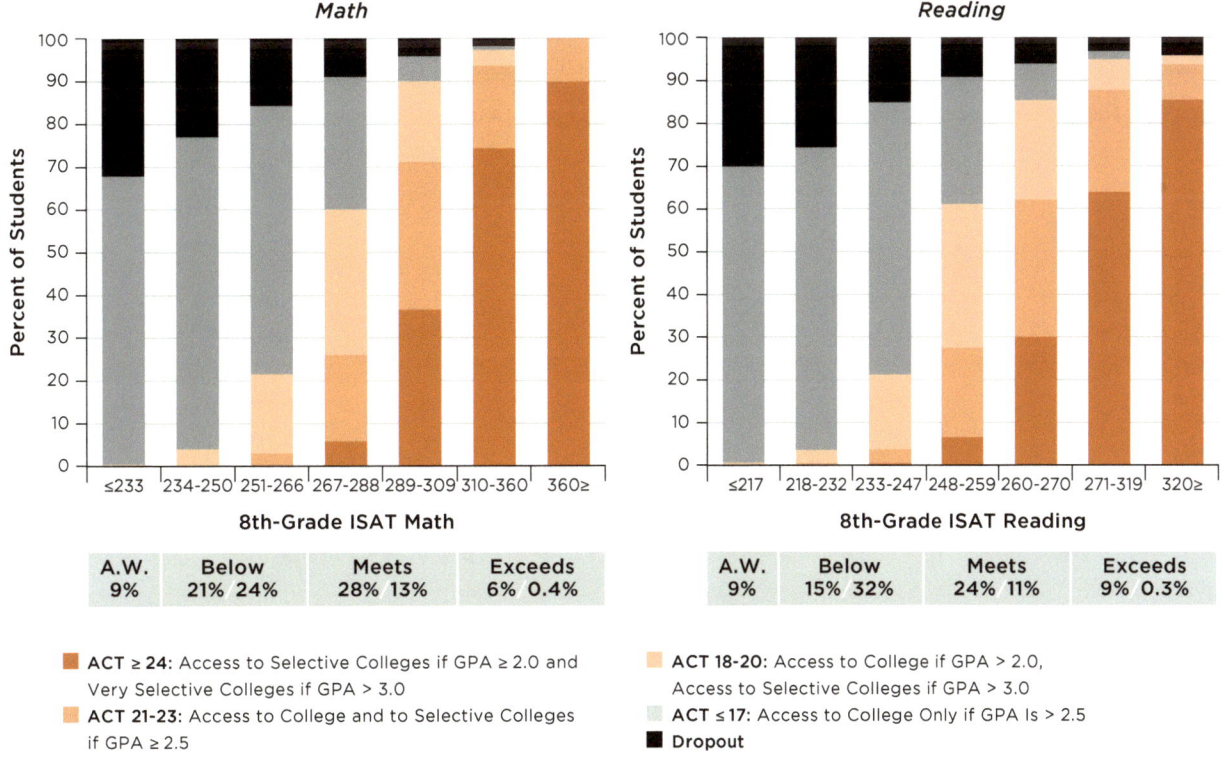

[59] High grades in math, science, and English are the strongest predictors of gains on those subject tests in a given year (Allensworth, Correa, and Ponisciak, 2008).

Summary

Parents, teachers, and students can gauge students' likely PLAN and ACT scores based on their ISAT performance and develop meaningful goals for learning based on college expectations before students begin high school. What those goals are for an individual student should depend not only on readiness benchmarks and standards but also on students' current level of academic skills.

Test scores are useful for parents and teachers to gauge students' level of academic skills; they provide information that can be used to guide further instruction and decisions about coursework. State standards and college-ready benchmarks provide a context for making meaning from scores. In practice, however, these benchmarks do not make good goals for the vast majority of students. For students exceeding eighth-grade standards in both reading and math, the ACT benchmarks provide targets that are too low to provide a good chance of attaining scholarships and getting into highly selective colleges. All other students have a very slim chance of meeting the ACT benchmark scores, potentially leading to frustration and disappointment on the part of students and school staff. Unless schools can figure out how to substantially increase the rates at which the students learn—given the resources they can make available—the benchmarks are not attainable for most students except by random chance. The goal should be to reach the highest attainable scores, even if those scores are below benchmarks. High PLAN scores will put students on a better path to reach high ACT composite scores; this, in combination with high GPAs, will help students to access more selective colleges, even if a student does not score at the benchmark.

What can be done before students reach high school? One strategy is to be discerning when advising students about applying to high school, since the previous chapter showed that students with the same middle grade scores make very different test score gains at different high schools. Another obvious answer is to assist students to attain higher levels of performance in the middle grades so that they have a better chance of getting good PLAN and ACT scores. There is a push to move all students to the *"exceeds"* range on the ISAT, and this year standards changed at the state level to more closely align with college expectations. These benchmarks are useful only if schools know how to improve students' test scores sufficiently to reach these levels of performance. Chapter 8 shows how much students' test scores grow in the middle grades; variation in growth is much smaller than most people believe, especially in reading. Currently, there are no schools that come close to moving students from just meeting standards to exceeding them.

CHAPTER 8

How Grades, Attendance, and Test Scores Change

As middle schools work to prepare students for high school, improving attendance, grades, and test scores are often their primary goals. This is in perfect alignment with the factors that are most predictive of high school outcomes. But how much do students' grades, attendance, and test scores change over the course of middle school? This chapter examines trends in students' grades, attendance, and test scores over the middle grade years, showing how much they change and the degree to which differences in growth vary across schools.

Chapter 3 showed that students' grades and attendance in earlier years are predictive of ninth-grade course performance. Seventh-grade GPA is almost as predictive as eighth-grade GPA, but seventh-grade attendance is less predictive. This suggests that students' attendance is less static during the middle grades years than GPA. Chapter 6 showed that students' sixth-grade ISAT scores are almost as predictive of their high school PLAN scores as their eighth-grade ISAT scores. If sixth-grade scores are as predictive of high school performance as eighth-grade scores, it suggests that there may be little change in students' scores—relative to other students—over the middle school years. If this is true, what should be the expectations for schools around improving students' scores in middle school? This chapter shows that reading scores, in particular, tend to grow at the same rate for almost all students. There is somewhat more variation in math score growth. Grades show more variation in growth over time than test scores, and attendance changes the most. This suggests that attendance depends more on students' specific experiences in the middle grades than do test scores.

> This chapter examines the degree to which students show different amounts of growth and decline in attendance, grades, and test scores over the middle grade years. It ends by estimating which indicators would have the biggest leverage for increasing students' educational attainment, if they could attain high levels of growth in any of these three areas.

Over the Middle Grades, Attendance Is Less Constant Than Grades, Which Are Less Constant than Test Score Ranks

Compared to grades or test scores, attendance is the factor that is most likely to change over time. As shown in **Table 12**, the correlation between seventh-grade attendance and eighth-grade attendance is strong (0.62), but not nearly as strong as the correlation of seventh-grade GPA with eighth-grade GPA (0.77) or seventh-grade ISAT with eighth-grade ISAT (0.81 for reading, 0.88 for math). Eighth-grade attendance is even less strongly correlated with attendance in sixth grade, and the correlation of eighth-grade attendance with fifth-grade attendance is just moderate (0.43). In contrast, eighth-grade ISAT scores are very highly correlated with fifth-grade ISAT scores (with correlations of 0.79 in reading and 0.82 in math). There is much less variation among students in the degree to which test scores change over time, relative to other students, than the degree to which attendance changes.

District-Wide, Average GPAs and Attendance Are Similar from Fifth through Eighth Grade in Chicago

On average in Chicago, attendance rates and grades are similar throughout the middle school years. Average attendance rates hover around 95 percent in fifth through eighth grade (**see Figure A**). Likewise, students' GPAs are similar across the middle grade years, hovering between 2.7 and 2.9, on average.

This does not mean that an individual student's attendance and grades are necessarily flat across the middle grades. It simply means that as many students show declines in attendance and grades as show improvements, so that the trends are fairly flat overall.

FIGURE A

Average Attendance and GPA During the Middle Grades

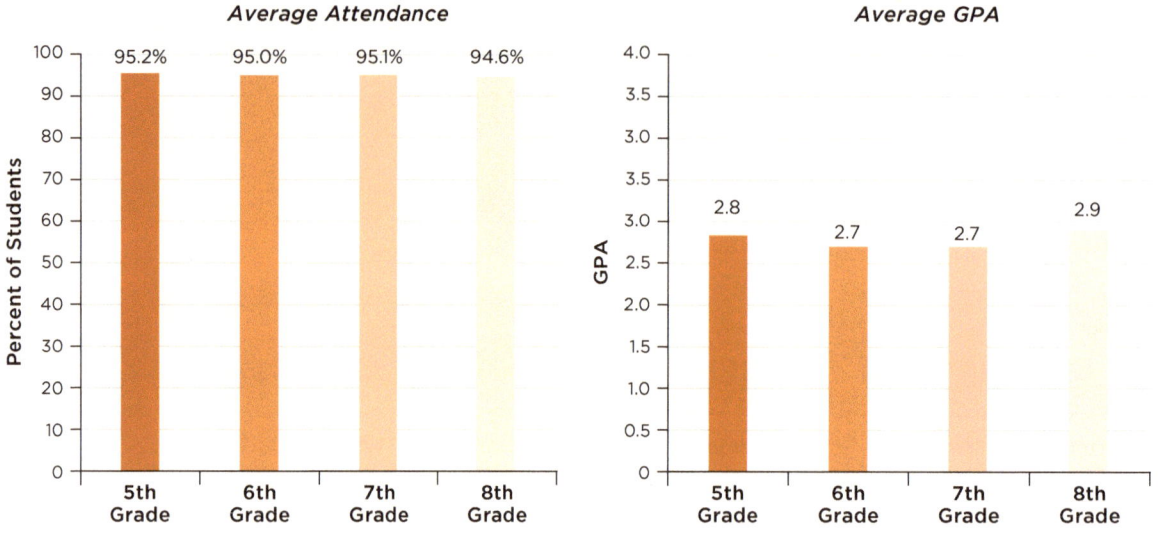

TABLE 12

Correlations of Eighth-Grade Attendance, Grades, and Test Scores with Their Attendance, Grades, and Test Scores in Earlier Years

Correlations Between Years	Attendance	Overall GPA	ISAT Reading and Math Combined	Grades		ISAT	
				English	Math	Reading	Math
	8th-Grade	8th-Grade	8th-Grade	8th-Grade	8th-Grade	8th-Grade	8th-Grade
7th Grade	0.62	0.77	0.90	0.67	0.59	0.81	0.88
6th Grade	0.52	0.66	0.88	0.58	0.48	0.80	0.84
5th Grade	0.43	0.62	0.86	0.55	0.46	0.79	0.82

FIGURE 32

Change in Attendance from Fifth Grade through Eighth Grade

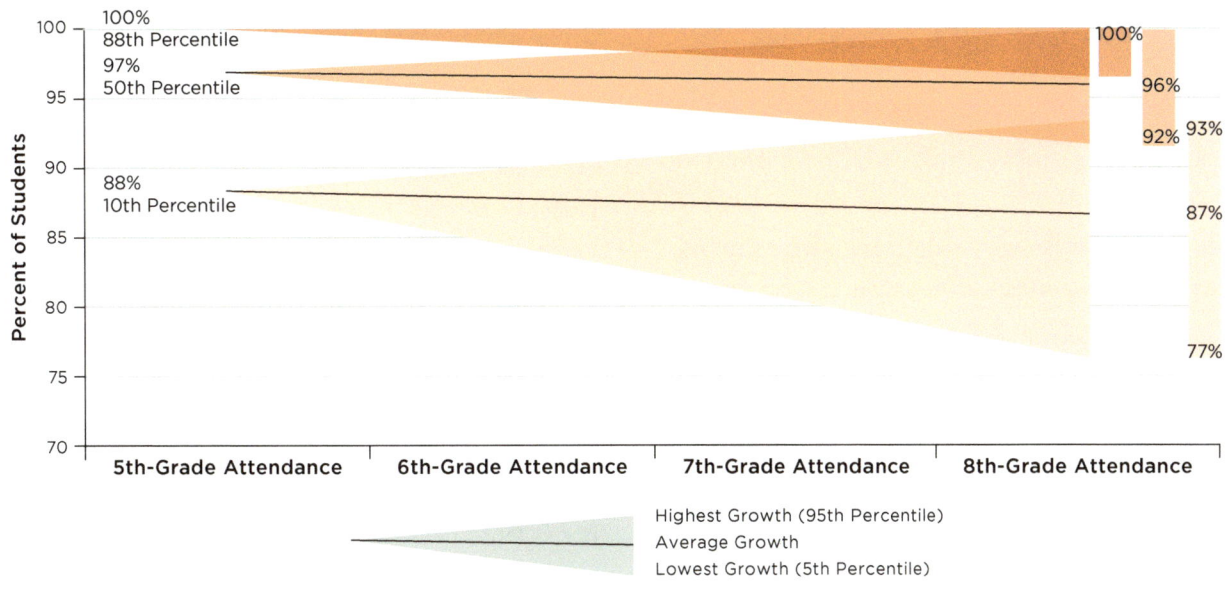

Note: Appendix C describes the methodology for calculating the growth trends. These growth trends are based on HLM models, nesting four observation points (grades five through eight) within students, and calculating a slope for each student. Variance in the Bayes estimates of the slope coefficients was inflated to match the model estimate of the true variance in slopes before graphing the distribution of growth trends.

The largest changes in attendance occur among chronically absent students, with some students showing large declines in attendance. Although attendance is more likely to change during the middle school years than either grades or test scores, attendance rates do remain about the same for many students during the middle grades. Students who have strong attendance in fifth grade are very likely to have strong attendance throughout the middle grade years. Among students with near-perfect attendance in fifth grade (99 to 100 percent), the greatest decline is just a percentage point a year—so that almost all end up with eighth-grade attendance of at least 97 percent (**see Figure 32**).

Most students who have weak attendance in fifth grade continue to have weak attendance throughout the middle grades. An earlier chapter suggested that students with very low attendance in eighth grade (below 90 percent) could already be identified in seventh grade as in need of substantial intervention efforts in order to be on-track for graduation from high school. The same is true at earlier grade levels. Except for a group whose attendance improves at the highest rate (nearly two points each year), students who are

FIGURE 33

Years of Chronic Absenteeism among Chronically Absent Eighth-Graders in 2011-12

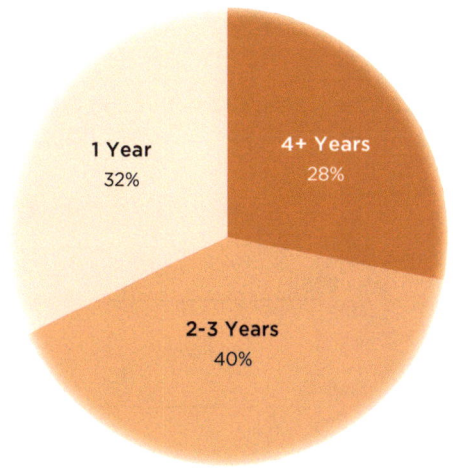

chronically absent in fifth grade are likely to be chronically absent in eighth grade. Only a third of chronically absent eighth-grade students experience chronic absenteeism for the first time in eighth grade (**see Figure 33**). All other chronically absent eighth-graders have experienced multiple years of chronic absenteeism during the middle grades, and over a quarter of these students have been chronically absent every year since fifth grade. This is a group that is in need of very substantial support if they are to eventually graduate from high school, and they can be identified very early. Even chronically absent fifth-graders whose attendance improves considerably over the middle grades still have below-average attendance in eighth grade (93 percent).

While many students with average attendance in fifth grade (97 percent) maintain this level of attendance over the middle grades, there also is a group that increasingly misses more days as they go through middle school and ends up with attendance rates that put students at risk of poor ninth-grade outcomes (ending with a 92 percent rate). This is a group for whom more modest intervention strategies might be effective to keep attendance from falling further. When attendance drops below 95 percent at any point in the middle grade years, it is a signal that students may be in need of assistance around attendance. Schools might try strategies to support students—reaching out to families, providing mentors, or appointing teachers for special monitoring and attention—to help these students maintain their attendance rates or improve them so that they are not at high risk of being off-track in ninth grade.

Some Students Show Growth or Decline in Grades by as Much as Half of a GPA Point

For many students, their course grades remain the same from year-to-year during the middle grade years. There are students, however, who show improvements while others show declines in their GPAs from fifth to eighth grade. Growth in GPA is highest among students who have the lowest GPAs in fifth grade; their GPAs can grow by as much as 0.8 over three years, so that they go from having a C- (1.8 GPA) in fifth grade to a C+/B- in eighth grade (2.6 GPA; **see Figure 34**). A 0.8 difference in GPAs may sound small, but it can make a big difference for later student outcomes. As shown in Chapter 3, a one-point difference in GPAs in eighth grade corresponds to a 20 percentage point difference in the likelihood of passing ninth-grade math (comparing eighth-grade students with a 1.5 GPA to those with a 2.5 GPA). A 2.6 GPA in eighth grade, however, is still nearly a full grade point below where students need to be to have any real chance of earning a B or better in ninth grade. Even students with typical grades in fifth grade (2.8 GPA) who improve their grades the most over the next three year do not quite make it to the 3.5 threshold (3.3 GPA).

FIGURE 34
Growth in GPA from Fifth Grade through Eighth Grade

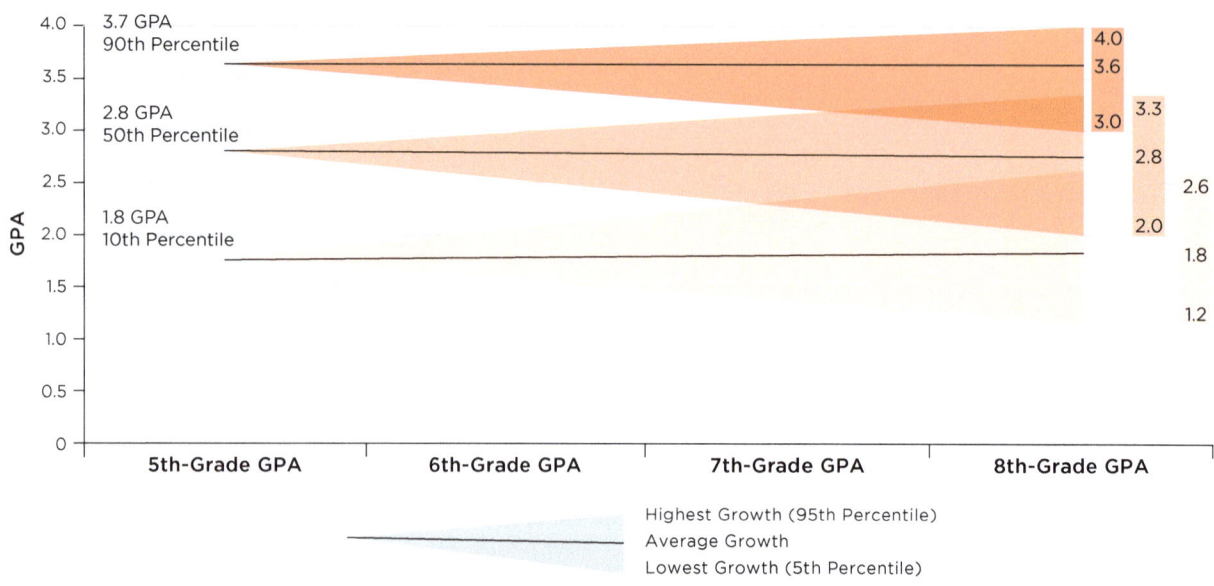

Note: Appendix C describes the methodology for calculating the growth trends, and the rationale for the methods that were used. These growth trends are based on HLM models, nesting four observation points (grades five through eight) within students, and calculating a slope for each student. Variance in the Bayes estimates of the slope coefficients was inflated to match the model estimate of the true variance in slopes before graphing the distribution of growth trends.

Differences in Test Score Growth Are Not Large Enough to Enable Low-Performing Students to Eventually Meet ACT Benchmarks

Almost all students make the same degree of progress on the reading ISAT from fifth to eighth grade. While there are substantial year-to-year fluctuations, these tend to even out over time so that students end up with about the same percentile rank in eighth grade as they had in fifth grade. **Figure 35 (top)** shows the ISAT reading growth patterns, based on their fifth-grade score, for students at the 10th percentile, with average scores, and at the 90th percentile. On average, students grow 10 points per year on the ISAT. There is some variation in that growth, but not much.[60] Students who start with lower scores tend to grow faster than average, averaging 12 points a year instead of 10 points a year, while students who start with higher reading scores grow eight points a year, on average. The variation in growth in reading scores mostly comes from where students start; there is very little difference in yearly growth rates among students who begin middle school with similar scores, once multiple years are averaged together.

Students at the 10th percentile in reading are well below meeting standards, and the 12 points per year of growth is not enough to make them close to meeting standards by eighth grade—even among students with the highest growth in this group. In eighth grade, these students score between the seventh and 11th percentile among eighth-grade students. Students at the 90th percentile in fifth grade reading grow the least on the reading tests. Nevertheless, their relative position remains very similar, between the 89th and 93rd percentiles in eighth grade.

Figure 35 (bottom) shows the patterns of math test scores growth over middle grades. There is similar variation in math growth (standard deviation of 2.3) as in reading, but the variation in growth is not as strongly determined by where students start. On average, students gain 13 points a year. Students at the 10th percentile in fifth grade gain a bit more than average (14 points), with average and high-scoring students in fifth grade gaining 13 and 12 points, respectively, per year.

High-scoring students show the most variation in their growth. Students scoring at the 90th percentile in fifth grade end up between the 81st and 95th percentile in eighth grade. Most students who start with very high scores in fifth grade, at the 90th percentile, gain over the middle grade years around 12 points and end up close to the exceeding range of scores by eighth grade. Low-scoring students, those at the 10th percentile, gain more, on average, than students who begin middle school with high math scores. The variability in their growth, however, is lower than the students at the 90th percentile—there are fewer differences among them in how much they grow. These low-performing students are not meeting standards in fifth grade and are unlikely in to meet standards in eighth grade.

Similar, but not identical patterns in test score growth can were observed in a study on middle grade students in New York. Variation in growth on tests in New York was also very small, relative to the variation in initial scores, and larger in math than in reading. The standard deviation of growth on the math test was 3 percent the size of the standard deviation of initial math scores, and 2 percent of in reading. Thus, students in New York also changed little in their rank order from year-to-year. Unlike Chicago, though, gains in the tests in New York were not strongly related to students' initial scores—students with lower initial scores made slightly higher gains in both reading and math (see Kieffer and Marinell, 2012).

While Test Growth Trends Are Similar When Averaged Over Multiple Years, Year-to-Year Gains Can Vary Substantially

Figure 35 shows students' annual test score growth, averaging their year-to-year gains over fifth, sixth, seventh, and eighth grades. These average gains are very different from the yearly gains that take place from one year to the next. Annual gains can reflect random events such as a particularly bad or good testing day on either the pre-test or the post-test. Students might have

---

60 The standard deviation of the growth estimate is 2.0 points. However, much of this variation can be accounted for by differences in growth rates for students who start with different levels of achievement.

FIGURE 35

Growth in Reading and Math Test Scores from Fifth Grade to Eighth Grade

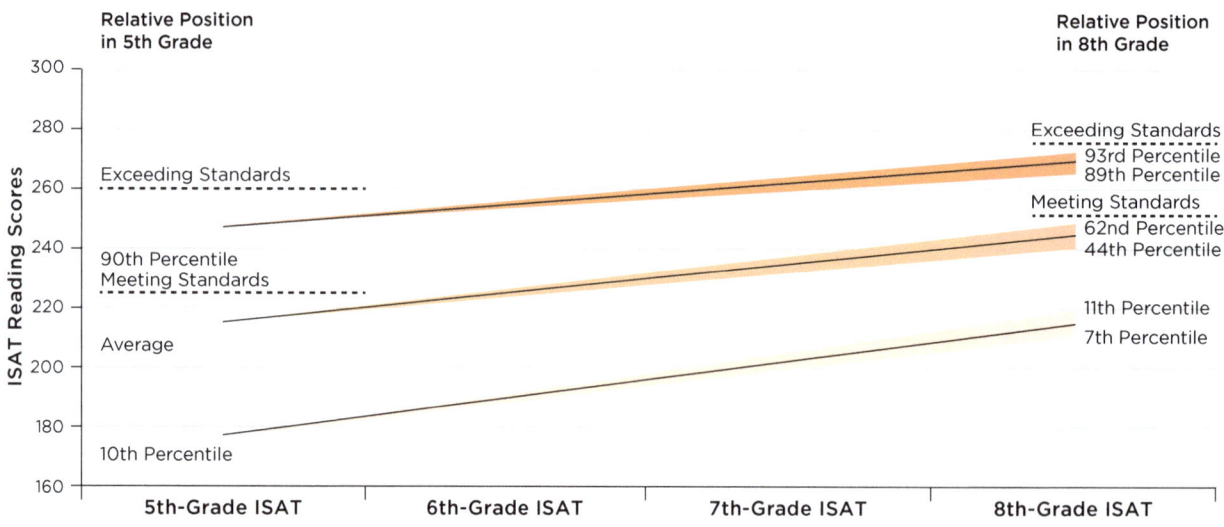

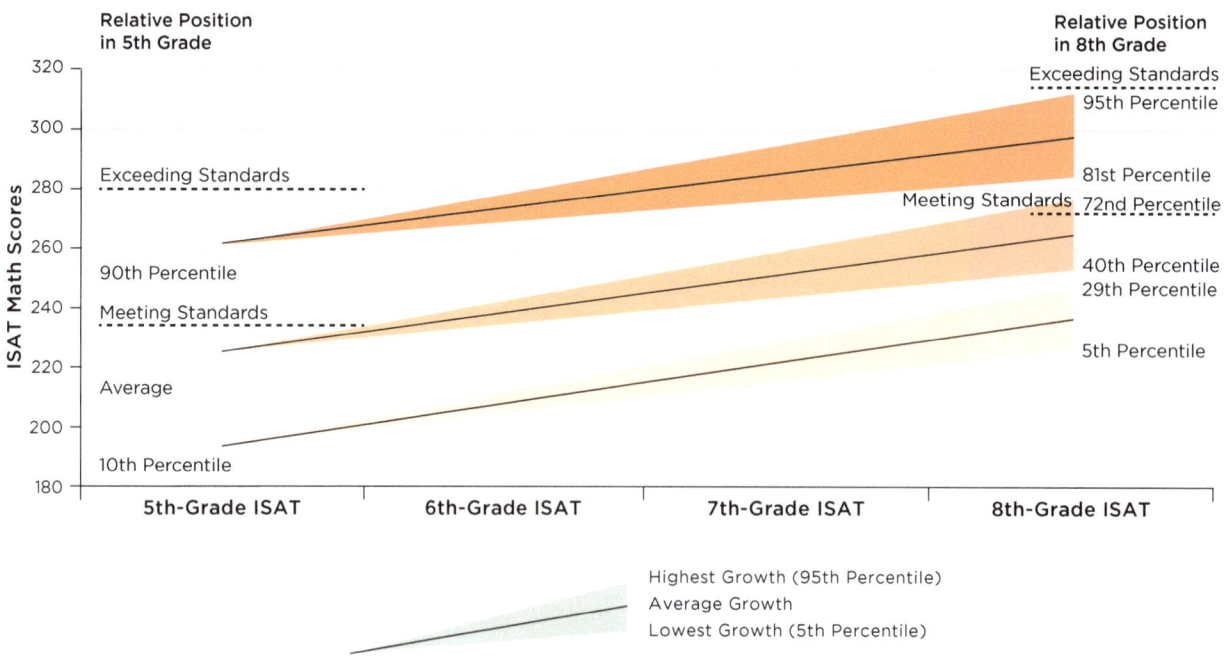

Note: Appendix C describes the methodology for calculating the growth trends and the rationale for the methods that were used. These growth trends are based on HLM models, nesting four observation points (grades five through eight) within students, and calculating a slope for each student. Variance in the Bayes estimates of the slope coefficients was inflated to match the model estimate of the true variance in slopes before graphing the distribution of growth trends. ISAT scores are vertically scaled so that a score has the same meaning at different grade levels (ISBE, 2012).

Are Certain Types of Students More Likely to Show Improving or Declining Grades, Attendance, and Test Scores Over the Middle Grade Years?

Changes over time in students' grades, attendance, and math test scores are not substantially different by students' race, gender, poverty, or disability status. As shown in Table A, no background factor is correlated at more than 0.08 with changes in attendance, grades, and math scores. The strongest relationship is with gender; boys' GPAs are slightly more likely to decline over the middle grade years than girls' GPAs. There are also some modest correlations of background factors with changing attendance, with attendance declining slightly less for Asian students than for African American, white, or Latino students.

Growth over the middle grade years in reading test scores is correlated with students' background characteristics, with students who are generally considered more disadvantaged showing higher average rates of growth. This occurs because reading test score growth in middle grades is highly negatively correlated with their test scores in fifth grade (at -0.92).[F] Students who start the middle grades with very weak reading scores show the most growth over the middle grade years; these may be students who were behind in basic literacy skills (e.g., decoding, vocabulary), versus more advanced skills (e.g., comprehension). A review of the What Works Clearinghouse shows that there are more successful programs available to schools to work on basic literacy than advanced literacy. Students with disabilities, male students, African American students, and students coming from neighborhoods with high poverty (more families below the poverty line and higher male unemployment) and low social status (with lower average levels of education and lower family incomes) show higher growth in reading test scores than other students. All of the correlations between reading ISAT trends with student characteristics shown in Table A are a reflection of how students score in fifth grade and the negative correlation between initial status in reading and subsequent growth. They no longer hold if we only compare students with similar ISAT scores in fifth grade.

TABLE A

Correlations of Change in Attendance, Grades, and ISAT with Background Factors

	Attendance Trend	GPA Trend	ISAT Trend	
			Reading	Math
White	0.01	0.05	-0.21	-0.03
Black	-0.06	-0.05	0.24	0.05
Asian	0.05	0.07	-0.15	0.02
Latino	0.04	-0.01	-0.07	-0.03
Male	-0.02	-0.08	0.12	-0.03
Concentration of Poverty (Students' Neighborhoods)	-0.05	-0.04	0.25	0.04
Social Status (Students' Neighborhoods)	0.02	0.05	-0.15	0.01
Cognitive Disability	-0.04	0.01	0.40	0.01

Note: All of the correlations over 0.01 are statistically significant because they are based on 99,300 cases for attendance and 61,791 cases for grades. The correlations for test scores are based on approximately 22,000 students.

[F] Math test scores in fifth grade and the growth from fifth to eighth grade are also negatively correlated; students with higher initial test scores tend to exhibit lower growth, but this correlation is much lower (-0.33) than the correlation of reading scores.

TABLE 13

Correlations of Test Score Gains in the Middle Grades in Different Years
Reading (in the top right of the table) and Math (in the bottom left of the table)

Gains	From 5th to 6th grade	From 6th to 7th grade	From 7th to 8th grade
From 5th to 6th grade		Reading -0.39	Reading 0.04
From 6th to 7th grade	Math -0.46		Reading -0.55
From 7th to 8th grade	Math -0.00	Math -0.42	

an exceptionally good or bad teacher one year, showing especially high or low gains in a given year that are very different from other years. Students might experience a developmental growth spurt one year that leads them to do better on a test, or experience a traumatic event that leads to lower performance. This year-to-year variation, however, tends to wash out over time. Students who have especially strong growth in one year tend to have especially weak growth in the next. The opposite is true as well; students who fall behind one year tend to make it up the next. **Table 13** shows the correlations between gains in test scores from one grade to the next. Gains from two consecutive years, from fifth to sixth grade and from sixth to seventh grade, are negatively correlated; the correlation is -0.39 in reading and -0.46 in math. Good years, in terms of gains, tend to be followed by low gains the following year, with the opposite also true.

Because high gains in one year are rarely followed by high gains in the next, there are few students who make exceptionally high gains over a three-year period. This is why it is difficult to move students into the "exceeds" range by eighth grade, unless they were close to exceeding standards in fifth grade. In reading, it seems like an impossible task. Something dramatically different, or at least very different, from what elementary schools are doing today, needs to happen in elementary schools to produce the kind of gains necessary in middle grades to put students within reach of the ACT benchmarks. To our knowledge, there is no known way to do this on a large scale.

Middle Schools Can Affect Whether Students' Grades, Attendance, and Test Scores Improve or Decline

About half of the differences in GPA and attendance growth and decline across students during the middle grades can be attributed to the school that they attend.[61] At some schools, it is typical for students' grades to improve by about a tenth of a GPA point each year over the middle grade years, ending up 0.3 points higher in eighth grade than in fifth grade; at other schools, GPAs tend to decline by about a tenth of a GPA point each year, ending up 0.3 points lower (comparing schools one standard deviation above the mean to schools one standard deviation below, in GPA growth). Thus, students' GPAs might end up as much as 0.6 points different by the eighth grade, based on which school they attend for the middle grade years. That is a sizable difference in terms of students' probability of passing their ninth-grade classes and getting good grades in high school.

At some schools, attendance tends to decrease by about one percentage point each year; at others, attendance tends to improve by about one percentage point each year (comparing schools one standard deviation above the mean to schools one standard deviation below, in attendance growth). This may seem small but, by the end of three years, students at some schools have improved their attendance by three percentage points, while others have shown a three percentage point decline. Thus, the school that a student attends may make a difference of six percentage points in their eighth-grade attendance. As shown in the previous

---

61 The variance in GPA trends comes from HLM models of students' GPAs, with observations (years) nested within students and nested within their eighth-grade schools. The standard deviation of the variance in GPA trends at the student level (within schools) is 0.089, while the standard deviation of the variance in GPA trends at the school level is 0.096. The variation in attendance trends comes from similar models, with the standard deviation of variance at the student level (within schools) at 0.013 and the standard deviation of variance in the trends between schools at 0.010.

chapter, six percentage points in attendance is very substantial in terms of students' probability of success in high school; a difference of 10 percentage points moves a student from perfect attendance (100 percent) to chronically absent (90 percent).

There are also differences across schools in the size of students' yearly gains on the ISAT; some schools show higher gains across the middle grade years than others. In reading, half of the differences in students' gains can be attributed to which school they attend. Among students at the 50th percentile, for example, students at schools with high growth gain 11 points a year, while those at schools with low growth gain nine points a year (comparing schools one standard deviation above the mean to schools one standard deviation below, in test score growth). In math, school differences account for more than half of the differences across students in yearly growth; students at schools with high growth gain 15 points a year, while those at schools with low growth gain 11 points a year. Despite the differences in what schools can contribute to growth, the gaps in test scores are so large from the start of middle school that no schools close those gaps in the middle grades.

Middle Grade GPA and Attendance Have the Greatest Potential for Improving High School Outcomes

As schools look for indicators that are likely to have high leverage for moving student outcomes, they need to consider two factors. First, they need to consider whether moving the indicator would likely move the later outcome they care about (e.g., high school and college graduation). Second, they need to consider the degree to which they can move the indicator with known strategies. The first factor depends on the degree to which the indicator is strongly and directly related to later outcomes. For high school graduation and college readiness, course grades are the most strongly related to later outcomes, followed by attendance, followed by ISAT scores; for ACT scores, ISAT scores are the strongest predictor.[62] The second factor depends on having known programmatic effects for moving the indicators, and evidence that differences in school practices result in differences in growth on the indicator. Variation in growth across students during the middle grades provides some indication of the degree to which there are known strategies to change the indicators during the middle grade years.

To put both of these factors together, **Figure 36** shows the predicted ninth-grade outcomes for a student that ended fifth grade with average attendance, grades, and test scores, but showed very high levels of growth on each of the indicators from fifth to eighth grade. **Figure 36** also shows the predicted ninth-grade outcomes for a student that had average performance in fifth grade, but showed little improvement throughout the middle grade years. While this is simply a simulation, and there are many factors that might influence students' actual performance, it provides an estimate of the degree to which students' high school outcomes could be influenced by what happens to their performance in the middle grades.

What happens in middle grades does seem to matter considerably for students' ninth-grade outcomes, especially their growth in grades and attendance. While students with average performance in fifth grade are unlikely to be at the top of their class in high school, their probability of being on-track goes from 54 to 95 percent, depending on whether their grades declined (from 2.8 to 2.0) or improved (from 2.8 to 3.3) during the middle grades. Likewise, their predicted ninth-grade GPA goes from 1.9 to 2.4, based on whether their grades declined or improved from fifth to eighth grade. Their predicted PLAN scores are also one point higher (16 compared to 15) if their grades improved, rather than declined, from fifth to eighth grade.

Changes in attendance over the middle grade years are also strongly associated with different ninth-grade outcomes. Students' probability of being on-track goes from 66 to 93 percent, depending on whether their

---

62 We cannot definitively test whether the observed relationships of the indicators with the outcomes are direct, indirect, or spurious, as there may be unmeasured variables that were not included in the models employed for Chapter 1 through Chapter 3. However, the methods employed to compare among the indicators were designed to determine which showed the largest direct relationships among the predictors that were available.

FIGURE 36

What Is the Predicted Ninth-Grade Outcome for Students with the Most and Least Improvement in Attendance, GPAs, and ISAT Scores in the Middle Grades?

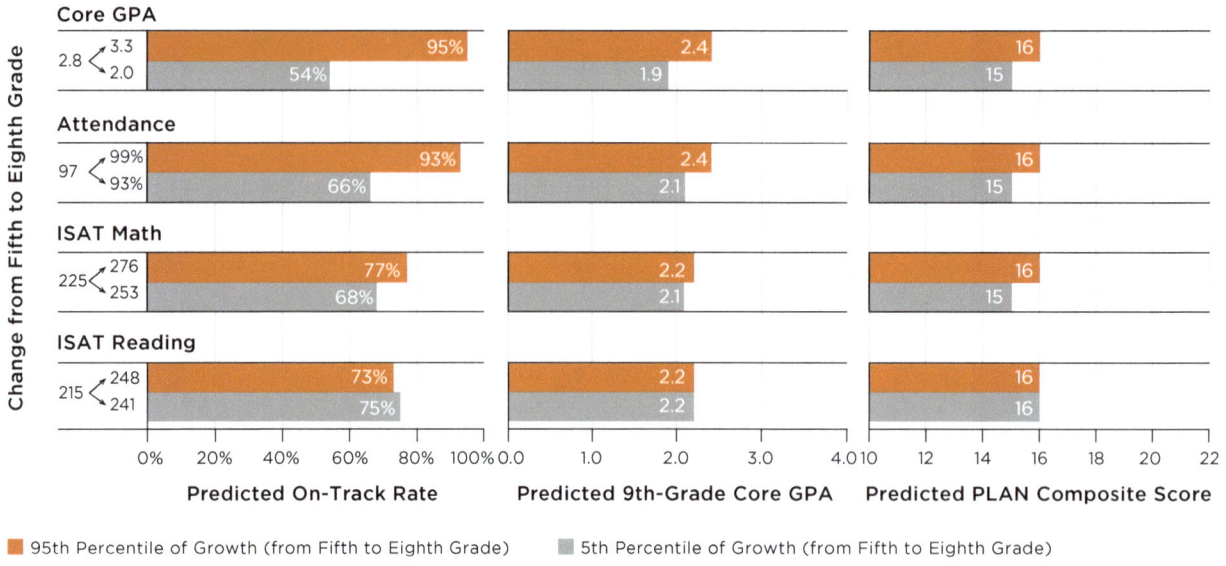

attendance declines (from 97 to 93 percent) or improves (from 97 to 99 percent) during the middle grades. Likewise, their predicted ninth-grade GPA goes from 2.1 to 2.4, based on whether their attendance declined or improved over time. Improving attendance in the middle grades is also associated with higher PLAN scores, as students who show the most improvements in attendance have average scores that are one point higher than students with the most decline in attendance—comparing students that had similar attendance and ISAT scores in fifth grade.

Larger improvements in students' ISAT math scores in the middle grades are associated with improvements in ninth-grade outcomes, but the differences are smaller than seen with improvements in attendance and grades. Students with the most improvement in their math scores in the middle grades are nine percentage points more likely to be on-track in ninth grade (77 percent compared to 68 percent) than students who showed the smallest math score gains—comparing students with similar test scores in fifth grade. Their ninth-grade GPAs are also higher by about 0.1 points, and their PLAN scores are higher by about one point.

Reading scores show little variation in growth across the middle grades. Students with the highest growth end up with eighth-grade scores that are only seven points higher than students with the lowest growth (e.g., 241 compared to 248, among students with a score of 215 in fifth grade). Thus, improving reading scores shows a much smaller relationship with ninth-grade outcomes than does improving math scores.

We cannot say whether changing middle school performance would result in better outcomes without conducting a study that is specifically designed to be able to make causal claims—showing that changing an earlier outcome results in a change in a later outcome. **Figure 35 on p.86**, simply shows what happened in high school to students who improved their middle school performance compared to those who declined. Students with improving performance in the middle grades had better high school outcomes than students who were similar to them in fifth grade but had declining attendance, grades, or math scores; this suggests that improving student performance in the middle grades has the potential to improve high school outcomes. These findings are very similar to the relationships found in New York between declining attendance and test scores and students' probability of graduating high school. Declining attendance in the middle grades was particularly strongly associated with a lowered probability of high school graduation. Declining test performance was also associated with a lower probability of graduating in New York, especially in math (Kieffer and Marinell, 2012).

Summary

For most students, attendance, grades, and test score ranks are fairly stable over the middle grades. However, some students show improvements in grades and attendance over the middle grade years; these students' ninth-grade outcomes are substantially higher than the ninth-grade outcomes of students who had similar achievement levels in fifth grade, but showed declining attendance and grades in middle school. There is less variation in growth in test scores across students than in grades or attendance because students who have high test score gains in one year tend to have low test score gains in the next, and vice-versa. About half of the differences in students' growth in attendance, grades, and test scores over the middle grades can be attributed to their school. Because attendance varies the most across the middle grade years, and because it is strongly related to ninth-grade course performance, improvements in attendance may have particularly high leverage for improving high school outcomes, compared to other indicators.

CHAPTER 9

Interpretive Summary

School districts across the country are trying to figure out what they can do to get all of their students to graduate from high school and be ready for success in college. There is recognition that these efforts need to begin prior to high school, but there is little guidance on what it is that schools should target in the middle grades to affect outcomes at the end of high school, and how to identify who is at risk for not succeeding in later years.

In this report, we show that students' risk of poor performance in high school—and their level of readiness to succeed—can be identified with just two or three key indicators of middle school performance. It is not necessary to put together complicated prediction models based on multiple indicators. Schools could use information on students' level of risk for different outcomes to design intervention strategies for individual students and for assessing which problems with readiness are most critical in particular schools.

The key indicator of readiness for passing classes, being on-track, and getting good grades in high school is students' overall core GPA in the middle grades. Students' GPA across all of their core courses is a better indicator of readiness for passing any one specific class (e.g., algebra, English) than their grades in that specific class in middle school. This is true in fifth grade, as well as in eighth grade. Often people think of grades as subjective and not good indicators of later performance. They may think that GPAs at early grade levels are particularly subjective. However, if grades were mostly subjective, they would not predict later outcomes. Grades are much better predictors of future performance than indicators that are considered more objective, such as test scores. Middle grade attendance is also predictive of high school course performance and improves the prediction of ninth-grade course

performance beyond students' grades alone. These two indicators by themselves can be used together in a simple indicator chart to show students' likelihood of success in their ninth-grade courses, based on their middle grade records.

There are other indicators that slightly improve the prediction of students' high school course performance. Among students with high grades in middle school, test scores can help predict who is likely to get As and Bs in high school. Indicator systems could also incorporate school effects, since students with similar middle grade performance (grades, attendance, and test scores) have different likelihoods of success, based on which middle school they attended and in which high school they enroll. While these additional factors improve the accuracy of the prediction, there is a trade-off in that they make calculations more complicated.

The key indicator of meeting benchmarks on the EPAS exams in high school (e.g., the PLAN taken at the start of tenth grade) is performance on standardized tests in middle grades—the ISAT reading and math exams. A student's score on either the reading or the math ISAT is a very good indicator of whether he or she will meet the college-readiness benchmark on any of the four subject-area tests on the PLAN. Combining the reading and math ISAT scores together, or combining ISAT scores from multiple years (e.g., students' seventh-grade score with their eighth-grade score), improves the prediction of students' PLAN score on any subject-specific test and on the composite score (the average of all of the subject-specific tests). The subject-specific tests are each very predictive of scores in other subjects, almost as predictive as tests within the same subject. This suggests that both the ISAT and the PLAN tests are measuring general knowledge and skills at least as much as knowledge and skills in any given subject area. In general, the more tests that are used to predict the high school test score (e.g., multiple subjects, multiple years), the more accurate the prediction.

Middle school performance can be used to identify students at high or very high risk of not performing well in high school—for being off-track, getting low grades, or not meeting benchmarks. However, there are many students at moderate risk of receiving low or failing grades whose performance could go either way. The change in school context from eighth to ninth grade makes it difficult to predict accurately the grades these students will receive in high school. For this reason, it is critical that student performance be monitored during the ninth-grade year to make sure students are performing up to their potential.

Implications for Addressing High School Dropout

Calls for ending high school dropout often call for early intervention. As shown in this report, early intervention will not solve all of the problems that lead students to drop out. It is during ninth grade that many students fall off-track to graduation. In Chicago, most future dropouts do not show strong signs of withdrawal until ninth grade. However, there are some students that can be identified as at high risk very early—students who need intervention before high school and across the transition—if they are to have a chance of graduating.

Many students can be identified as at very high risk of not graduating at least as early as fifth grade, based on their attendance and grades. The same levels of the same indicators identify students with an extremely high risk of not graduating in Chicago as in Philadelphia—attendance less than 80 percent or a final year grade of F in their math or language arts class puts students at extremely high risk of failure (with a greater than 75 percent chance).[63] This suggests that there are common underlying patterns in the factors that can be used to identify future dropouts in middle school. One key difference between Philadelphia and Chicago is that a larger proportion of eventual dropouts can be identified earlier in Philadelphia than in Chicago. This could be caused by the structure of schools in Chicago versus schools in Philadelphia—most elementary schools in Chicago serve students in grades K-8 and students do not face a middle school transition. It is possible that students fall off-track to graduation earlier when their major school transition occurs in the middle grades instead of high school.[64] In Chicago, just focusing on students with very high risk of dropout based on middle school indicators would only capture a very small number of future dropouts. Different cities face different challenges and need to develop strategies with the indicators that meet their own circumstances.

For students with 80 percent or lower attendance in the middle grades or a GPA of less than 1.0 in the middle grades, interventions are strongly warranted while they are in middle school. These students are extremely likely to drop out of school, with a risk greater than 75 percent, unless they experience a substantial change in the way in which they are engaging with school. Students earning a mix of Cs and Ds or below, or who attend less than 90 percent of the time in middle school, have less than a 50 percent chance of being on-track when they get to high school. Moderate interventions might be sufficient to get them to succeed in high school.

In general, students whose middle school attendance is below 95 percent have not developed strategies to get to school every day, despite whatever obstacles they face. Ninety percent attendance is considered chronic absenteeism, and students who are chronically absent in the middle grades are more likely to be off-track

---

63 Neild and Balfanz (2006); Balfanz, Herzog, and MacIver (2007).

64 Achievement tends to decline during transitions to middle school and high school (Alspaugh, 1998; Barber and Olsen, 2004; Eccles, Lord, and Midgely, 1991).

than on-track when they get to high school. In the less-supportive high school environment, chronic absence is likely to drop to intermittent attendance, and moderate attendance is likely to drop to chronic absence. While the group of students with less than 95 percent attendance may be too large for intensive interventions, moderate efforts to reach out to families or provide community support to help students address barriers to school attendance might actually have considerable pay-off later on.

In the summer before ninth grade, high schools can use students' grades and attendance from middle school to identify students for whom it is most critical to establish trusting relationships. Students with eighth-grade attendance less than 90 percent or a GPA of less than 2.0 in eighth grade are very likely to need support during the ninth-grade year. Schools could reach out to these students and their parents to establish positive connections before problems occur. Some schools in CPS have used Freshman Watchlists for this purpose in the past, reaching out to particular students during the summer through the district's Freshmen Connection program.

Once students are in high school, schools can put students on the right path toward graduation by closely monitoring their attendance and grades. Many schools that have used ninth-grade "success reports" to identify students in need of support have shown substantial improvements in their ninth-grade on-track rates and progress toward graduation.[65]

Efforts to improve students' attendance and grades could have benefits for improving not only high school graduation rates but also college outcomes. The factors that are important for high school graduation—grades and attendance—are also important for college readiness. Often efforts to improve high school graduation are seen as separate from efforts at improving college readiness—one targets low-achieving students, while the other targets high-achieving students. However, the two goals are complementary. Getting more students ready for college requires substantial improvements in students' grades and attendance in the middle grade years.

Implications for Improving College Readiness

Almost all students want to go to college, but the vast majority of students who leave eighth grade in Chicago do not even have a 1-in-4 chance of finishing high school with the qualifications that indicate they will succeed in college. *The biggest stumbling block is students' grades.* Despite all of the attention on test scores, high school grades are the strongest predictors of college graduation and middle school grades are the strongest predictors of high school grades. Yet, only a quarter of CPS students earn the grades that indicate they will succeed in college.

Grades are a reflection of students' work effort—coming to class, getting assignments completed, participating, studying, and delivering high-quality work day after day. These academic behaviors are what matter for college success. They are also some of the same behaviors that employers look for in workers. Preparing for college requires students to work hard in their classes; by putting in effort around challenging work, students develop the strategies and skills they will need at higher levels of education. Students may not remember the Pythagorean Theorem down the line, but working hard to understand and apply it helps them build the cognitive frameworks and study habits that allow them to conquer math problems later on. Putting together an excellent term paper may teach students something new about the world, but it also teaches them how to organize their thinking and put information together in new ways. It is the process of working hard on academic work that gets students ready for college. While students and their parents may know that grades and work effort matter for college, they may not realize how important they are or how high they need to be for students to be on a path to college readiness.

Students need to know that college readiness means at least B-level work, starting at least in the middle grades. Grades do not usually get better when work gets harder and students are given more responsibility. Instead, grades tend to decline as students move into

---

65 See Allensworth (2013) for a description of the ways in which high schools used indicators to improve on-track rates.

and through high school. If students do not have at least a B average in the middle grades, they are extremely unlikely to end high school with at least a B average. Students with lower than a 3.0 high school GPA have a slim chance of graduating from college, and they will be ineligible to attend many colleges or receive most scholarships. Families should not have to wait until the junior year in high school to realize this. Middle schools can reach out to families of students who are not making high grades to let them know that they are not on-track to be ready for college. They can make sure that teachers are keeping up with their grading in the parent portal and have clear grading policies, so that students and parents always know where their grades stand and can notice if they slip. For some students, this knowledge may be enough to motivate higher work effort. For others, it may take support from teachers, mentors, or support staff to reach out, determine why students' grades are low, and then develop strategies to support their particular needs.

The ways that teachers structure their classes can influence whether students put in strong or weak work effort. Teaching is a complex task. Teachers need to design methods for engaging students around challenging academic work, even though students enter their class with different skill levels, different histories of success, and their own issues and priorities. The ways in which teachers implement their lessons have implications for the degree to which their students put in effort. As discussed in the report, *Teaching Adolescents to Become Learners*,[66] students put more effort into their classes when they have positive mindsets about the work—when they feel like they can be successful, that they belong in the class, that the work has value and will lead them to have stronger skills. A host of factors can undermine positive mindsets. For example, being at the bottom of the class in skill levels can make students feel they cannot succeed and do not belong.[67] Lessons without clear goals can keep students from seeing the value in the work they are asked to do. Clear grading standards and constant feedback can provide motivation to keep up with work.[68]

Mindsets are not set in stone. They change as students move across different contexts—different classes, different schools. Teachers can modify their instruction and their interactions with students to encourage positive mindsets about the work. The fact that non-cognitive factors, such as study habits and grit in eighth grade, are not predictive of ninth-grade performance provides evidence that they are context-specific, rather than just a feature of individuals. When a student is not putting in effort, a teacher or other adult could find out why they are putting in little effort—what it is about the class or about students' own experiences and skills that is preventing strong performance. Teachers also can design courses so that they intentionally develop students' learning strategies, such as metacognitive skills and study habits, as part of teaching their course subject. Explicitly teaching strategies to do better in class can pay off with better success on tests and assignments in that class and in future work. Other research at UChicago CCSR has found that students' grades are higher the more teachers monitor their performance and provide help as soon as they start to fall behind.[69]

Teachers can also reach out to students who miss class as soon as they are absent to make sure they start attending regularly and do not fall behind in their work. If students miss multiple days, it is important to find out why and figure out strategies to help students get to school. Students should have close to 100 percent attendance to be on a path to be ready for college.

Attendance is critical, at least as important as test performance. It may seem like a low bar—get students to come to school every day. But if students are not in school, they cannot learn. Even among students with high grades and test scores, those with very strong attendance in middle school (98 percent or higher) get much better grades in high school than those with moderate attendance (e.g., 94 percent). By the time students are in high school, and in college, they need to know how to get themselves to class. Efforts aimed at 100 percent attendance could actually have substantial pay-off in students' eventual success in college and careers, but problems with attendance are often dismissed as being of low importance compared to progress on tests.

Figuring out how to get to school when other factors may interfere—from family sickness and transportation issues, to the pull of more interesting activities—is not of secondary importance to improving test scores. This is more difficult for some schools than others, as schools serving many students in poverty will struggle with issues around transportation, health care, safety, and residential instability. But there is no reason to think that these schools would be less successful at improving attendance than at improving test scores, which are also hard to address in highly impoverished communities.

Schools and the public are concerned about meeting ACT benchmarks, but reaching benchmark scores is less important for college readiness than maximizing learning growth and getting good grades. There is a strong focus on raising test scores to reach ACT benchmark scores. However, while all students' scores grow as they move through the middle grades and high school, they do not grow at rates that are different enough to make up for the initial differences in scores across students. This makes benchmarks irrelevant for all but a subset of students, because they are too high for some students and too low for others. Setting one testing goal for all students sets up many students and schools for failure and does not push students at the high end to meet their potential. It gives a false sense of success for schools serving students with high test scores to begin with, while setting impossible standards for schools serving students with the weakest skills.

All schools have reading and math improvement as a priority, and the differences between schools in the instruction that students receive are not enough to make up for the large differences that exist before they enter the middle grades. This is not only true in Chicago but it also can be inferred from research in many other places.[70] Getting high gains on tests may take more resources—smaller classes, more time, more individualized assistance—for students with weak skills than are currently available to most schools.[71] The good news is that students can have success in high school and college despite test scores that are well below ACT's benchmarks. In fact, students who score well below ACT's benchmark scores do not have a substantially lower probability of success in college classes than students who meet the benchmark. For example, while the probability of earning at least a B in a college social science class for students at the benchmark reading score of 21 is 50 percent, the probability of earning at least a B for students with a score of 16 is 40 percent.[72]

Even students who have high test scores and strong GPAs in the middle grades do not necessarily perform well in high school; many students fall off the path to college readiness in high school. In schools serving low-income minority students, it is particularly important that those students who have a chance of success get opportunities that will allow them to be competitive with students from more advantaged schools. Students need classroom environments that encourage them to put in strong effort, earn high grades, and show high rates of learning growth. If students are coming into high school with strong middle school records and not performing well, high schools need to find out why.

Research has shown that students learn more when they are in orderly environments with high expectations.[73] Schools can achieve this in multiple ways. For academically strong students, they can run honors classes, IB programs, and advanced classes.[74] Or they can put sufficient support staff in place in mixed-ability classes so that expectations are high for all students, and so that teachers are able to provide differentiated instruction in an orderly environment.[75] They can make sure that students with low achievement have sufficient support, time for learning, and student-

---

66 Farrington et al. (2012).
67 Nomi and Allensworth (2013).
68 Rosenkranz et al. (2014).
69 Allensworth et al. (2014).
70 As noted in Chapter 4, tests in early grades are extremely predictive of test scores in later grades, suggesting that there is little variation in long-term growth on tests taken (e.g., in California): see Zau and Betts (2008); Kurlaender, Reardon, and Jackson (2008); New York: Kieffer and Marinell (2012): or on ACT's EPAS system: ACT, Inc. (2008).
71 For example, evidence suggests that struggling adolescent readers can show improvements in literacy with intensive, individualized interventions (Kamil et al., 2008). But individualized interventions require additional resources for students.
72 See the figures in Allen and Sconing (2005), the report used to set the original ACT benchmark scores.
73 See Gates Foundation (2010); Allensworth et al. (2014).
74 In general, high-achieving students have higher test score gains when in classes that are sorted by skills. See Nomi and Allensworth (2009, 2012, 2013); Collins and Gan (2013); Argys, Rees, and Brewer (1996); Loveless (1999).
75 We found that all students' achievement improved in algebra classes where students with below-average skills received an extra period of instruction simultaneously to their primary algebra class (Nomi and Allensworth, 2012).

Chapter 9 | Interpretive Summary

centered pedagogy to enable them to be engaged and successful in challenging classes.[76] Students tend to put in more effort and earn higher grades when teachers are attuned to their academic needs and provide support as soon as they start to struggle. Monitoring systems can make it easier for educators to identify students who need help so they can reach out as soon as a student's performance starts to slip or is below their potential.

Monitoring systems could help students get the right level and kinds of support to keep them on-track for high school and college graduation. High schools in Chicago have made extraordinary progress over the last five years in improving student performance in the ninth grade by using early warning indicators to support student performance in their classes. Ninth-grade on-track rates have increased from around 59 percent to close to 85 percent in just a few years. In many high schools, educators have designed systems for reaching out to ninth-grade students whose absences are high or grades are low to find out why they are struggling and figure out ways to help them perform better. Schools are setting goals around particular groups of students, identifying them, and tracking the progress of their intervention plans. They are using data on grades and attendance to have difficult, but important, conversations about how they could better support their students to make progress towards high school graduation. Most of these systems have focused on getting students on-track to graduation. Similar systems could be designed around students who are falling off-track to college readiness. The success of data-driven practices around grades and attendance in high schools suggests that similar efforts in schools serving the middle grades might do much to further improve CPS students' educational attainment.

---

[76] When Chicago implemented its double-algebra policy, it provided support for teachers and twice as much instructional time for students. The challenge and instructional quality in algebra classes improved for students with below-average test scores, and they learned more math (Nomi and Allensworth, 2009, 2012).

References

ACT, Inc. (2008).
The forgotten middle. Iowa City, IA: ACT. Retrieved from http://www.act.org/research/policymakers/pdf/ForgottenMiddle.pdf.

ACT, Inc. (2012).
The condition of college & career readiness. Iowa City, IA: ACT. Retrieved from http://media.act.org/documents/CCCR12-NationalReadinessRpt.pdf?_ga=1.256103106.857372413.1414731200.

Alexander, K.L., Entwisle, D.R., and Kabbani, N.S. (2001).
The dropout process in life course perspective: Early risk factors at home and school. *Teachers College Record, 103*(5), 760-822.

Allen, J., and Sconing, J. (2005).
Using ACT assessment scores to set benchmarks for college readiness. ACT Research Report Series 2005-3. Retrieved from http://www.act.org/research/researchers/reports/pdf/ACT_RR2005-3.pdf.

Allen, J. (2013).
Updating the ACT college readiness benchmarks. ACT Research Report Series 2013 (6). Retrieved from http://www.act.org/research/researchers/reports/pdf/ACT_RR2013-6.pdf.

Allensworth, E. (2006).
Update to: From High School to the Future: A First Look at Chicago Public School Graduates' College Enrollment, College Preparation, and Graduation from Four-Year Colleges Chicago, IL: University of Chicago Consortium on Chicago School Research.

Allensworth, E. (2013).
The use of ninth-grade early warning indicators to improve Chicago schools. *Journal of Education for Students Placed at Risk, 18*(1), 68-83.

Allensworth, E., Correa, M., and Ponisciak, S. (2008).
From High School to the Future: ACT Preparation—Too Much, Too Late. Chicago, IL: University of Chicago Consortium on Chicago School Research.

Allensworth, E., and Easton, J.Q. (2005).
The On-Track Indicator as a Predictor of High School Graduation. Chicago, IL: University of Chicago Consortium on Chicago School Research.

Allensworth, E., and Easton, J.Q. (2007).
What Matters for Staying On-Track and Graduating in Chicago Public High Schools: A Close Look at Course Grades, Failures, and Attendance in the Freshman Year. Chicago, IL: University of Chicago Consortium on Chicago School Research.

Allensworth, E., Gwynne, J., Pareja, A.S., Sebastian, J., and Stevens, W.D. (2014).
Free to Fail or On-Track to College: Setting the Stage for Academic Rigor: Without Classroom Control and Student Support, a Challenging Curriculum Falls Flat. Chicago, IL: University of Chicago Consortium on Chicago School Research.

Alliance for Excellent Education (2011).
The High Cost of High School Dropouts: What the Nation Pays for Inadequate High Schools. Washington, DC: Alliance for Excellent Education.

Alspaugh, J.W. (1998).
Achievement loss associated with the transition to middle school and high school. *The Journal of Educational Research, 92*(1), 20-25.

Argys, L.M., Rees, D.I., and Brewer, D.J. (1996).
Detracking America's schools: Equity at zero costs? *Journal of Policy Analysis and Management, 15*(4), 623-645.

Balfanz, R., Herzog, L., and MacIver, D.J. (2007).
Preventing student disengagement and keeping students on the graduation path in urban middle-grades schools: Early identification and effective interventions. *Educational Psychologist, 42*(4), 223-235.

Ballou, D. (2007).
Magnet schools and peers: Effects on student achievement [PowerPoint document]. Retrieved from schoolchoice.uconn.edu/assets/PPT/4B_Ballou.ppt.

Baltimore Education Research Consortium (BERC) (2011).
Destination Graduation: Sixth-Grade Early Warning Indicators for Baltimore City Schools: Their Prevalence and Impact. Baltimore, MD: BERC.

Barber, B.K., and Olsen, J.A. (2004).
Assessing the transitions to middle and high school. *Journal of Adolescent Research,* 19(1), 3-30.

Benner, A.D. (2011).
The transition to high school: Current knowledge, future directions. *Educational Psychology Review,* 23(3), 299-328.

Bowen, W.G., Chingos, M.M., and McPherson, M.S. (2009).
Crossing the Finish Line: Completing College at America's Public Universities. Princeton, NJ: Princeton University Press.

Bowers, A.J., Sprott, R., and Taff, S.A. (2013).
Do we know who will drop out? A review of the predictors of dropping out of high school: Precision, sensitivity, and specificity. *The High School Journal, 96*(2), 77-100.

Collins, C.A., and Gan, L. (2013).
Does sorting students improve scores? An analysis of class composition. NBER Working Paper No. 18848. Cambridge, MA: National Bureau of Economic Research. Retrieved from http://www.nber.org/papers/w18848.

Dale, S., and Krueger, A. (2012).
Estimating the return to college selectivity over the career using administrative earnings data. NBER Working Paper No. 17159. Cambridge, MA: National Bureau of Economic Research. Retrieved from http://www.nber.org/papers/w17159.

Davis, J.A. (1985).
The Logic of Causal Order. Newbury Park, CA: Sage.

Day, J.C., and Newburger, E.C. (2002).
The big payoff: Educational attainment and synthetic estimates of work-life earnings. Washington, DC: U.S. Census Bureau (P23-210).

Duckworth, A.L., and Seligman, M.E.P. (2005).
Self-discipline outdoes IQ in predicting academic performance of adolescents. *Psychological Science, 16*(12), 939-944.

Duckworth, A.L., and Seligman, M.E.P. (2006).
Self-discipline gives girls the edge: Gender in self-discipline, grades, and achievement test scores. *Journal of Educational Psychology, 98*(1), 198-208.

Duckworth, A.L., Peterson, C., Matthews, M.D., and Kelly, D.R. (2007).
Grit: Perseverance and passion for long-term goals. *Journal of Personality and Social Psychology, 92*(6), 1087-1101.

Dweck, C., Cohen, G., and Walton, G. (2011).
Academic tenacity. An unpublished white paper prepared for the Bill & Melinda Gates Foundation.

Eccles, J.S., Lord, S., and Midgley, C. (1991).
What are we doing to early adolescents? The impact of educational contexts on early adolescents. *American Journal of Education, 99*(4), 521-542.

Farkas, G., Sheehan, D., and Grobe R.P. (1990).
Coursework mastery and school success: Gender, ethnicity, poverty groups within an urban school district. *American Educational Research Journal, 27*(4), 807-827.

Farrington, C.A., Roderick, M., Allensworth, E., Nagaoka, J., Keyes, T.S., Johnson, D.W., and Beechum, N.O. (2012).
Teaching Adolescents to Become Learners: The Role of Noncognitive Factors in Shaping School Performance. Chicago, IL: University of Chicago Consortium on Chicago School Research.

Gamoran, A. (1996).
Student achievement in public magnet, public comprehensive, and private city high schools. *Educational Evaluation and Policy Analysis, 18*(1), 1-18.

Gates Foundation. (2010).
Learning about teaching: Initial findings from the measures of effective teaching project. Retrieved from http://www.metproject.org/downloads/Preliminary_Findings-Research_Paper.pdf.

Geiser, S., and Santelices, V. (2007).
Validity of High School Grades in Predicting Student Success Beyond the Freshman Year: High-School Record versus Standardized Tests as Indicators of Four-year College Outcomes. Berkeley, CA: University of Berkeley Center for Studies in Higher Education.

Heckman, J.J., and LaFontaine, P.A. (2007).
The American high school graduation rate: Trends and levels. NBER Working Paper No. 13670. Cambridge, MA: National Bureau of Economic Research. Retrieved from http://www.nber.org/papers/w13670.

Heppen, J.B., and Therriault, S.B. (2008).
Developing Early Warning Systems to Identify Potential High School Dropouts. Washington, DC: National High School Center. Retrieved from http://www.betterhighschools.org/pubs/documents/IssueBrief_EarlyWarningSystemsGuide.pdf.

Hoxby, C.M. (2001).
The return to attending a more selective college: 1960 to the present. In M. Devlin and J. Meyerson (Eds.), *Forum Futures: Exploring the Future of Higher Education, 2000 Papers* (pp. 13-42). Forum Strategy Series, Volume 3. Oxford, OH: Jossey-Bass.

Illinois State Board of Education. (2008).
Illinois Standards Achievement Test 2008 Technical Manual. Springfield, IL: Illinois State Board of Education Assessment Division. Retrieved from http://www.isbe.net/assessment/pdfs/isat_tech_2008.pdf.

Illinois State Board of Education. (2011).
Interpretive Guide 2011 Illinois Standards Achievement Test. Springfield, IL: Illinois State Board of Education. Retrieved from http://www.isbe.net/assessment/pdfs/ISAT_Interpr_Guide_2011.pdf.

Illinois State Board of Education. (2012).
Illinois Standards Achievement Test 2012 Technical Manual. Springfield, IL: Illinois State Board of Education Assessment Division. Retrieved from http://www.isbe.net/assessment/pdfs/isat_tech_2012.pdf.

Kamil, M.L., Borman, G.D., Dole, J., Kral, C.C., Salinger, T., and Torgesen, J. (2008).
Improving adolescent literacy: Effective classroom and intervention practices: A practice guide (NCEE #2008-4027). Washington, DC: National Center for Education Evaluation and Regional Assistance, Institute of Education Sciences, U.S. Department of Education. Retrieved from http://ies.ed.gov/ncee/wwc/pdf/practice_guides/adlit_pg_082608.pdf.

Kelly, S. (2008).
What types of students' effort are rewarded with high marks? *Sociology of Education, 81*(1), 32-52.

Kieffer, M.J., and Marinell, W.H. (2012).
Navigating the Middle Grades: Evidence from New York City. New York, NY: Research Alliance for New York City Schools.

Koretz, D. (2005).
Alignment, high stakes, and the inflation of test scores. *Yearbook of the National Society for the Study of Education, 104*(2), 99-118.

Koretz, D. (2008).
Measuring Up: What Educational Testing Really Tells Us. Cambridge, MA: Harvard University Press.

Kurlaender, M., Reardon, S.F., and Jackson, J. (2008).
Middle School Predictors of High School Achievement in Three California School Districts. Santa Barbara, CA: University of California, California Dropout Research Project.

Lehr, C.A., Sinclair, M.F., and Christenson, S.L. (2004).
Addressing student engagement and truancy prevention during the elementary school years: A replication study of the Check and Connect model. *Journal of Education for Students Placed at Risk (JESPAR), 9*(3), 279-301.

Loveless, T. (1999).
The Tracking Wars: State Reform Meets School Policy. Washington, DC: Brookings Institution Press.

Luppescu, S., Allensworth, E., Moore, P., de la Torre, M., and Murphy, J., with Jagesic, S. (2011).
Trends in Chicago's Schools Across Three Eras of Reform. Chicago, IL: University of Chicago Consortium on Chicago School Research.

National Center for Education Statistics. (2007).
The condition of education (NCES 2007-064). U.S. Department of Education. Washington, DC: National Center for Education Statistics.

Neild, R.C., and Balfanz, R. (2006).
Unfulfilled promise: The dimensions and characteristics of Unfulfilled Promise: The Dimensions and Characteristics of Philadelphia's Dropout Crisis, 2000-05. Philadelphia, PA: Philadelphia Youth Transitions Collaborative.

Nomi, T., and Allensworth, E. (2009).
"Double-dose" algebra as an alternative strategy to remediation: Effects on students' academic outcomes. *Journal of Research on Educational Effectiveness, 2*(2), 111-148.

Nomi, T., and Allensworth, E. (2012).
Sorting and supporting: Why double-dose algebra led to better test scores but more course failures. *American Educational Research Journal, 50*(4), 1-33.

Nomi, T., and Allensworth, E. (2014).
Skill-Based Sorting in the Era of College Prep for All: Costs and Benefits. Chicago, IL: University of Chicago Consortium on Chicago School Research.

Raudenbush, S., and Bryk, A.S. (2002).
Hierarchical Linear Models: Applications and Data Analysis Methods. Newbury Park, CA: Sage.

Roderick, M., Coca, V., Moeller, E., and Kelley-Kemple, T. (2013).
From High School to the Future: The Challenge of Senior Year in Chicago Public Schools. Chicago, IL: University of Chicago Consortium on Chicago School Research.

Roderick, M., Nagaoka, J., Allensworth, E., Coca, V., Correa, M., and Stoker, G. (2006).
From High School to the Future: A First Look at Chicago Public School Graduates' College Enrollment, College Preparation, and Graduation from Four-Year Colleges. Chicago, IL: University of Chicago Consortium on Chicago School Research.

Roderick, M., Nagaoka, J., Coca, V., Moeller, E., Roddie, K., Gilliam, J., and Patton, D. (2008).
From High School to the Future: Potholes on the Road to College. Chicago, IL: University of Chicago Consortium on Chicago School Research.

Rosenkranz, T., de la Torre, M., Stevens, W.D., and Allensworth, E. (2014).
Free to Fail or On-Track To College: Why Grades Drop When Students Enter High School and What Adults Can Do About It. Chicago, IL: University of Chicago Consortium on Chicago School Research.

Rumburger, R., and Lim, S.A. (2008).
Why Students Drop Out of School: A Review of 25 Years of Research. Santa Barbara, CA: California Dropout Research Project.

Sinclair, M.F., Christenson, S.L., and Thurlow, M.L. (2005). Promoting school completion of urban secondary youth with emotional or behavioral disabilities. *Exceptional Children, 71*(4), 465-482.

Sum, A., Khatiwada, I., and McLaughlin, J. (2009). *The Consequences of Dropping Out of High School: Joblessness and Jailing for High School Dropouts and the High Cost for Taxpayers.* Boston, MA: Center for Labor Market Studies (Northeastern University).

Tough, P. (2011). What if the secret to success is failure? *New York Times.* Retrieved from http://www.nytimes.com/2011/09/18/magazine/what-if-the-secret-to-success-is-failure.html?scp=2&sq=the%20character%20test&st=cse.

Zau, A.C., and Betts, J.R. (2008). *Predicting Success, Preventing Failure: An Investigation of the California High School Exit Exam.* San Francisco, CA: Public Policy Institute of California.

Appendix A
Students' College Access and Graduation Rates, Based on High School Performance

In a 2006 study, UChicago CCSR examined the college-going patterns of CPS students, and compared the colleges students attended with their qualifications upon leaving high school, to determine what types of ACT scores and GPAs students needed to have a chance of attending colleges of different selectivity levels (Roderick et al., 2006). While colleges often provide guidelines of qualifications in their application materials, the analysis showed that the students were often able to gain admission with lower qualifications than were stated. **Table A.1** shows the types of colleges that students potentially could access, based on their qualifications, given the colleges at which students with such qualifications actually enrolled. The selectivity categories are based on Barron's ratings.

The same study also examined CPS students' college graduation rates, based on their high school qualifications. Students' high school GPA turned out to be the strongest predictor of college graduation. **Figure A.1** comes from an update to that report, and shows the relationship between students' high school GPAs and their college graduation rates, among students who enrolled in a four-year college. Only students with at least a 3.0 high school GPA had at least a 50 percent chance of graduating from college, among those who enrolled in a four-year college. In their study of North Carolina colleges Bowen, Chingos, and McPherson (2009) also found that students' high school GPA was a stronger predictor of college graduation than their SAT score, particularly after controlling for which college students attended. As was found in Chicago, they found that a 3.0 GPA was the point at which students' probability at graduating reached 50 percent, among students in their North Carolina sample. For this reason, this report focuses on a GPA of 3.0 or above as a primary indicator of readiness to succeed in college.

TABLE A.1
Categories for Access to College Types Based on CPS Juniors' GPAs and ACT Scores

Unweighted GPA in Core Courses (By the End of Junior Year)

Composite ACT Score	Less than 2.0	2.0–2.4	2.5–2.9	3.0–3.4	3.5–4.0
Missing ACT	Two-Year Colleges	Nonselective Four-Year Colleges	Somewhat Selective Colleges	Selective Colleges	Selective Colleges
Less than 18	Two-Year Colleges	Nonselective Four-Year Colleges	Somewhat Selective Colleges	Somewhat Selective Colleges	Selective Colleges
18–20	Nonselective Four-year Colleges	Somewhat Selective Colleges	Somewhat Selective Colleges	Selective Colleges	Selective Colleges
21–23	Somewhat Selective Colleges	Somewhat Selective Colleges	Selective Colleges	Selective Colleges	Selective Colleges
24 or Higher	Somewhat Selective Colleges	Selective Colleges	Selective Colleges	Very Selective Colleges	Very Selective Colleges

Note: Roderick et al. (2006)

FIGURE A.1

College Graduation Rates by Unweighted High School GPA

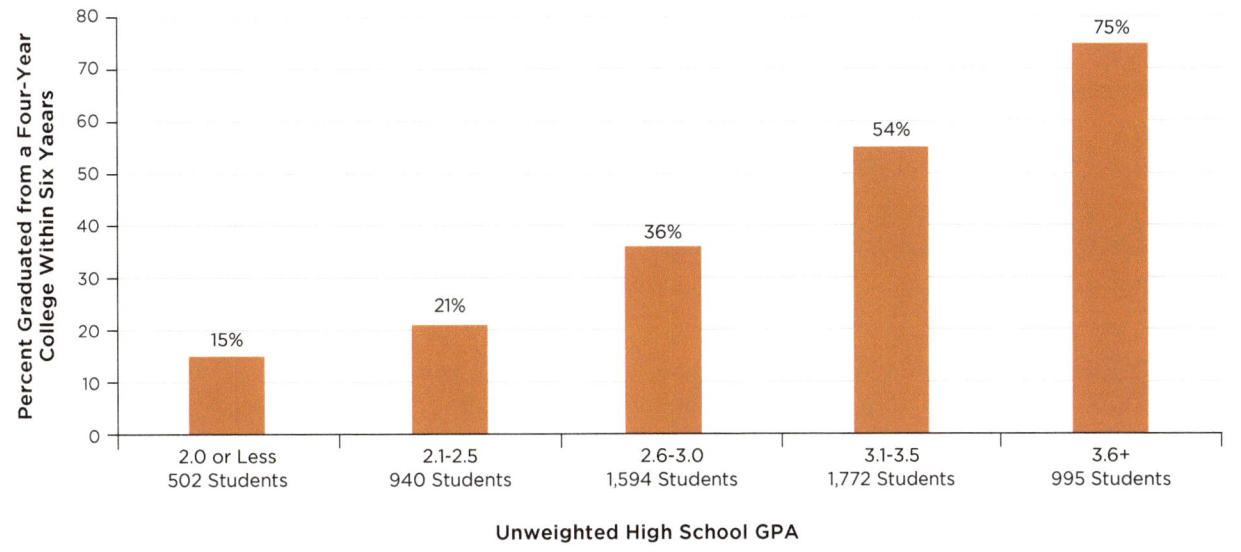

Note: These were CPS alumni who enrolled full-time in a four-year college by spring following their high school graduation and enrolled in a college for which we have graduation information. Allensworth (2006).

Appendix A

Appendix B
Data Definitions

Sample Used for the Indicator Analysis (Chapters 3 through 7)

The indicator analysis is based on the cohort of students who were first-time freshmen in the fall of 2009. The students in the analytic sample attended either a neighborhood, vocational, magnet school, or an Academic Preparatory Center (APC) in ninth grade. Charter school students are also included in the analysis of test scores (see Chapters 6 and 7). Students' transcripts are not available for charter schools, which is why they are not included in the analysis of ninth-grade on-track rates or grades. Alternative school students are not included in the analysis. Alternative schools do not follow the same curriculum and graduation requirements as other schools. Students were included if they enrolled for at least 120 days during the prior year (2008-09 school year) out of a school year of 170 days total.

- In Chapters 3 through 5, the analysis is based on students with data on ninth-grade GPA and eighth-grade GPA, attendance, and ISAT scores. This cohort comprised 19,963 students.

- In Chapters 6 and 7, the analysis is based on students with data on tenth-grade PLAN and eighth-grade GPA and attendance, and ISAT scores in eighth, seventh, and sixth grade. This cohort comprised 20,356 students (including students in charter high schools).

Sample Used for the Growth Analysis in Chapter 8

Growth analyses were done in different ways for grades and attendance than for test scores. To examine test score growth, we used one cohort of students over four years—the same 2009 ninth-grade cohort used for all other analyses in the report. For the analysis of grades and attendance, we did not have data on grades and attendance for this cohort as far back as fifth grade, since these data just became available in 2007. Therefore, we used later cohorts of students to examine growth over time in grades and attendance—students who were in fifth grade in 2007-09.

- **Change in attendance** from fifth to eighth grade was examined using data from three cohorts of students: those who were in fifth grade in the fall of 2007, 2008, or 2009. This cohort comprised 99,300 students. The samples used in the analyses of attendance and also GPA trends differ from the sample used to validate middle grade indicators and analyze ISAT trends because of limited data from the middle grade years for students who were first-time ninth-graders in 2009. The first year in which attendance and GPA data were available for students in elementary and middle schools was 2007-08, meaning there were only two years of middle grade data for the cohort of students used in the rest of the report.

- **Change in GPA** from fifth to eighth grade was examined using data from two cohorts of students: those who were in fifth grade in the fall of 2007 or 2008. Eighth-grade GPA data were not yet available for the fifth-graders in 2009 when the analysis was performed. This cohort comprised 61,791 students. Only two cohorts of fifth-grade students were used in the GPA analysis, instead of the three cohorts used in the attendance analysis because at the time the analysis was done we had not yet received GPA data files from 2012 or beyond when most of the fifth-graders from 2009-10 would have been in seventh grade or higher.

- **Change in test scores** from fifth to eighth grade was examined using students who were ninth-graders in the fall of 2009. Students form this cohort with test scores in any of those years are used to calculate test scores growth. This cohort comprised just over 27,300 students.

Variables Considered as Potential Middle Grade Indicators

- **Core GPA** is the average of grades earned in the following subjects: English, math, science, and social science on a 4-point scale where A=4 regardless of level (e.g., Honors).
    - **Growth in GPA**: the average yearly growth or decline in GPA that students experienced between fifth to eighth grade
- **Failures** is a count of the number of semester failures in eighth-grade core subjects (English, math, science, and social science).
- **Misconducts** include infractions of severity 4 or higher. We did not include lower levels of misconducts because they are less likely to be reported consistently across schools. Higher-level infractions are reported more consistently than lower-level infractions because they are usually accompanied by a suspension.
- **Suspensions** is a count of the number of days a student spent out of school due to suspension.
- **Grit** (reliability=0.86) is a measure constructed from students' responses to the following questions on UChicago CCSR's annual survey of CPS students. It is based on a scale developed by Duckworth et al. (2007):
    - I finish whatever I begin
    - I am a hard worker
    - I continue steadily towards my goals
    - I don't give up easily
- **Study Habits** (reliability=0.73) is a measure constructed from students' responses to the following questions on UChicago CCSR's annual survey of CPS students:
    - I set aside time to do my homework and study
    - I try to do well on my schoolwork even when it isn't interesting to me
    - If I need to study, I don't go out with my friends
    - I always study for tests
- **Background Characteristics** include indicators of race/ethnicity, gender, special education status, neighborhood concentration of poverty and social status, free/reduced-priced lunch status, and whether a student was older than 14 when entering high school. Neighborhood concentration of poverty is based on data from the 2000 U.S. Census on the census block group in which students lived. Students' home addresses were used to link each student to a particular block group within the city, which could then be linked to census data on the economic conditions of the student's neighborhood. Two indicators were used to construct these variables, the log of the percentage of household above the poverty line and the log of the percentage of men employed in the block group. Neighborhood social status is based on data from the 2000 U.S. Census on the census block group in which students lived. Students' home addresses were used to link each student to a particular block group within the city, which could then be linked to census data on the economic conditions of the student's neighborhood. Two indicators were used to construct these variables, the average level of education among adults over age 21 and the log of the percentage of men in the block group employed as managers or executives.

- **Attendance** is a proportion of the number of days attended out of the number of days enrolled.
  - **Growth in attendance:** the average yearly growth or decline in attendance rate that students experienced between fifth and eighth grade.
- **Illinois Standard Achievement Test (ISAT)** measures individual student achievement relative to the Illinois Learning Standards. Students in grades three through eight take the ISAT in reading and math. Information on the ISAT is available in ISBE (2012).
  - **Subscales:** scores in the reading test in eighth grade in the areas of vocabulary development, reading strategies, reading comprehension, literature, and extended-response results. Scores in math test in eighth grade in the areas of number sense, measurement, algebra, geometry, data analysis, statistics and probability; and extended-response results for mathematical knowledge, strategic knowledge, and explanation results.
  - **Gains over middle grades:** gains were calculated annually over the middle grades (from fifth to sixth grade, from sixth to seventh grade, and from seventh to eighth grade) and averaged.
  - **Relative class rank:** relative rank in reading/math score from average of eighth-grade peers in the same school.

High School Outcomes

- **PLAN and ACT tests** are tests taken by CPS students as part of the Educational Planning and Assessment System (EPAS): the EXPLORE in the fall of eighth and ninth grade; PLAN in the fall of tenth grade; and ACT in the spring of eleventh grade. These tests measure student achievement in English, reading, mathematics, and science. The four subject-area scores are averaged together to calculate a composite score. The PLAN test scores range from 1 to 32. For each subject, ACT has defined a college-readiness benchmark; this is the score at which ACT has determined that students have a 50 percent chance of earning a B or better and a 75 percent chance of earning a C or better in corresponding college courses. Appendix D lists the benchmarks for the PLAN and ACT. Information about the EPAS system tests is available at ACT's website: www.act.org.
- **Ninth-grade on-track** is an indicator of whether students are making the basic level of progress in ninth grade to be on-track to graduating within four years. Ninth-graders are on-track if they have at least five full-year credits and have failed no more than one semester in a core course by the end of their first year of high school. Students who are on-track at the end of their freshman year are nearly four times more likely to graduate from high school than their classmates who are not on-track (Allensworth and Easton, 2005).
- **Eleventh-grade on-track** is an indicator of whether students have made sufficient progress to be on-track to graduate from high school within four years by the end of their third year of high school. Students are considered on-track in eleventh grade if they have at least 17 credits by the end of their third year of high school. Students are considered off-track in eleventh grade if they do not have at least 17 credits by the end of their third year of high school, regardless of whether they are officially designated as eleventh-graders or not.
- **GPA** is the average of grades earned on a 4-point scale where A=4 regardless of level (e.g., Honors). Core GPA takes the average of English, math, science, and social science; Math GPA is based on grades from only math classes; and English GPA is based on grades from only English classes.
- **Passing Math** is an indicator of whether students passed all semesters of math class. Put another way, this variable indicates whether or not students received exactly zero semester Fs in math classes.
- **Passing English** is an indicator of whether students passed all semesters of English class. Put another way, this variable indicates whether or not students received exactly zero semester Fs in English classes.

Appendix C
Research Methodology

Methods for Comparing Indicators in Chapters 3 and 6

The process of examining potential indicators of high school success involved several steps. We examined, in the following order: 1) which indicators showed strong relationships with later outcomes, and how predictive they were individually; 2) the shape of the relationship among those indicators that were strongly predictive; 3) which indicators were predictive above and beyond others—adding new information to the prediction; 4) how the indicators functioned together to predict later outcomes; and 5) whether predictions varied by school. These steps were performed separately for each high school outcome.

We began by gauging the general strength of the relationship of each potential indicator with each outcome through bivariate correlations. For dichotomous outcomes (those that can be characterized as success versus failure—such as being on-track, passing math, meeting the benchmark—we also calculated the sensitivity and specificity of predictions using each potential indicator as a predictor of each outcome, with 50 percent probability as the point for classifying each case as a success or failure on the outcome. The bivariate relationships and prediction statistics of each potential indicator with high school outcomes are provided in **Tables E.1 and E.2 in Appendix E**.

For those indicators that showed moderate to strong relationships with high school outcomes, we examined the shape of the relationship—whether there was a steady improvement in the outcome for each unit of improvement in the indicator, or whether the indicator was related to the outcome at just high or low levels, etc. The relationships were examined through simple charts that graphed levels of the outcome at different levels of the predictor. These figures are not included in the report, but the nature of relationships of the variables can be seen through figures that graph each outcome by the predictors; for example, **Figures 7 and 8** show that the relationship between eighth-grade GPA and the probability of earning As and Bs in high school is strongest among students with high eighth-grade GPAs.

We then conducted a series of analyses in which we examined combinations of potential indicators for each high school outcome. With each outcome, we started with the indicator that had the strongest bivariate relationship, and then we added additional predictors one at a time to determine whether each added new information to improve the prediction. We used regression models (or logistic regression models for dichotomous outcomes), comparing the R-square (pseudo-R-square), percent correct prediction, sensitivity, and specificity derived from each model. We focused on model statistics, rather than coefficients associated with individual variables, to discern whether inclusion of each additional potential indicator in the model improved the prediction of the high school outcome beyond the prediction of a simpler model without that potential indicator. The model statistics from select combinations of predictors—those with the greatest potential for improving the prediction—are displayed in the bottom of **Tables 3 and 7** in Chapters 4 and 7 and in the tables in **Appendix E**.

Once we discerned the indictors that provided unique information to the prediction model, we examined the ways in which the different indicators together predicted the outcomes; for example, whether an indicator provided information at all levels of the other predictor or whether its relationship with the outcome depended on levels of the other predictor. **Figures 7 and 8** provide an example of a case when a predictor (attendance or ISAT scores) improves the prediction of the outcome (earning As and Bs) only at particular levels of another indicator (among students with high eighth-grade GPAs).

The figures displayed in Chapter 3 show the contribution of attendance and test scores for predicting on-track rates and high grades among students with similar middle school GPAs. We chose those displays because middle grade GPAs had the strongest bivariate relationship with the high school outcomes. An alternative approach would be to group students by test scores and then examine the contribution of grades or attendance for predicting high school outcomes among students with the same test scores. **Figures C.1 through C.4** show this. Students are more likely to be on-track in ninth grade or earn high grades if they have high test scores. However, the probability of being on-track or earning high grades depends considerably on attendance and middle grade GPAs among students with similar test scores. In contrast, as shown in the figures in Chapter 3, test scores only modestly add to the prediction of high school grades, beyond students' middle grade GPAs.

Methods for Calculating School Effects in Chapters 3 and 6

In studying school effects, we wanted to know if students who looked like they should have the same levels of success in high school, based on their middle school qualifications, had different levels of success depending on which middle or high school they attended. To

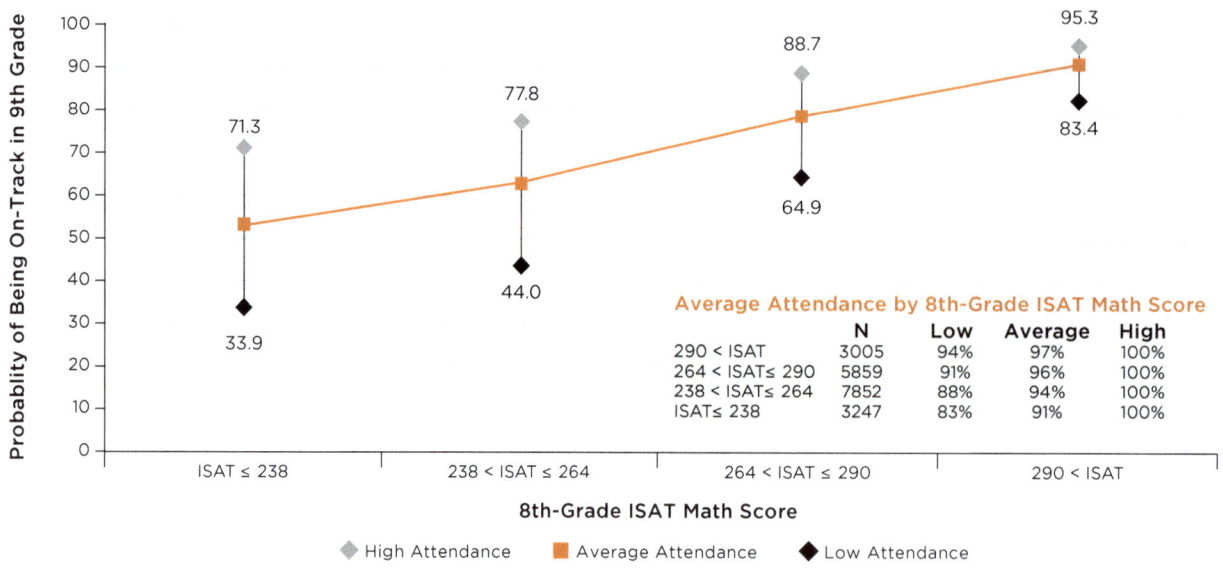

FIGURE C.1
On-Track Rates by ISAT Math Scores and Eighth-Grade Attendance Rates

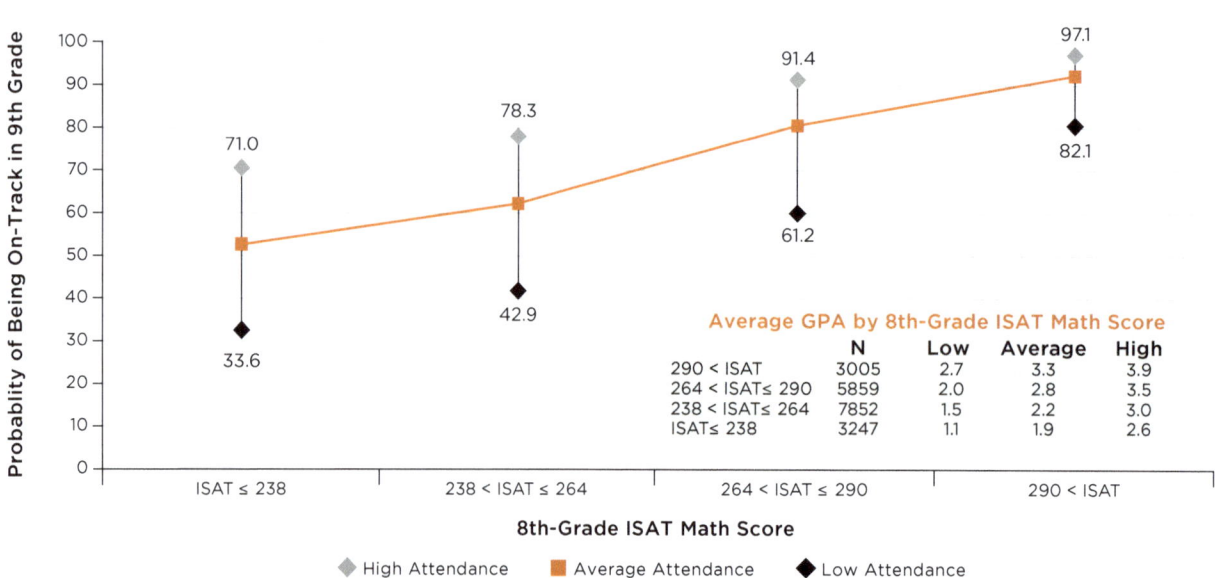

FIGURE C.2
On-Track Rates by ISAT Math Scores and Eighth-Grade Core GPA

do this, we used two stages of prediction models: one model to estimate each student's likely outcome, based only on their individual qualifications at the end of middle school, and another to determine whether students from each school had actual outcomes that were higher or lower than predicted based on their individual qualifications.

The first stage of analysis determined each student's predicted outcome (or probability of success for dichotomous outcomes), based only on their middle school performance, using eighth-grade GPA, attendance, and test scores—these were the predictor variables most strongly related to the ninth-outcomes. This predicted value (ŷ) was entered as a predictor in the school-effects model to represent all of a student's individual qualifications. Combining all prior records into one variable that represents a student's predicted outcome made it easier to interpret the school effects in the second stage of analysis than a model with multiple student parameters. It also attributes all shared variance that may exist between individual characteristics and schools to individual characteristics, assuring that any school effects

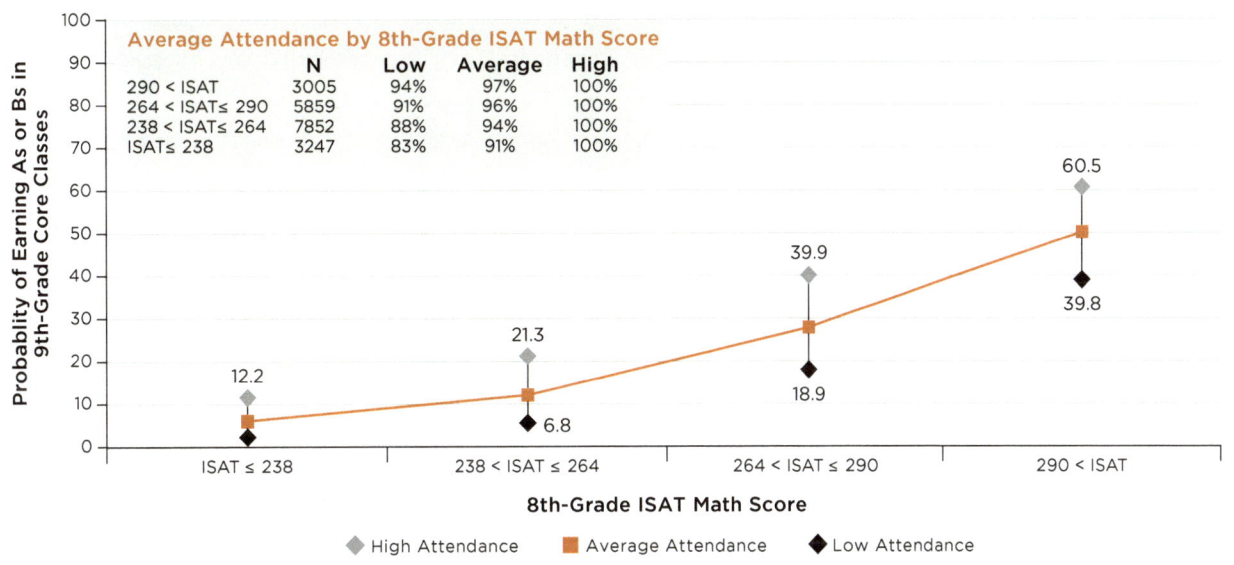

FIGURE C.3
Probability of Earning As or Bs by ISAT Math Scores and Eighth-Grade Attendance

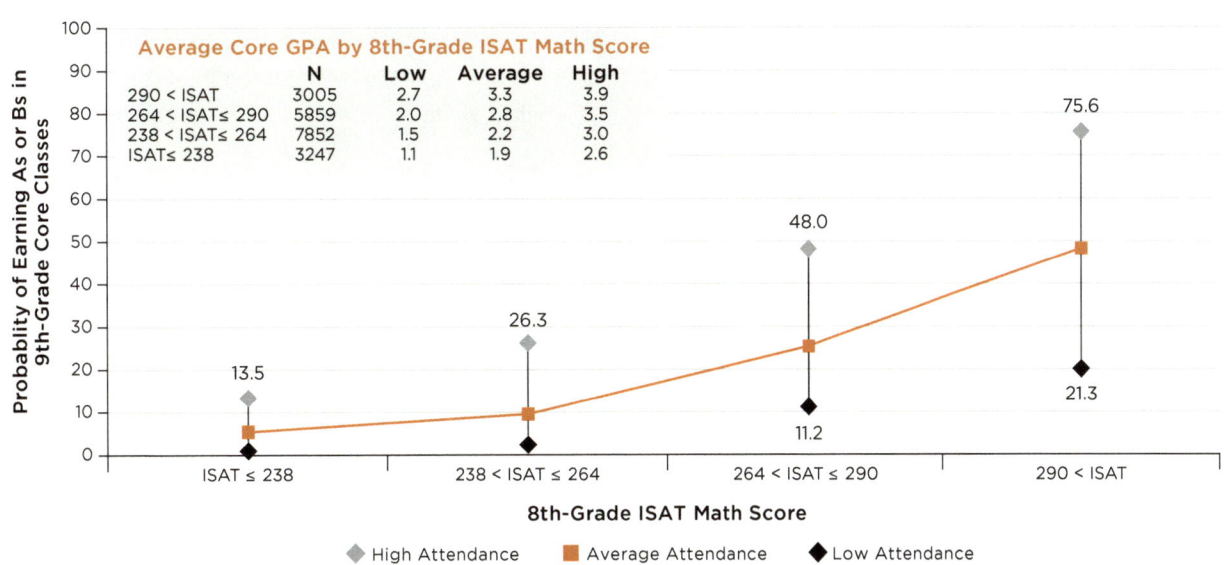

FIGURE C.4
Probability of Earning As or Bs by ISAT Math Scores and Eighth-Grade Core GPA

Appendix C

that are discerned do not result simply from the selection of students with particular achievement levels into specific schools. For this reason, we may be underestimating school effects, but we are certain that any school effects that are identified actually can be attributed to schools rather than to individuals.

School effects were calculated through cross-nested models, with students nested simultaneously in their eighth-grade school and their ninth-grade school. For each outcome, the predicted value of the outcome from the first stage analysis (ŷ) controls for students' qualifications (see models below). The extent that students from particular middle schools or high schools have outcomes that are higher or lower than the predicted values are captured with the school effects (b_{00} and c_{00}). Cross-nesting students in both schools allows us to capture middle school and high school effects net of each other.

LEVEL-1 MODEL

outcome = $\pi_0 + \pi_1*(\hat{y})$

LEVEL-2 MODEL

(students nested simultaneously in their middle and high school)

$\pi_0 = \theta_0 + b_{00} + c_{00}$
$\pi_1 = \theta_1$

After determining the middle and high school effects, net of each other, we ran hierarchical models with students nested in their middle grade school only to determine the middle school effects incorporating high school effects. These models attribute high school effects to middle schools, showing the actual effect of attending a particular middle school, given the sending/receiving patterns that exist between schools.

Methods for Calculating Growth Over Time in Chapter 8

We begin by discussing the analysis of growth trends on the ISAT; attendance and grade models were similar, but had some differences, as discussed below. Growth trends on ISAT scores were based on the population of students who were first-time ninth-graders in the fall of 2009. For the ISAT trends, data comes from the tests students took in the spring of 2006, 2007, 2008, and 2009. If students had data at any point in time in those four years they were included in the analysis. We included all schools and all students with test data, regardless of whether they were receiving special education or bilingual services.

We modeled trends in ISAT scores over time using a two level HLM model in which annual ISAT scores at level 1 were nested within students at level 2. Students' scores at level 1 were modeled as a function of students' grade level (centered at grade eight), and also whether a student had been retained in that year or had skipped a grade that year. Because there were only four points to the trend, and preliminary models had shown that the quadratic term was very small in these models, we did not include a nonlinear term in the model for simplicity when estimating school effects. We also looked for anomalies from linear growth at specific grade levels, which are discussed further below. The models for reading and math ISAT scores, attendance, and grades were basically the same:

LEVEL-1

ISAT Score = $\pi_0 + \pi_1*$(Grade − Centered Grade 8) + π_2*(Old for Grade) + π_3*(Retained) + π_4*(Skipped Grade) + e

LEVEL-2

$\pi_0 = \gamma_{00} + u_0$
$\pi_1 = \gamma_{10} + u_1$
$\pi_2 = \gamma_{20}$
$\pi_3 = \gamma_{30}$
$\pi_4 = \gamma_{40}$

where:

- grade is the growth trajectory slope, centered around grade 8, so that it is 0 when grade=8, -1 when grade=7, etc.

- old for grade is 1 if student was old for grade at the first data point they appear in the data

- retained is 0 if never retained in grade at that point, 1 if retained that year and for each year after that, 2 the second time retained and 2 after that, and so on if there are multiple years of grade retention

- skipped grade is 0 if never skipped a grade, 1 if they skipped a grade and after that, 2 the second time and so on.

The retention variables allow students to have multiple observations for a given grade, accumulating additional growth for the extra year of instruction through the retained variable, rather than through the trend variable. The extra year of instruction is accounted for in the retained variable for all subsequent observations. The skipped grade variable has the opposite function, so that a move of two grade levels does not count as two years in the trend calculation. The gap in learning from the year that did not occur is subtracted out of all subsequent years.

The intercept and slope are allowed to vary randomly at the student level, and residuals from these models were used to calculate Empirical Bayes estimates of growth for each student. The model was also run with a set of dummy variables for different grades to see if there were systematic differences in particular grades. These are discussed further below. The ISAT growth trends without school effects are shown in **Table C.1**.

Students grow around 10 points per year in reading (see the grade coefficient), with a 2.0 standard deviation in trends across students (see u_0 for reading). Their scores grow about 13 points per year in math, with a standard deviation of 2.3 points across students. The retention and skipped grade variables are about half the size of the yearly growth trend reflecting smaller growth in the retained year than in years when students are promoted, and an acceleration in growth in the years that students skip grades, both of about half a year.

In reading, the growth parameter and the intercept (ISAT score in eighth grade) are highly negatively correlated, meaning that students with high scores tend to grow less than students with low scores. In math, this is not true; there is a very small but positive correlation between growth and the ISAT score in eighth grade.

Scores at some grade levels do not conform to a strict linear trend. Grades six and seven tend to be under-predicted by the linear trajectory in reading; grades five and seven tend to be over-predicted by the linear trajectory in math. **Figures C.1 and C.2** show these trends. In reading (**see Figure C.5**), notice that high-scoring students improve their scores more from sixth (2007) to seventh (2008) grade than in the previous year, and then improve less from seventh to eighth grade. This

TABLE C.1
HLM Analyses for ISAT Growth Trends

	Reading	Reading With Grade Dummies	Math	Math With Grade Dummies
Intercept	246.7**	245.6**	266.5**	266.2**
Grade (Centered Around Grade 8)	10.2**	10.2**	13.1**	12.0**
Old for Grade	-16.4**	-16.4**	-18.2**	-18.3**
Retained in Grade (Cumulative)	6.5**	6.7**	6.3**	6.8**
Skipped Grade (Cumulative)	-7.1**	-6.8**	-8.4**	-7.6**
Grade 4~		2.0		-2.6
Grade 5		-0.4		-4.7*
Grade 6		2.4*		0.1
Grade 7		2.3**		-1.5*
Variance-Covariance (Standard Deviations) Components				
Level-1 (e)	124.0 (11.1)**	120.8 (11.0)**	105.0 (10.2)**	101.4 (10.1)**
u_0 (int)	378.9 (19.5)**	379.0 (19.5)**	578.7 (24.1)**	580.6 (24.1)**
u_1 (grd_c8)	4.0 (2.0)**	4.9 (2.2)**	5.4 (2.3)**	6.1 (2.5)**
Corr (u_0, u_1)	-0.70	-0.65	0.11	0.10
Observations				
Level 1/Level 2	98,103/ 27,366	98,103/ 27,366	98,312/27,509	98,312/27,509

Note: *p<.05 **p<.001
~ Some students were in fourth grade when the tests took placed in the spring of 2006.

might be due to the fact that it is seventh-grade scores that count for applications to selective enrollment schools in Chicago—high-achieving students might put extra effort into their performance in seventh grade for this reason. However, the same pattern is not observed in math (**see Figure C.6**), so this may be an anomaly. Students in the not meeting range and low meets range grew the most (also student in exceeds range grew quite a bit but the number of students in this group is very small). That is why there is a negative correlation between the ISAT scores in eighth grade and growth. In math, the picture is different; the higher the scores the higher the growth (positive correlation between eighth-grade score and growth).

Table C.2 shows the estimates of growth trajectories allowing for variation at the school level. The basic model is the same as described earlier where we fit a linear growth trajectory where the observations over time (level 1) are nested within students (level 2) and then each student is nested within the schools they attended in the year 2009 (level 3):

LEVEL-1

ISAT Score = $\pi_0 + \pi_1$*(Grade–Centered Grade 8) + π_2*(Old for Grade) + π_3*(Retained) + π_4*(Skipped Grade) + e

LEVEL-2

$\pi_0 = \gamma_{00} + r_0$
$\pi_1 = \gamma_{10} + r_1$
$\pi_2 = \gamma_{20}$
$\pi_3 = \gamma_{30}$
$\pi_4 = \gamma_{40}$

LEVEL-3

$\gamma_{00} = \eta_{000} + u_{00}$
$\gamma_{10} = \eta_{100} + u_{10}$
$\gamma_{20} = \eta_{200}$
$\gamma_{30} = \eta_{300}$
$\gamma_{40} = \eta_{400}$

The variation in scores (intercept) and annual growth (GRD_C8) in test scores is now divided among students (r_0 and r_1) and schools (u_{00} and u_{01}). The estimates from *reading* scores indicate that half of the variation in test score growth comes from middle schools (the variance is 2.1 at the student level and 1.9 at the school level). Schools explain more than half the variation in the *math* test score growth (the variance is 1.8 at the student level and 3.7 at the school level). This suggests that schools have greater influence on growth in math scores than growth in reading.

FIGURE C.5
Average ISAT Reading Scores Grouped by 2009 Grade Scores

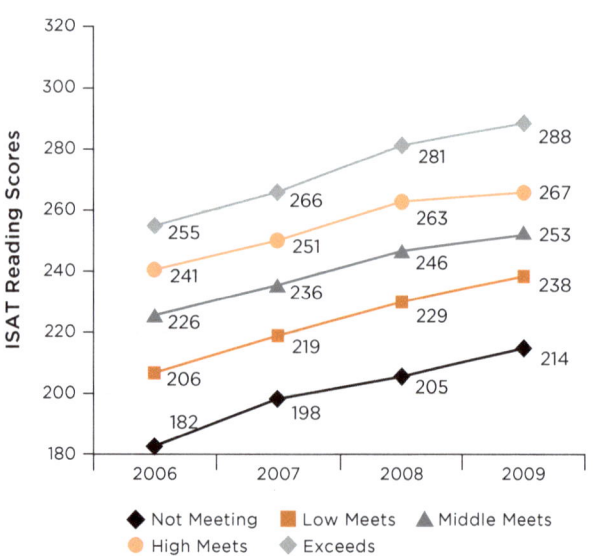

FIGURE C.6
Average ISAT Math Scores Grouped by 2009 Grade Scores

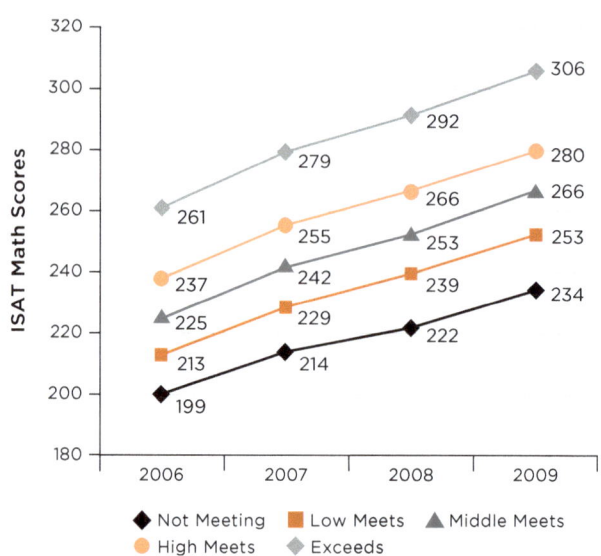

We used a similar approach for analyzing trends in attendance and GPA from fifth through eighth grade. However, the analysis of attendance trends was based on three cohorts of students who were in fifth grade in 2007-08, 2008-09, or 2009-10. It also included students who joined one of these cohorts by enrolling in a CPS school at some point during sixth through eighth grade. The total sample size is 99,300. The analysis of GPA trajectories was based on two cohorts of fifth-graders from 2007-08 and 2008-09 and also includes students who joined these cohorts between sixth and eighth grade. The sample size for the GPA analysis is 61,791. As we described in Appendix B, the samples used in the analyses of attendance and also GPA trends differ from the sample used to validate middle grade indicators and analyze ISAT trends because of limited data from the middle grade years for students who were first-time ninth-graders in 2009.

We ran two sets of analyses to look at trajectories in attendance and GPA. The first analysis used a two level model in which observations of either GPA or attendance from fifth through eighth grade are nested within students.

LEVEL-1

Attendance or GPA = $\pi_0 + \pi_1*(\text{TREND}) + \pi_2*(\text{RETAINED}) + e$

LEVEL-2

$\pi_0 = \gamma_{00} + u_0$
$\pi_1 = \gamma_{10} + u_1$
$\pi_2 = \gamma_{20}$

where:

- **TREND** is the growth trajectory slope, centered around grade 5, so that it is 0 when grade=5, 1 when grade=6, etc.

- **RETAINED** is 0 if never retained in grade at that point, 1 if retained that year and for each year after that, 2 the second time retained and 2 after that, and so on if there are multiple years of grade retention. Like the analysis of ISAT trends, the RETAINED variable allows students to have multiple observations for a given grade. It accounts for whether GPA or attendance is different in retained years, compared to the first time at a grade level.

The intercept and slope (TREND) are allowed to vary randomly at the student level while RETAINED is fixed. On average, fifth-grade students have an attendance rate of 95 percent, and their attendance drops only slightly, by 0.002 each year, through eighth grade (**Table C.3**). For students who are retained, attendance is 2.2 percentage points lower than in non-retained

TABLE C.2
HLM Analyses for ISAT Growth Trends Estimating School Variation

	Reading	Math
	Estimates From a 3-Level Model	Estimates From a 3-Level Model
Intercept	246.2**	265.3**
GRD_C8	10.3**	13.2**
FDPOLDFG	-12.8**	-12.9**
CUMRET	6.7**	6.2**
CUMSKIP	-7.9**	-8.9**
Variance-Covariance (Standard Deviations)		
r_0 (int)	294.6 (17.2)**	421.6 (20.5)**
r_1 (grd_c8)	2.1 (1.4)**	1.8 (1.3)**
u_{00} (int)	90.9 (9.5)**	176.1 (13.3)**
u_{10} (grd_c8)	1.9 (1.4)**	3.7 (1.9)**
Level 1/	96,433 observations	96,539 observations
Level 2/	/26,528 students	/26,635 students
Level 3	/472 schools	/472 schools

TABLE C.3
Two-Level HLM Analyses of Attendance and GPA Trends

	Attendance	GPA
Intercept	0.952	2.754
TREND	-0.002***	-0.002-
RETAINED	-0.022***	0.041***
Variance and (Standard Deviations)		
Level-1 (e)	0.0016 (0.040)	0.133 (0.365)
u_0 (Intercept)	0.0024*** (0.049)	0.393*** (0.627)
u_1 (TREND)	0.0002*** (0.014)	0.016*** (0.127)
Observations		
Level 1/Level 2	319,879 observations/ 99,300 students	184,407 observations/ 61,791 students

Note: *p<.05 **p<.001 ***p<.0001

years. Average GPA for fifth-graders is around 2.8. Between fifth and eighth grade, GPAs drop only slightly, by 0.002 each year. GPAs are nearly half a point higher in retained years than in non-retained years (**Table C.3**).

The second analysis uses a three-level model in which observations are nested within students who are nested within schools. This allows us to determine how much variation in growth in attendance and GPA can be attributed to students and how much can be attributed to school. Schools explain about a third of the variance in attendance growth and a little more than half of the variance in GPA growth (**Table C.4**).

LEVEL-1

Attendance or GPA = $\pi_0 + \pi_1 *\text{TREND} + \pi_2 *(\text{RETAINED}) + e$

LEVEL-2

$\pi_0 = \gamma_{00} + r_0$
$\pi_1 = \gamma_{10} + r_1$
$\pi_2 = \gamma_{20}$

LEVEL-3

$\gamma_{00} = \eta_{000} + u_{00}$
$\gamma_{10} = \eta_{100} + u_{10}$
$\gamma_{20} = \eta_{200}$

TABLE C.4

Three-Level HLM Analyses of Attendance and GPA Trends

	Attendance	GPA
Intercept	0.947	2.69
TREND	-0.003***	0.001
RETAINED	-0.019***	0.043
Variance and (Standard Deviations)		
Level-1 (e)	0.0016 (0.040)	0.133 (0.364)
r_0 (Intercept)	0.0020*** (0.045)	0.260*** (0.510)
r_1 (TREND)	0.0002*** (0.013)	0.008*** (0.089)
u_0 (Intercept)	0.0005*** (0.022)	0.141*** (0.376)
u_1 (TREND)	0.0001*** (0.009)	0.009*** (.096)
Observations		
Level 1/ Level 2/ Level 3	319,879 observations/ 99,300 students/ 554 schools	184,407 observations/ 61,791 students/ 545 schools

Note: *p<.05 **p<.001 ***p<.0001

Why we used Bayesian estimates with inflated variance to demonstrate growth in attendance, grades, and test scores over time in Chapter 8.

After running the models described above, we then developed Bayesian estimates of growth in attendance, grades, and test scores for each student, and inflated the variance among the estimates to match model-based standard deviations of growth trends. The rationales for these growth measures are described below, along with details on the models and resulting coefficients. The two-level hierarchical linear models (observations nested within students) were used to create the estimates of each student's growth when comparing indicators, and used to estimate the growth trends in **Figures 32, 33, and 34** in Chapter 8.

To understand the degree to which students' test scores, grades, and attendance change over time, we wanted to be sure that random fluctuation would not inflate our assessment of the variation to which student achievement changed over time. At the same time, we did not want to minimize variance in growth/change that really occurred through overly stringent statistical adjustments. This issue was a particular concern with test scores, which are based on just one score obtained on one day in the year, while grades and attendance are based on performance over the entire school year. There is considerable error in any given test score; a student's score on any given test may be high or low for random reasons—a good or bad testing day, feeling ill, lucky guesses, misreading a question. In fact, the measurement error associated with any one score is larger than the average growth that students make from year-to-year. For example, on the ISAT reading test, students gain about 10 points a year, on average. But a typical score has a standard error of around nine points, which means that a student's true ability is very likely within 18 points of their measured score (two times the standard error).[77] If a student's measured score was randomly higher by 10 points one year than it should have been,
it would look like he had gained an entire extra year

---

77 Standard errors on the ISAT reading test range from eight to 47 points, depending on the score and grade level. For a seventh grade student with a typical score of 246, the standard error is nine points. On the ISAT math test, standard errors range from six to 49 points; for a typical seventh-grade score of 265 the standard error is seven points (ISAT 2008 Technical Manual, Illinois State Board of Education Division of Assessment).

worth of skills when he had not. We examined a number of potential methods of estimating growth in test scores, and the variance in test score growth over time, described below. We then applied the same methods to examine changes in grades and attendance over the middle grade years.

A simple method for calculating the average growth that students make from fifth to eighth grade on the ISAT exam is to estimate a growth trajectory (slope) for each student using OLS regression models fit to each student's data. This method gives the average gain made over three years (four time points) for each student. However, scores that are much higher or lower than the student's real ability can make it look like gains are smaller or larger than they really are. This is especially true if a score with substantial error occurs at the beginning or end of the time series, in fifth or eighth grade. As a first, simple examination of whether this should be a concern, we calculated the growth trajectory for each student through OLS models, and plotted students' scores against their estimated growth trajectory, for a random sample of students. We could easily see that this did seem to be a problem for some students, as their estimated slope was overly influenced by scores that were substantially lower or higher than other points.

An alternative method of calculating growth was to get Empirical Bayes estimates of each student's average yearly growth through hierarchical linear models (HLM) that nested observations within students (Raudenbush and Bryk, 2002). The Bayesian estimates minimize variance introduced by scores that are exceptionally high or low, compared to a student's scores in other years, given the typical growth trajectory. If scores are inconsistent relative to typical growth, the trend is adjusted to reflect the most likely true growth trajectory—given the patterns observed in other students. However, this method has the potential to reduce the differences between students in their growth trends beyond what is true variation.

We decided to test which method produced the most accurate estimates of students' abilities at the end of eighth grade (OLS growth estimates or Bayes growth estimates), given where they started in fifth grade. If the OLS estimate inflated or deflated growth based on poor measurement in some years, the eighth-grade score estimated based on the OLS trajectories should be incorrectly lower or higher than their true score. If the Bayesian estimate reduced true differences in students' growth, the eighth-grade score estimated based on the Bayesian trajectories should also be incorrectly lower or higher than their true score. We then compared those estimated scores to students' scores on a different exam, the EXPLORE, which is taken at the start of the ninth-grade year. Students' performance on the EXPLORE should be strongly predicted by their true skills at the end of the eighth-grade year.

All things being equal, we expected that, unless they were substantially better estimates of growth than the OLS estimates, the Bayesian estimates should have had a weaker correlation with EXPLORE scores since their variance was constrained. However, this was not the case. The eighth-grade scores that were estimated based on the Bayesian growth estimates were more predictive of ninth-grade EXPLORE test scores, even though there was less total variation (**see Table C.5**). This convinced us that much of the variance in the OLS estimates was noise, not true growth in skills, especially on the reading test where there were much larger differences between the trends calculated through OLS and HLM.

However, we were concerned that representing the Bayes estimates of growth as the true variance in growth would not be accurate in terms of the total variation in growth. Variation in the empirical Bayes estimates is known to be reduced beyond the true variance, as each estimate is pulled towards the group mean based on the number of observations used to construct the estimate.[78] In this case, each estimate was based on only a small number of test observations (four each). Therefore, we inflated the variance among the Bayes estimates based on the maximum likelihood estimate of

---

[78] Raudenbush and Bryk (2002).

TABLE C.5

Prediction of EXPLORE Test Score Based on Different Estimates of Eighth-Grade Scores
R-squares from models predicting EXPLORE scores in ninth grade as a function of fifth-grade ISAT data growth trend predicted form OLS versus HLM models

	Prediction of EXPLORE Test Score in Ninth Grade			
	Composite	Reading	English	Math
Using estimated eighth-grade **reading** scores based on:				
OLS slopes	0.6872	0.5373	0.6106	0.5454
HLM slopes	0.6968	0.5485	0.6309	0.5436
Using estimated eighth-grade **math** scores based on:				
OLS slopes	0.6970	0.4535	0.5535	0.6769
HLM slopes	0.6994	0.4557	0.5556	0.6784

the variance of the true slopes, obtained from the model statistics. In this way, the variance of the growth trends represented the best estimate of the true variation of growth trends, rather than the shrunken variation from the Bayesian estimates.

Methods for Producing Figures 32, 34, and 35 from the HLM Models

Figures 32, 34, and 35 in Chapter 8, visually display the average growth in student performance (i.e., attendance, GPA, and ISAT scores) from fifth to eighth grade, and the variation in growth, for students that started out with low, medium and high achievement in fifth grade. These figures show the extent to which some students might be catching up to students with higher initial achievement (i.e., attendance, GPA, and ISAT scores), or falling further behind.

For each measure of student achievement (attendance, GPA, ISAT scores), we selected three groups of students: those whose fifth-grade data on that performance indicator placed them at the 10th, 50th, and 90th percentile. For the attendance figure, which used multiple cohorts of students, there were 1,007 students at the 10th percentile, 1,328 at the 50th percentile, and 1,047 at the 88th percentile.[79] For the GPA figure, there were 626 students at the 10th percentile, 628 at the 50th percentile, and 738 at the 90th percentile. For the ISAT reading score figure, there were 288 students at the 10th percentile, 714 at the 50th percentile, and 558 at the 90th percentile. For the ISAT math score figure, there were 396 students at the 10th percentile, 458 at the 50th percentile, and 250 at the 90th percentile.

We then determined the variation in growth for students in each group. To do this, we used the Bayesian estimates of growth that were calculated for each student from the HLM models, but we modified them to adjust for the reduction in variance associated with Bayesian estimates. Because the variance in Bayesian estimates is smaller than the estimated true variance that exists in the population, we inflated the variance of the growth estimates to match the maximum likelihood estimate of the variance in growth, obtained from the model statistics. We used the SAS procedure PROC STANDARD, which allows the standard deviation for a variable to be specified, forcing the standard deviation of the Bayesian estimates to match the estimated true standard deviation (tau) from the model.

Using these modified Bayesian estimates of growth, we then determined what low, average, and high growth was within each of the three groups of students that were defined based on their fifth-grade performance (students at the 10th, 50th, and 90th percentiles in fifth grade). The standard deviation of growth for each of these sets of students was similar to the standard deviation from the model statistics, except for the growth in reading. For example, the standard deviation of math growth from the model across all students was 2.3 (**see Table C.1 on p.113**), while the standard deviation of growth was

---

[79] For attendance, the 88th percentile was the highest percentile group in fifth grade; students in this group had 100 percent attendance in fifth grade.

2.0 among students at the 10th percentile, 2.3 among students at the 50th percentile, and 2.8 among students at the 90th percentile. Because there is a large negative covariance between initial reading test score and growth on the reading tests, the standard deviation of growth for each set of students with particular reading scores in fifth grade was smaller than the overall variation. This is because much of the variation in growth overall is determined by students' initial status. The standard deviation of growth in each group was about one-third the size of the standard deviation for the population.

The figure graphs the growth that corresponded to the 5th, 50th, and 95th percentiles for each group of students. In this way, the figures show the range of growth observed for students that started out initially with low, medium and high performance. By using this method we can see the differences in growth based on initial status that could not be discerned by the overall estimates. For example, it shows that students that started with initially low attendance had the largest decline in attendance. We did not include quadratic terms in the models because there were only four points of time used to construct the slopes and the nonlinear coefficients were very small when included.

Methods for Calculating Figure 36

To create **Figure 36**, we first regressed each ninth-grade outcome on the corresponding fifth-grade value for that outcome; in other words, ninth-grade GPA was regressed on fifth-grade GPA, ninth-grade on-track was regressed on fifth-grade GPA and tenth-grade math PLAN scores were regressed on fifth-grade math ISAT scores. The residuals from this regression represent how different the ninth-grade outcome is conditional on the fifth-grade values. The residuals from each of those analyses are then regressed on each of the primary eighth-grade indicators (GPA, attendance, ISAT math, and ISAT reading) to discern the prediction based on eighth-grade data conditional on the values of fifth grade. Using the coefficients from both set of regressions, we calculated what the value of each ninth-grade outcome would be given an eighth-grade GPA of 2.0 or 3.3 for students with a fifth-grade GPA of 2.5; eighth-grade attendance of 93 percent or 99 percent with a fifth-grade attendance of 97 percent; math ISAT scores of 253 or 276 and reading ISAT scores of 241 or 248 with fifth-grade test scores of 225 in math and 215 in reading.

Appendix D
ISAT Standards and EPAS Benchmarks

TABLE D.1

Scale Score Ranges That Defined Student Performance Levels on the ISAT in 2009

	Academic Warning	Below Standards	Meets Standards	Exceeds Standards
Reading Grade Level				
3	120-155	156-190	191-226	227-329
4	120-157	158-202	203-236	237-341
5	120-160	161-214	215-246	247-351
6	120-166	167-219	220-256	257-360
7	120-173	174-225	226-266	267-369
8	120-179	180-230	231-277	278-364
Math Grade Level				
3	120-162	163-183	184-223	224-341
4	120-171	172-199	200-246	247-355
5	120-179	180-213	214-270	271-369
6	120-193	194-224	225-275	276-379
7	120-206	207-234	235-280	281-392
8	120-220	221-245	246-287	288-410

Source: Guides to the Illinois State Assessment (ISBE, 2011). Retrieved from http://www.isbe.net/assessment/pdfs/ISAT_Interpr_Guide_2011.pdf.

TABLE D.2

Scale Score Ranges That Defined Student Performance Levels on the ISAT in 2013

	Academic Warning	Below Standards	Meets Standards	Exceeds Standards
Reading Grade Level				
3	120-159	160-206	207-235	236-329
4	120-174	175-216	217-248	249-341
5	120-192	193-227	228-260	261-351
6	120-201	202-236	237-266	267-360
7	120-202	203-238	239-270	271-369
8	120-217	218-247	248-270	271-364
Math Grade Level				
3	120-172	173-213	214-254	255-341
4	120-190	191-223	224-266	267-355
5	120-200	201-234	235-279	280-369
6	120-213	214-246	247-291	292-379
7	120-220	221-256	257-301	302-392
8	120-233	234-266	267-309	310-410

Source: Retrieved from http://www.isbe.state.il.us/assessment/htmls/isat-cut-scores13.htm.

The ACT college-readiness benchmarks are scores on the ACT test that represent the level at which students have a 50 percent likelihood of earning at least a B in a corresponding first-year college course. ACT has also established college readiness benchmarks for EXPLORE and PLAN, based on a student's likelihood of meeting the ACT benchmarks, given normal progress in grades nine through eleven.

TABLE D.3

ACT's College-Readiness Benchmarks

Test	EXPLORE	PLAN	ACT
English	14	15	18
Math	18	19	22
Reading	17	18	22
Science	19	20	23

Source: *The Forgotten Middle: Ensuring that All Students Are on Target for College and Career Readiness before High School*, ACT (2008).

Appendix E
Relationships of All Potential Indicators with High School Outcomes

Course Performance

TABLE E.1

Relationships of Middle Grade Indicators with Course Performance

Middle Grade Indicators	9th-Grade On-Track (Pseudo-R^2)	Passing 9th-Grade English (Pseudo-R^2)	Passing 9th-Grade Math (Pseudo-R^2)	Earning As or Bs in 9th-Grade Classes (Pseudo-R^2)	Earning As or Bs in 9th-Grade English (Pseudo-R^2)	Earning As or Bs in 9th-Grade Math (Pseudo-R^2)
ISAT Score indicators						
8th-Grade Reading ISAT	0.05	0.04	0.03	0.09	0.08	0.05
8th-Grade Math ISAT	0.08	0.06	0.06	0.11	0.09	0.10
7th-Grade Reading ISAT	0.05	0.04	0.03	0.08	0.07	0.05
7th-Grade Math ISAT	0.07	0.05	0.05	0.10	0.08	0.09
6th-Grade Reading ISAT	0.05	0.04	0.02	0.07	0.07	0.05
6th-Grade Math ISAT	0.06	0.05	0.05	0.10	0.08	0.09
% Correct Vocabulary Development (8th-Grade ISAT)	0.03	0.02	0.02	0.04	0.04	0.02
% Correct Reading Strategies (8th-Grade ISAT)	0.03	0.03	0.02	0.05	0.04	0.03
% Correct Reading Comprehension (8th-Grade ISAT)	0.05	0.04	0.03	0.08	0.08	0.05
% Correct Literature (8th-Grade ISAT)	0.03	0.03	0.02	0.06	0.05	0.04
Reading Extended Response Points (8th-Grade ISAT)	0.03	0.03	0.02	0.05	0.05	0.03
% Correct Number Sense (8th-Grade ISAT)	0.05	0.03	0.04	0.08	0.06	0.07
% Correct Measurement (8th-Grade ISAT)	0.06	0.04	0.04	0.08	0.07	0.08
% Correct Algebra (8th-Grade ISAT)	0.07	0.05	0.05	0.10	0.08	0.09
% Correct Geometry (8th-Grade ISAT)	0.05	0.03	0.03	0.07	0.05	0.07
% Correct Data Analysis, Statistics and Probability (8th-Grade ISAT)	0.06	0.04	0.04	0.08	0.07	0.07
Math Extended Response Points—Mathematical Knowledge (8th-Grade ISAT)	0.03	0.02	0.02	0.04	0.04	0.04

TABLE E.1: *CONTINUED*

Relationships of Middle Grade Indicators with Course Performance

Middle Grade Indicators	9th-Grade On-Track (Pseudo-R^2)	Passing 9th-Grade English (Pseudo-R^2)	Passing 9th-Grade Math (Pseudo-R^2)	Earning As or Bs in 9th-Grade Classes (Pseudo-R^2)	Earning As or Bs in 9th-Grade English (Pseudo-R^2)	Earning As or Bs in 9th-Grade Math (Pseudo-R^2)
ISAT Score indicators						
Math Extended Response Points—Strategic Knowledge (8th-Grade ISAT)	0.03	0.02	0.02	0.04	0.04	0.03
Math Extended Response Points—Explanation (8th-Grade ISAT)	0.04	0.03	0.03	0.06	0.05	0.04
ISAT Reading Gains Over Middle Grades	0.00	0.00	0.00	0.00	0.00	0.00
ISAT reading Growth Over Middle Grades (Removing Influence of Starting Point)	0.00	0.00	0.00	0.00	0.00	0.00
Relative Class Rank Based on ISAT Reading	0.04	0.03	0.02	0.06	0.06	0.04
ISAT Math Gains Over Middle Grades	0.00	0.00	0.00	0.00	0.00	0.00
ISAT reading Growth Over Middle Grades (Removing Influence of Starting Point)	0.00	0.00	0.00	0.00	0.00	0.00
Relative Class Rank Based on ISAT Math	0.06	0.04	0.05	0.08	0.06	0.08
Grade-Based Indicators						
8th-Grade English GPA	0.15	0.13	0.10	0.18	0.18	0.12
8th-Grade Math GPA	0.14	0.11	0.10	0.15	0.14	0.13
8th-Grade Core GPA	0.18	0.15	0.12	0.21	0.20	0.15
8th-Grade Number of Fs	0.10	0.09	0.07	0.08	0.08	0.06
7th-Grade Core GPA	0.17	0.14	0.12	0.18	0.18	0.14
Behavior-Based indicators						
8th-Grade Attendance	0.12	0.09	0.08	0.08	0.09	0.07
8th-Grade Suspensions	0.06	0.04	0.04	0.04	0.04	0.03
8th-Grade Misconducts	0.03	0.02	0.02	0.02	0.02	0.01
8th-Grade Grit	0.01	0.01	0.00	0.00	0.00	0.00

TABLE E.1: *CONTINUED*

Relationships of Middle Grade Indicators with Course Performance

Middle Grade Indicators	9th-Grade On-Track (Pseudo-R^2)	Passing 9th-Grade English (Pseudo-R^2)	Passing 9th-Grade Math (Pseudo-R^2)	Earning As or Bs in 9th-Grade Classes (Pseudo-R^2)	Earning As or Bs in 9th-Grade English (Pseudo-R^2)	Earning As or Bs in 9th-Grade Math (Pseudo-R^2)
Behavior-Based indicators						
8th-Grade Study Habits	0.02	0.01	0.01	0.03	0.03	0.02
7th-Grade Attendance	0.08	0.06	0.05	0.07	0.06	0.05
Background Characteristics						
Race, Gender, Old-for-Grade, Neighborhood Poverty, Neighborhood Social Status, Special Education Status	0.06	0.05	0.03	0.09	0.09	0.06
Combinations of Indicators						
8th-Grade ISAT Math & Reading + 7th-Grade ISAT Math & Reading	0.08	0.06	0.06	0.12	0.10	0.11
8th-Grade Core GPA + Attendance	0.21	0.17	0.14	0.22	0.21	0.16
8th-Grade Core GPA + 7th-Grade Core GPA	0.20	0.17	0.14	0.22	0.22	0.16
8th-Grade Core GPA + ISAT Math & Reading	0.18	0.15	0.13	0.21	0.20	0.17
8th-Grade Core GPA + Attendance + 7th-Grade Core GPA	0.23	0.18	0.16	0.23	0.23	0.17
8th-Grade Core GPA + Attendance + ISAT Math & Reading	0.21	0.17	0.15	0.22	0.22	0.18
All Student-Level Indicators	0.22	0.18	0.16	0.25	0.24	0.20
School Effects						
School Effects (Fixed Effects of Middle and High Schools)	0.14	0.13	0.12	0.13	0.13	0.13
All + School Effects (Fixed Effects)	0.33	0.29	0.28	0.34	0.34	0.31

Test Scores

This section shows adjusted-R^2 for models predicting PLAN test scores and pseudo-R^2 for PLAN benchmarks for all the potential middle grade indicators used in the analyses. **Table E.2** shows the prediction fit for subject-specific scores, as well as composite scores.

As with composite scores, the PLAN subject-specific scores are predicted almost as well with sixth-grade scores as with eighth-grade scores. In some cases, PLAN English and reading scores are best predicted by middle grade reading scores, while PLAN math and science scores are best predicted by middle grade math scores. Combining two test scores helps improve the prediction of any PLAN scores. For PLAN English and science, the best prediction comes from combining eighth-grade reading and math scores; for PLAN reading the best prediction comes from combining seventh- and eighth-grade reading scores; and for PLAN math, the best prediction comes from combining seventh- and eighth-grade math scores. Adding core GPA or students' background characteristics only slightly improves the fit of the models. Knowing the middle school and high school that students attend can help with the prediction of PLAN subject-specific scores. The same findings apply to whether students reach the benchmarks in each subject.

TABLE E.2

Relationships of Middle Grade Indicators with PLAN Scores

Middle Grade Indicators	English		Reading		Math	
	PLAN Scores (Adjusted-R^2)	Reaching Benchmark (Pseudo-R^2)	PLAN Scores (Adjusted-R^2)	Reaching Benchmark (Pseudo-R^2)	PLAN Scores (Adjusted-R^2)	Reaching Benchmark (Pseudo-R^2)
ISAT Score Indicators						
8th-Grade Reading ISAT						
Linear Term	0.50	0.36	0.43	0.33	0.41	0.23
Linear & Squared Terms	0.50	0.36	0.44	0.33	0.41	0.24
8th-Grade Math ISAT						
Linear Term	0.50	0.34	0.37	0.26	0.61	0.35
Linear & Squared Terms	0.50	0.34	0.37	0.26	0.61	0.35
7th-Grade Reading ISAT						
Linear Term	0.51	0.35	0.43	0.31	0.40	0.22
Linear & Squared Terms	0.51	0.35	0.44	0.31	0.40	0.23
7th-Grade Math ISAT						
Linear Term	0.49	0.33	0.36	0.26	0.60	0.34
Linear & Squared Terms	0.49	0.33	0.36	0.26	0.60	0.34
6th-Grade Reading ISAT						
Linear Term	0.50	0.34	0.43	0.30	0.39	0.22
Linear & Squared Terms	0.51	0.34	0.44	0.31	0.39	0.22
6th-Grade Math ISAT						
Linear Term	0.47	0.32	0.35	0.25	0.55	0.31
Linear & Squared Terms	0.47	0.32	0.35	0.25	0.55	0.31
% Correct Vocabulary Development (8th-Grade ISAT)	0.31	0.23	0.26	0.21	0.23	0.14
% Correct Reading Strategies (8th-Grade ISAT)	0.24	0.18	0.20	0.15	0.20	0.11
% Correct Reading Comprehension (8th-Grade ISAT)	0.44	0.33	0.37	0.30	0.35	0.22
% Correct Literature (8th-Grade ISAT)	0.30	0.22	0.25	0.20	0.24	0.13
Reading Extended Response Points (8th-Grade ISAT)	0.17	0.12	0.14	0.10	0.14	0.07
% Correct Number Sense (8th-Grade ISAT)	0.32	0.21	0.24	0.18	0.39	0.25
% Correct Measurement (8th-Grade ISAT)	0.37	0.25	0.27	0.20	0.44	0.29
% Correct Algebra (8th-Grade ISAT)	0.42	0.29	0.32	0.23	0.48	0.30
% Correct Geometry (8th-Grade ISAT)	0.30	0.20	0.21	0.16	0.38	0.23
% Correct Data Analysis, Statistics and Probability (8th-Grade ISAT)	0.36	0.26	0.27	0.21	0.40	0.26
Math Extended Response Points—Mathematical Knowledge (8th-Grade ISAT)	0.23	0.17	0.17	0.14	0.25	0.14

Science		Composite	
PLAN Scores (Adjusted-R^2)	Reaching Benchmark (Pseudo-R^2)	PLAN Scores (Adjusted-R^2)	Reaching Benchmark (Pseudo-R^2)
0.37	0.15	0.56	0.38
0.38	0.16	0.58	0.38
0.43	0.18	0.63	0.39
0.44	0.18	0.63	0.39
0.36	0.15	0.56	0.35
0.38	0.16	0.57	0.35
0.43	0.18	0.62	0.38
0.44	0.18	0.62	0.38
0.35	0.15	0.55	0.35
0.37	0.16	0.57	0.35
0.39	0.16	0.58	0.36
0.40	0.17	0.58	0.36
0.19	0.09	0.33	0.22
0.15	0.07	0.26	0.17
0.29	0.15	0.48	0.35
0.19	0.09	0.33	0.21
0.11	0.04	0.19	0.11
0.26	0.014	0.40	0.27
0.31	0.15	0.46	0.31
0.33	0.16	0.52	0.34
0.25	0.12	0.38	0.25
0.28	0.13	0.44	0.31
0.17	0.07	0.27	0.17

Appendix E

TABLE E.2: *CONTINUED*

Relationships of Middle Grade Indicators with PLAN Scores

Middle Grade Indicators	English		Reading		Math	
	PLAN Scores (Adjusted-R^2)	Reaching Benchmark (Pseudo-R^2)	PLAN Scores (Adjusted-R^2)	Reaching Benchmark (Pseudo-R^2)	PLAN Scores (Adjusted-R^2)	Reaching Benchmark (Pseudo-R^2)
ISAT Score Indicators						
Math Extended Response Points—Strategic Knowledge (8th-Grade ISAT)	0.23	0.18	0.17	0.15	0.25	0.15
Math Extended Response Points—Explanation (8th-Grade ISAT)	0.19	0.16	0.14	0.12	0.20	0.10
ISAT Reading Gains Over Middle Grades	0.05	0.04	0.04	0.03	0.02	0.01
Relative Class Rank Based on 8th-Grade ISAT Reading	0.34	0.26	0.30	0.23	0.26	0.14
ISAT Math Gains Over Middle Grades	0.00	0.00	0.00	0.00	0.00	0.00
Relative Class Rank Based on 8th-Grade ISAT Math	0.35	0.25	0.26	0.19	0.42	0.25
Grade-Based Indicators						
8th-Grade English GPA	0.24	0.17	0.20	0.16	0.21	0.14
8th-Grade Math GPA	0.18	0.13	0.14	0.11	0.21	0.14
8th-Grade Core GPA	0.26	0.19	0.22	0.17	0.25	0.16
Number of Fs in 8th-Grade	0.05	0.04	0.04	0.04	0.05	0.04
Behavior-Based Indicators						
8th-Grade Attendance	0.04	0.03	0.03	0.02	0.05	0.03
8th-Grade Suspensions	0.02	0.03	0.02	0.02	0.02	0.02
8th-Grade Misconducts	0.01	0.01	0.01	0.01	0.01	0.01
8th-Grade Grit	0.00	0.00	0.00	0.00	0.00	0.00
8th-Grade Study Habits	0.00	0.00	0.00	0.00	0.00	0.00
Background Characteristics						
Race, Gender, Old-for-Grade, Neighborhood Poverty, Neighborhood Social Status, Special Education Status	0.27	0.19	0.21	0.15	0.27	0.14
Combinations of Indicators						
Combination ISAT Tests						
7th- and 8th-Grade Reading	0.55	0.39	0.47	0.36	0.44	0.26
7th- and 8th-Grade Math	0.52	0.35	0.39	0.27	0.63	0.36
8th-Grade Reading and Math	0.57	0.40	0.46	0.34	0.62	0.35
7th- and 8th-Grade Reading and Math	0.61	0.41	0.49	0.36	0.64	0.36
Two ISAT Tests* + Core GPA	0.58	0.40	0.48	0.36	0.63	0.37
Two ISAT Tests* + Background Characteristics	0.58	0.41	0.49	0.37	0.63	0.37

Science		Composite	
PLAN Scores (Adjusted-R^2)	Reaching Benchmark (Pseudo-R^2)	PLAN Scores (Adjusted-R^2)	Reaching Benchmark (Pseudo-R^2)
0.16	0.07	0.27	0.19
0.13	0.04	0.22	0.13
0.02	0.00	0.04	0.30
0.23	0.09	0.38	0.24
0.00	0.00	0.00	0.00
0.29	0.12	0.44	0.28
0.17	0.08	0.27	0.19
0.15	0.06	0.23	0.16
0.20	0.09	0.31	0.22
0.04	0.02	0.06	0.05
0.03	0.01	0.05	0.03
0.02	0.01	0.02	0.02
0.01	0.00	0.01	0.01
0.00	0.00	0.00	0.00
0.00	0.00	0.00	0.00
0.22	0.10	0.32	0.18
0.38	0.17	0.61	0.41
0.44	0.19	0.66	0.41
0.46	0.19	0.69	0.44
0.48	0.21	0.72	0.46
0.45	0.20	0.69	0.45
0.46	0.21	0.70	0.44

Appendix E

TABLE E.2: *CONTINUED*

Relationships of Middle Grade Indicators with PLAN Scores

Middle Grade Indicators	English		Reading		Math	
	PLAN Scores (Adjusted-R^2)	Reaching Benchmark (Pseudo-R^2)	PLAN Scores (Adjusted-R^2)	Reaching Benchmark (Pseudo-R^2)	PLAN Scores (Adjusted-R^2)	Reaching Benchmark (Pseudo-R^2)
Combinations of Indicators						
All (Two ISAT Tests* + Background Characteristics + Core GPA + Attendance + Suspensions + Number of Fs + Misconducts + Relative Class Rank)	0.59	0.41	0.50	0.37	0.64	0.37
School Effects						
School Effects (Fixed Effects of Middle and High Schools)	0.40	†	0.33	†	0.41	†
All + School Effects (Fixed Effects)	0.63	†	0.52	†	0.67	†

Note: Sample size was kept the same for most analyses to make comparisons easier, except when data from surveys were analyzed. In those cases the sample sizes get smaller. That is the case when grit and study habits are part of the analysis.

* For English and science PLAN test, as well as composite scores, the two tests are eighth-grade reading and math ISAT tests. For Reading PLAN test the two tests are eighth- and seventh-grade reading ISAT tests. For math PLAN test the two tests are eighth- and seventh-grade math ISAT tests.

** Given the data for this cohort and analyses, a model with no explanatory variables would be able to predict correctly 51.7 percent of students in English by assigning all of them to not reaching the benchmark, 69.6 percent in reading, 83.8 percent in math, 93.5 percent in science benchmarks, and 77.2 percent for the composite score of 18 and above.

†Given the low variability in whether or not students reach benchmarks by middle and high school, these models could not be run.

As was the case with PLAN composite, it is easier to correctly predict which students are at risk of not reaching benchmarks than which students will reach the benchmarks, because so few students are successful. But there are big differences among the subject-specific tests. In English the proportion of student correctly classified at risk is 80 percent, the lowest; in reading it goes up to 91 percent, while in math and science it is above 96 percent. **Figure E.1** shows the proportion of students correctly classified as not reaching benchmarks in the Y-axis and the proportion of students incorrectly classified as not reaching benchmarks in the X-axis for models with different explanatory variables for the four PLAN subject-specific tests.

In general, most subjects can have a large proportion of students misclassified as at risk of not reaching benchmarks when they actually do. This number is especially high for science, 64 percent of students who do reach the benchmark are identified as at risk of not doing so using middle grade reading and math test scores. Even though the proportion is large, there are only 6.5 percent of students in our sample who reach the science benchmarks. In reading and math the proportion of students identified as at risk when they actually reach the benchmark is 40 percent, and in English it is 23 percent.

Science		Composite	
PLAN Scores (Adjusted-R^2)	Reaching Benchmark (Pseudo-R^2)	PLAN Scores (Adjusted-R^2)	Reaching Benchmark (Pseudo-R^2)
0.47	0.21	0.71	0.45
0.39	†	0.50	†
0.53	†	0.75	†

Appendix E

FIGURE E.1

Correct versus Incorrect Classification of Students Not Meeting Benchmarks

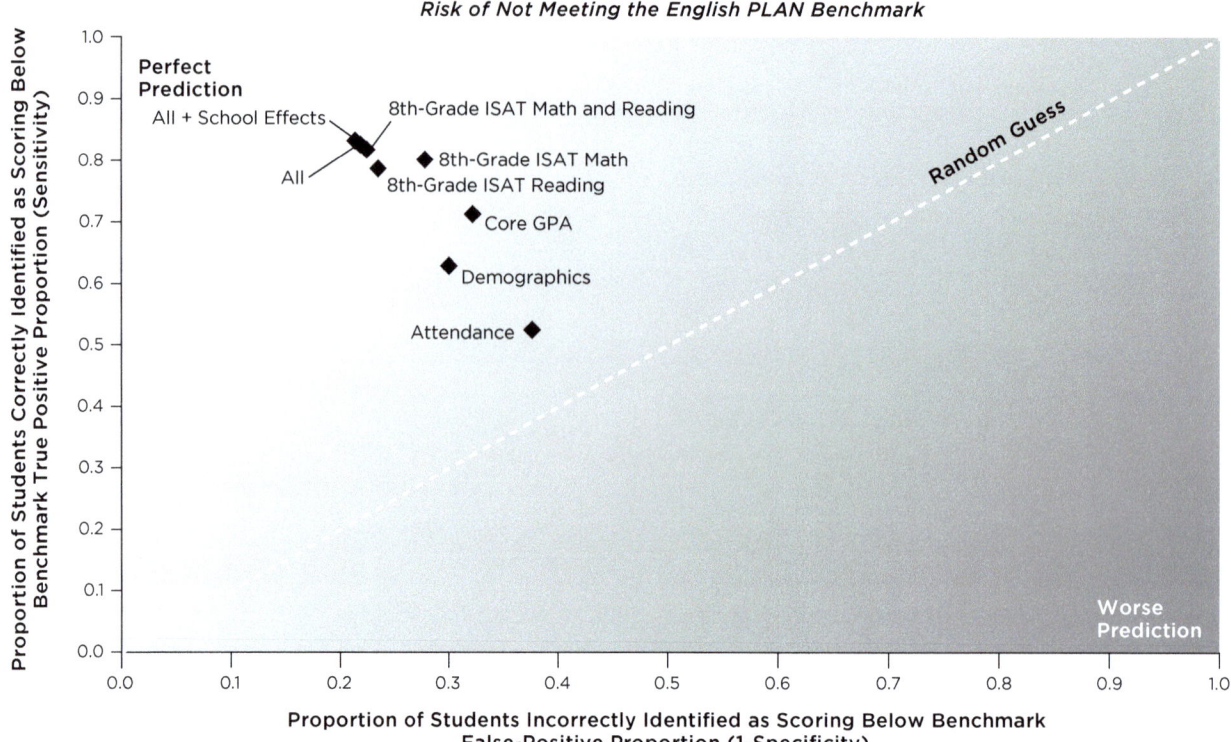

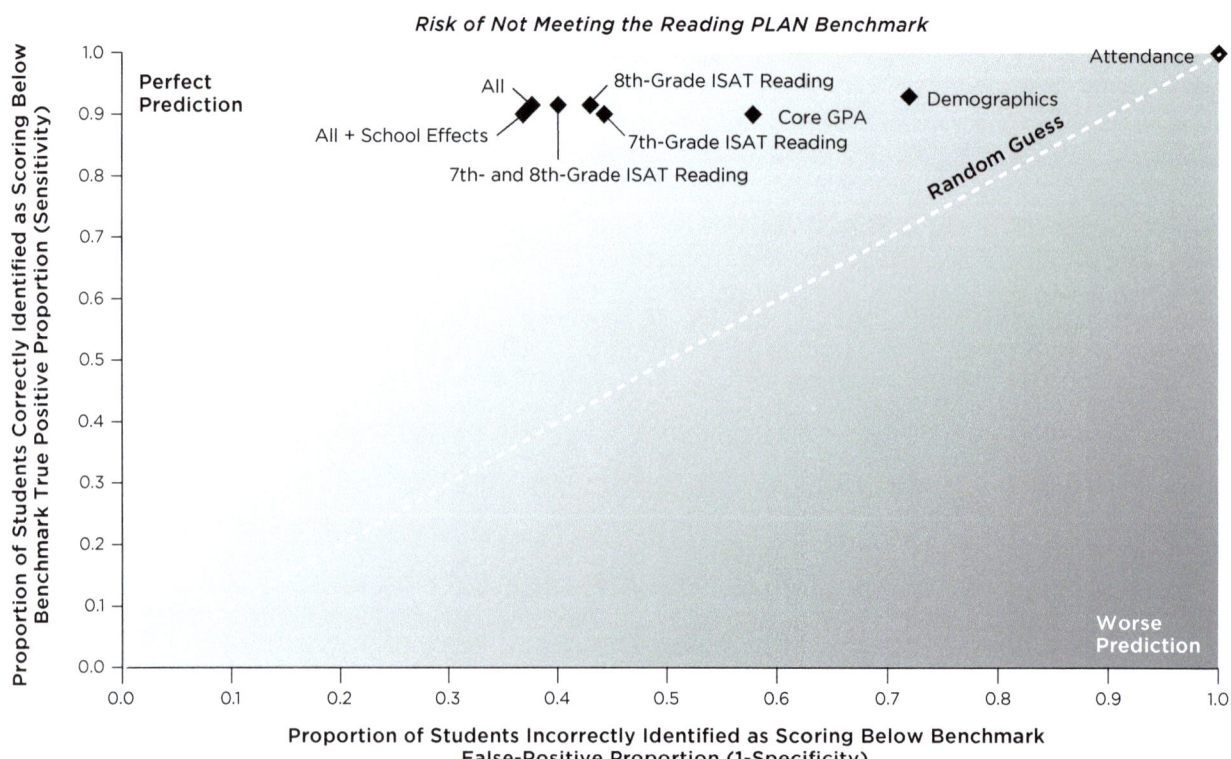

FIGURE E.1

Correct versus Incorrect Classification of Students Not Meeting Benchmarks

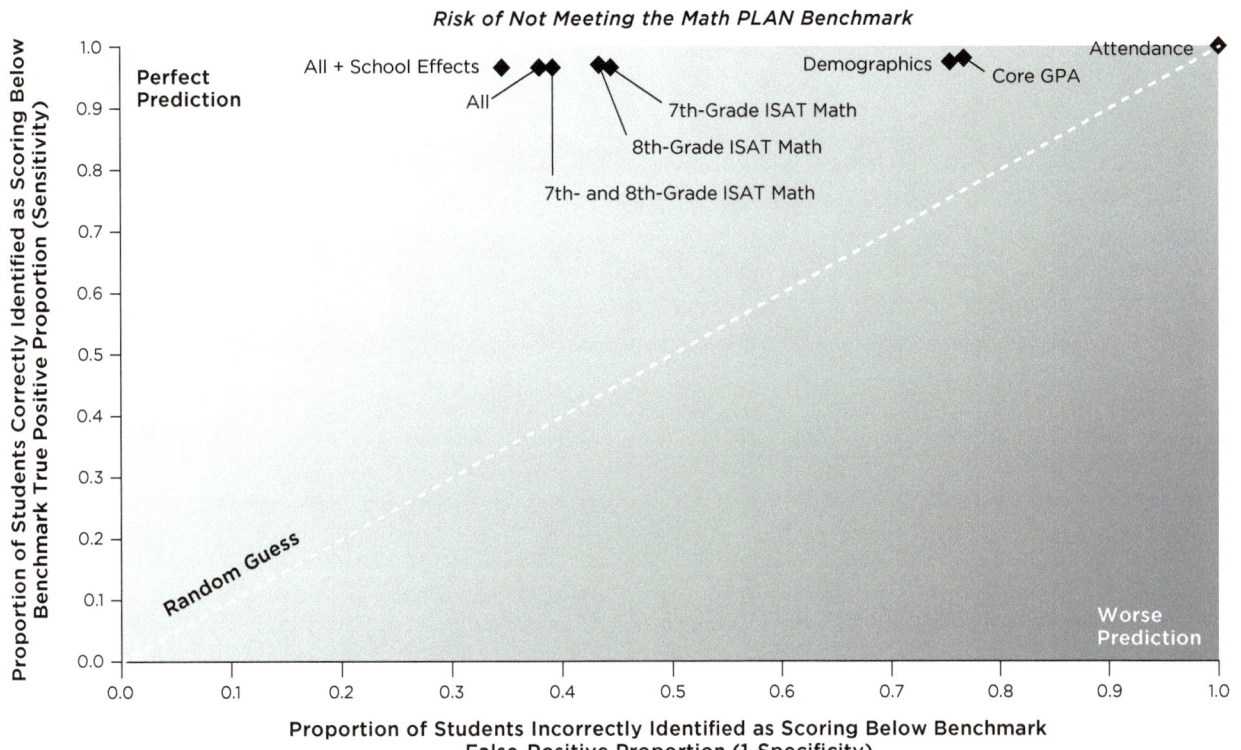

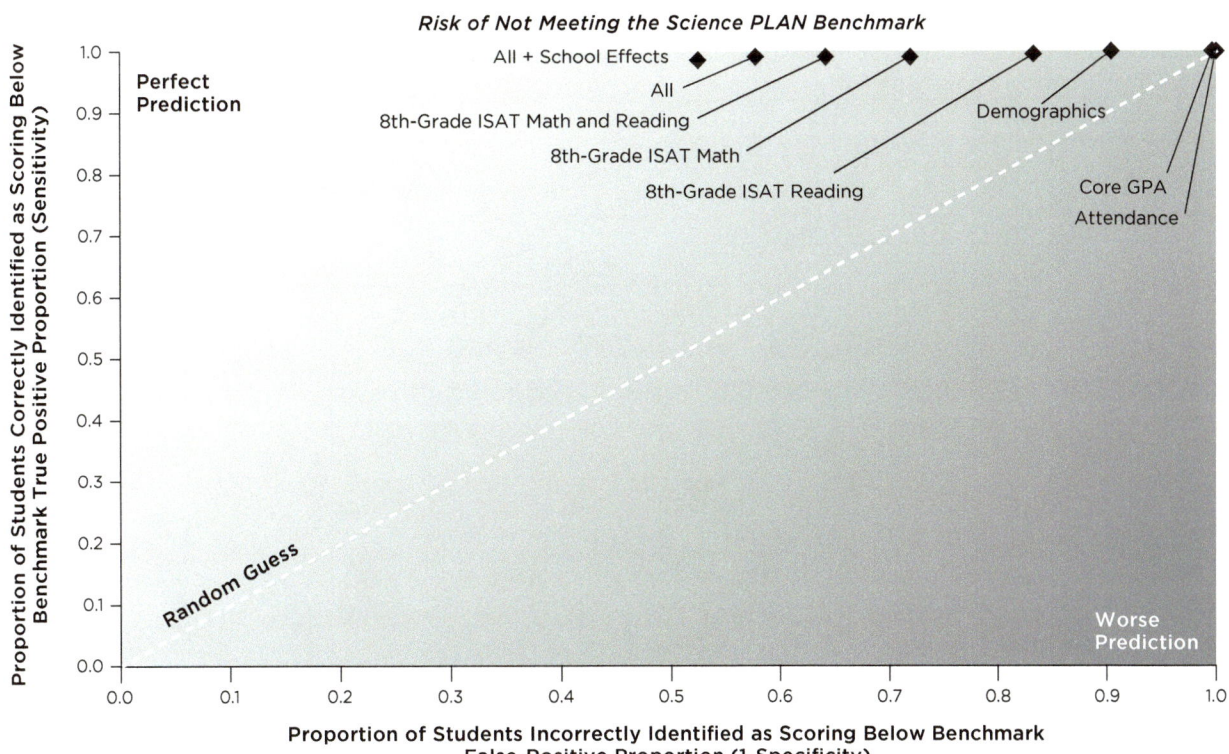

Appendix E

ABOUT THE AUTHORS

ELAINE M. ALLENSWORTH is the Lewis-Sebring Director at UChicago CCSR where she has conducted research on educational policy for the last 15 years. She is best known for her studies of high school graduation and college readiness, and also conducts research in the areas of school leadership and school organization. Her work on early indicators of high school graduation has been adopted for tracking systems used in Chicago and other districts across the country. She is one of the authors of the book *Organizing Schools for Improvement: Lessons from Chicago*, which provides a detailed analysis of school practices and community conditions that promote school improvement. Dr. Allensworth holds a PhD in Sociology and an MA in Urban Studies from Michigan State University. She was once a high school Spanish and science teacher.

JULIA A. GWYNNE is a Senior Research Analyst at UChicago CCSR. Her current work focuses on early warning indicators of high school and college readiness and the use of indicators with groups such as English Language Learners and students with disabilities. In addition, she has conducted research on student mobility, school closings, and classroom instructional environments. She received her doctoral degree in sociology from the University of Chicago.

PAUL MOORE is a Research Analyst at UChicago CCSR and is in the process of completing an MA in the social sciences at the University of Chicago. His research interests include quantitative modeling and methodology. Moore is studying the effects of attending higher performing schools on students' academic performance and noncognitive skills. He earned a BS in mathematics and education science from Vanderbilt University.

MARISA DE LA TORRE is the Director for Internal Research Capacity at the Consortium on Chicago School Research. She is very familiar with Chicago Public Schools' policies and part of her work involves studying them. She was the author of two studies on the effects of policies aimed at the lowest-performing schools in the district. One, *Turning Around Low-Performing Schools in Chicago*, investigates the effects of these policies on whether schools see improvements after the reform. The other report deals with the effect of school closings on students' academic outcomes, *When Schools Close: Effects on Displaced Students in Chicago Public Schools*, which has been widely cited in the press. This work prompted Chicago Public Schools to create a Student Bill of Rights for students affected by school closings. She is also familiar with the high school choice process in Chicago Public Schools and one of her studies was published in *School Choice and School Improvement*, a book edited by Mark Berends, Marisa Cannata, and Ellen B. Goldring. She is currently studying the impact that attending higher-performing high schools have on students' academic and non-academic outcomes. Before joining UChicago CCSR, she worked for the Chicago Public Schools in the Office of Research, Evaluation, and Accountability. She received a master's degree in economics from Northwestern University.

This report reflects the interpretation of the authors. Although UChicago CCSR's Steering Committee provided technical advice, no formal endorsement by these individuals, organizations, or the full Consortium should be assumed.

UCHICAGO CCSR

CONSORTIUM ON CHICAGO SCHOOL RESEARCH

Directors

ELAINE M. ALLENSWORTH
Lewis-Sebring Director

EMILY KRONE
Director for Outreach and Communication

JENNY NAGAOKA
Deputy Director

MELISSA RODERICK
Senior Director
Hermon Dunlap Smith Professor
School of Social Service Administration

PENNY BENDER SEBRING
Founding Director

SUE SPORTE
Director for Research Operations

MARISA DE LA TORRE
Director for Internal Research Capacity

Steering Committee

KATHLEEN ST. LOUIS CALIENTO
Co-Chair
Spark, Chicago

KIM ZALENT
Co-Chair
Business and Professional People for the Public Interest

Ex-Officio Members

TIMOTHY KNOWLES
Urban Education Institute

Institutional Members

JOHN R. BARKER
Chicago Public Schools

CLARICE BERRY
Chicago Principals and Administrators Association

AARTI DHUPELIA
Chicago Public Schools

CHRISTOPHER KOCH
Illinois State Board of Education

KAREN G.J. LEWIS
Chicago Teachers Union

SHERRY J. ULERY
Chicago Public Schools

Individual Members

VERONICA ANDERSON
Communications Consultant

JOANNA BROWN
Logan Square Neighborhood Association

CATHERINE DEUTSCH
Illinois Network of Charter Schools

RAQUEL FARMER-HINTON
University of Wisconsin, Milwaukee

KIRABO JACKSON
Northwestern University

CHRIS JONES
Stephen T. Mather High School

DENNIS LACEWELL
Urban Prep Charter Academy for Young Men

LILA LEFF
Umoja Student Development Corporation

RUANDA GARTH MCCULLOUGH
Loyola University, Chicago

LUISIANA MELÉNDEZ
Erikson Institute

CRISTINA PACIONE-ZAYAS
Latino Policy Forum

PAIGE PONDER
One Million Degrees

LUIS R. SORIA
Chicago Public Schools

BRIAN SPITTLE
DePaul University

MATTHEW STAGNER
Mathematica Policy Research

AMY TREADWELL
Chicago New Teacher Center

ERIN UNANDER
Al Raby High School

ARIE J. VAN DER PLOEG
American Institutes for Research (Retired)

www.ingramcontent.com/pod-product-compliance
Lightning Source LLC
Chambersburg PA
CBHW041522220426
43669CB00002B/22